AMERICAN FOLKSONGS
OF PROTEST

American Folksongs of Protest

by John Greenway

OCTAGON BOOKS

A DIVISION OF FARRAR, STRAUS AND GIROUX

New York   1977

Reprinted 1970
by special arrangement with the University of Pennsylvania Press

Second Octagon printing 1971

Third Octagon printing 1977

OCTAGON BOOKS

A DIVISION OF FARRAR, STRAUS & GIROUX, INC.
19 Union Square West
New York, N.Y. 10003

LIBRARY OF CONGRESS CATALOG CARD NUMBER: 75-111635
ISBN 0-374-93254-9

Manufactured by Braun-Brumfield, Inc.
Ann Arbor, Michigan
Printed in the United States of America

TO RUTH

Preface

The songs of the working people have always been their sharpest statement, and the one statement that cannot be destroyed. You can burn books, buy newspapers, you can guard against handbills and pamphlets, but you cannot prevent singing.

For some reason it has always been lightly thought that singing people are happy people. Nothing could be more untrue. The greatest and most enduring songs are wrung from unhappy people—the spirituals of the slaves which say in effect—"It is hopeless here, maybe in heaven it will be better."

Songs are the statement of a people. You can learn more about people by listening to their songs than any other way, for into the songs go all the hopes and hurts, the angers, fears, the wants and aspirations.

—JOHN STEINBECK.

From the earliest periods of American history the oppressed people forming the broad base of the social and economic pyramid have been singing of their discontent. What they have said has not always been pleasant, but it has always been worth listening to, if only as the expression of a people whose pride and expectation of a better life have traditionally been considered attributes of the American nation. Yet the more literate persons to whom the songs of protest have frequently been directed have stopped their ears, allowing many worth-while and often noble songs to vanish with the memories of the folk who made them.

The purpose of this study is to stimulate the inception of a corrective movement which will consider, evaluate, and preserve those songs still remaining to us. It is, therefore, an introduction rather than a scientific analysis, an impressionistic panorama rather than a blueprint. While it has been impossible to achieve completeness in a work designed to open a previously unexploited vein of American folk culture, I am confident that the picture of our singing protest presented by the songs, stories, and descriptions that I have selected as representative of thousands of others necessarily omitted is not an inaccurate one.

For those good things which readers may find in this study I am indebted to many people. To Professor MacEdward Leach, who persuaded me to abandon my share of those inhibitions which have denied these songs the scholarly consideration they have deserved, and who supervised the work with a faith in its value transcending my own, I am especially grateful. My gratitude is due also to University of Pennsylvania professors Matthias Shaaber, Sculley Bradley, Edgar Potts, and Wallace E. Davies, who read the manuscript and offered suggestions for its improvement; to Pete Seeger, Dr. Charles Seeger, Dr. Wayland Hand, Lawrence Gellert, Irwin Silber, Dr. Philip S. Foner, Alan Lomax, and Dr. Herbert Halpert, who led me to much material I might otherwise have overlooked; to Moses Asch, for allowing me to quote freely from his copyright holdings of recorded material; to the gracious and ever-patient library workers, particularly those at Brown University and the American Antiquarian Society, who made available to me numerous broadsides and songsters from the early years of our nation; and most of all, to Aunt Molly Jackson, Woody Guthrie, Harry McClintock, Joe Glazer, and the hundreds of nameless composers who wrote this book, and whom I served in the office of a sometimes presumptuous amanuensis. And of course to my wife, who ministered with unflagging good humor to a bear in the house during the composition of this book.

Contents

Musical transcriptions by EDMUND F. SOULE

AMERICAN FOLKSONGS
OF PROTEST

Introduction

THE POSITION OF SONGS OF PROTEST
IN FOLK LITERATURE

When the lowborn ballad maker composed his lyrical descriptions of lords and ladies in the dazzling splendor of their rich red velvet robes and silken kirtles and habiliments worth a hundred pounds, did he ever look down upon his own coarse garments? Did his wife ever look at her own red rough hands as she sang about the lily-white fingers of her mistress? When the varlet polished the knight's sollerets, did he ever think about their weight on his back? After the groom had put away the golden saddle and led to its stall his master's berry-brown steed, did he ever look at his own bed in the straw and reflect upon the similarity of the beast's estate and his own? If we are to judge by the English and Scottish ballads that have come down to us, these inequalities never occurred to the medieval peasantry; they ac-

1

cepted the kicks, curses, and deprivations of their station in abject servility, and sang only in admiration of the heaven-appointed aristocracy. But folksong cannot be dissociated from sociology; and the social history of the Middle Ages proves that the common man was aware of the injustice of aristocratic oppression, that he revolted against it and, furthermore, that he sang against it. On June 14, 1381, the peasant army that Wat Tyler led against London buoyed its determination with the couplet

> *When Adam delved and Eve span*
> *Who was then the gentleman?*

which is congeneric to the refrains that nearly six centuries later are being sung on picket lines. There are other modern analogues that support the inference that there was considerable vocal protest against social and economic inequalities in the folk expression of the Middle Ages. The medieval folk who, in their desperate need for militant champions, adopted and idealized such a dubious altruist as Robin Hood, established a tradition that their distant posterity continue with ballads about Jesse James, Pretty Boy Floyd, Matthew Kimes, and other criminals whose only identity with the cause of the oppressed was their temporarily succcessful flouting of laws the poor often found discriminatory. Present-day subversive political organizations have ancient analogues in the medieval witch cults that in all probability were seeking objectives beyond the dissolution of the Church, and which had songs full of potential symbolism.[1] And John Ball's exhortations to his followers to persist in "one-head" are only linguistically different from the appeals of modern labor leaders who reiterate the necessity for union.

The traditional ballads provide evidence to show that they arose from an area of social enlightenment sufficiently well developed to have produced songs of more overt protest than those extant; "Glasgerion," "The Golden Vanity," "Lord Delamere," "Botany Bay," "Van Diemen's Land," "The Cold Coast of Greenland," and many similar pieces are pregnant with social significance that could not conceivably have escaped the consciousness of their singers. But except for these hints of social consciousness

---

[1] Cf. "The Cutty Wren," p. 110, in which the wren is possibly a symbol of the people under feudal tyranny.

and some possible symbolic protest deeply imbedded in the traditional songs and ballads, and a few scattered manuscripts of pieces like "The Song of the Husbandman," nothing remains of the songs of protest that must have been produced by the social upheaval resulting from the decline of the feudal aristocracy and the rise of merchant capitalism, two movements that ground the working class between them. Unquestionably these songs disappeared for the same reasons that the body of song represented by the selections in this collection will not survive.

The first of these reasons is that man has been blessed with a potential of happiness that enables him not only to keep going under apparently intolerable present circumstances, but to forget the bitterness of past trials. Things never look so bad in retrospect, and the songs that were sung in anguish are likely to sound humiliating in time of serenity. Songs of protest also are usually spontaneous outbursts of resentment, composed without the careful artistry that is a requisite of songs that become traditional. And doubtless some songs of protest have been let die by early scholars who were likely to be less tolerant toward songs of social unrest than are modern collectors; protest songs are unpleasant and disturbing, and some feel that they and the conditions they reflect will go away if no attention is paid to them. But they cannot be ignored by anyone who realizes that folksongs are the reflection of people's thinking, and as such are affected by times and circumstances, cultural development, and changing environment. The poor we have always with us, and the discontent of the poor also, but the protest of the poor so rarely disturbs the tranquillity of social relationships over a long period of time that popular histories, concerned as they are largely with catastrophic events, are likely to underemphasize such constants as the discontent of the lower classes. This is one reason society again and again has felt that the flaws in the structure were at last widening into cracks, and that the world was going to ruin. It is easy to feel in such circumstances that a rash of protest song among the discontented is an abnormal phenomenon, unprecedented in ages past, and therefore possibly caused by the infiltration of guileful men who use folk expression to further their own insidious ends. The contemporary body of songs of discontent, which will have vanished by the time the next generation composes its expressions of protest, prompted one writer to observe that

... there seems ... to be a new movement, a kind of ground swell, inspired by David-like motives: "everyone in distress, everyone that was in debt, and everyone that was discontented, gathered themselves unto him, and he became a captain over them." Those that have a complaint are being brought together under the guise of an interest in the several folk arts, as being the folk, who banded together and uttering their lamentations can change our social picture. The truest values of folklore, which are entertainment for the participants, or as the materials for cultural studies by the scholar, are completely lost or perverted.[2]

It will generally be agreed that entertainment is the great constant in the production of folksay, but there are variables also operative in the process. To understand the people who produce folksongs, and thereby to understand the songs themselves, it is essential to consider all the songs that emanate from them, the disturbing as well as the complacent, those that carry a message as well as those written simply for diversion. To conclude that the need for entertainment is the only force that inspires the composition of folksong is to hold a very unworthy opinion of the folk.

Many songs of protest have been and are being lost because of the insufficiency of a definition. The 226 of these songs now reproduced in full or in fragment in this collection have been selected from more than two thousand similar pieces of American origin. What part of the extant songs of protest is represented by these two thousand is difficult to estimate; possibly one-third, possibly one-tenth. Every day of even desultory search turns up a few more. What percentage they represent of the songs that have been lost is impossible even to guess. There can be no question that many thousands of songs of social and economic protest have existed, and do exist, but except for parenthetical mention no cognizance has been taken of them by the scholars who collect and codify productions of the folk and of the conscious artist. Every song, poem, or piece of prose must be classified either as folk or conscious art, but these songs are in the position of an

[2] Thelma G. James, "Folklore and Propaganda," *Journal of American Folklore*, vol. 61 (1948), p. 311.

illegitimate child, unrecognized and unwanted by either group. They are not literature, in the strict sense of the term; indeed, few could be considered even infra-literary. There is no quarrel therefore with literary historians who fail to class them with productions of conscious art. But since they emanate from the same people who have written and sung and preserved ballads like "Young Charlotte" and "The Little Mohea," it is not preposterous to group them with folksong; yet only a handful have appeared in recognized collections. When uncounted thousands of songs current among the folk are permitted to vanish because they do not qualify under the terms of a definition, it is time to question the usefulness of that definition.

Folklorists do not agree on what constitutes folksong (and that in itself casts doubt on the validity of traditional definitions), but most attempts to arrive at a definition embody the criteria of these examples:

Folk song is a body of song in the possession of the people, passed on by word of mouth from singer to singer, not learned from books or from print.[3]
. . . the term "folk" may not justly be applied to a song unless that song shows evidence of having been subjected to the processes of oral tradition for a reasonable period of time. The appearance of a song in different versions or variants, textual or musical, in the absence of any suspicion of self-conscious altering or tampering would generally be accepted as pretty conclusive proof that a song is a genuine folk-song.[4]
Genuine folk songs are not static, but are in a state of flux; they have been handed down through a fair period of time, and all sense of their authorship and origin has been lost.[5]

A conflate definition of folksong to which most authorities would subscribe would contain as essentials the following qualifications: that the song have lost its identity as a consciously composed piece; that it have undergone verbal changes during oral transmission; and that it have been sung for an appreciable period of time, let us say two generations. This would be a defini-

[3] Robert Winslow Gordon, *Folk Songs of America*, New York, 1938, p. 3.
[4] Arthur Kyle Davis, *Traditional Ballads of Virginia*, Cambridge, 1929, p. xxii.
[5] Louise Pound, *American Ballads and Songs*, New York, 1922, p. xiii.

tion of considerable liberality, for earlier definitions were even
more restrictive. For example, as late as 1915 John Lomax wrote:

> Have we any American ballads? Let us frankly confess that, accord-
> ing to the definitions of the best critics of the ballad, we have none
> at all.[6]

It is hardly necessary to demonstrate the inadequacy of a definition that would deny America any native folk ballads, but the
inadequacy of the more generally accepted definitions is less
obvious, though scholars are continually aware of it. For instance,
Mellinger Henry, finding a number of pieces current among the
Southern mountain folk that did not meet the requirements
imposed by traditional definitions of folksong, discarded the term
altogether and titled his collection *Songs Sung in the Southern
Appalachians.*[7]

Early in the process of assembling this study, the obstacle of
definition had to be faced, since one or more of the criteria
of traditional interpretations of folksong disqualified most of the
songs chosen as illustrations. Songs of protest are by their very
nature ephemeral; most are occasional songs that lose their meaning when the events for which they were composed are forgotten,
or displaced by greater crises. Since many are parodies of well-
known popular songs or adaptations of familiar folk melodies,
they forfeited another attribute of traditional songs—at least one
widely known identifying tune. Except for the very simple ones
("We Shall Not Be Moved") and the very best ones ("Union
Maid") they are likely to become forgotten quickly because it is
easier to set to the basic tune new words more relevant to immediate issues and circumstances than it is to remember the old.
And the songs cannot lose their sense of authorship, because they
rarely outlive their composers.

Expediency—in this case, avoidance of contention—recommended abandoning the term "folk" in identifying the status of
these songs. But evading so fundamental a question is both impracticable and pusillanimous. If there is a choice to be made
between rejecting a definition which excludes so great a body of
material and rejecting the songs, there can be no hesitation in

[6] "Some Types of American Folk Song," *Journal of American Folklore,* vol. 28
(1915), p. 1.
[7] London, 1934.

deciding which must go. But rejecting an established definition simply because it will not work with a particular class of song is indefensible; the definition must be demonstrably fallacious. The mere fact that it does exclude so many songs proceeding from the folk is sufficient reason for questioning its validity, but there are other reasons for considering it insufficient. The requirement of persistence—that a song must be sung by the folk for a "reasonable" or "fair" period of time—is a gauge of popularity, not of authenticity. It excludes from folksong nearly all Negro secular songs, which are so slight that they have no more chance than a scrap of conversation to become traditional. A song may become traditional by remaining popular among the folk for a number of years, but its status as a folksong in most cases was determined the day it was composed. The folk may receive a popular song composed by a conscious artist and take possession of it, and thus it may become a folksong by adoption. "The Kentucky Miners' Dreadful Fight" became a folksong the moment Aunt Molly Jackson scribbled it on a piece of paper;[8] "Barbara Allen" was not a folksong until the folk had worn off its music-hall veneer. The requirement of transmissional changes is hardly more convincing than that of persistence. Many if not most of the changes that a folksong undergoes as it is passed from one singer to another are the result of imperfect hearing. If a thoughtless singer reproduces "pipe in his jaw" as the senseless "pips in his paw" or "the strong darts of Cupid" as "streamlets dark acoople,"[9] should his carelessness be accepted—even required—as a hallmark of genuine folksong? By this reasoning Shakespeare was on his way to becoming a folk artist the afternoon the pirates first spirited out of the Globe those stol'n and surreptitious texts that Heminges and Condell complained about. Like the qualification of oral transmission, the requirement of transmissional changes is valid only as a proof that the folk have taken possession of a song; it should not be considered as a criterion in itself.

A new definition must be made which will include evanescent Negro songs, hillbilly songs like Jimmie Rodgers' blue yodels which the folk have accepted, sentimental pieces like "The Fatal

[8] If the folk are in complete possession of a song, the mere fact that it is written down does not revoke its authenticity.

[9] Emelyn Elizabeth Gardner and Geraldine Jencks Chickering, *Ballads and Songs of Southern Michigan*, Ann Arbor, 1939, p. 22 f.

Wedding,"[10] and songs of social and economic protest. It must
be a definition of greater flexibility than traditional interpretations of "folk," yet rigid enough to distinguish folksong from
material on the lowest level of conscious art, like popular song.
It must be built on the solid base that folksongs are songs of the
folk; its qualifications should be seen as nothing more than tests
by which full folk possession can be determined. "This is what a
folk song realy is the folks composes there own songs about there
own lifes an there home folks that live around them," writes
Aunt Molly Jackson, cutting ruthlessly away the pedantry that
has confused most learned definitions. There is little that can be
added to Aunt Molly's definition of folksong except a clarification
of terms. "The folks composes": if an individual is the sole author
of a folksong he must speak not for himself but for the folk community as a whole, and in the folk idiom; he must not introduce
ideas or concepts that are uncommon, nor may he indelibly im-
press his own individuality upon the song. His function is not
that of a consciously creative artist, but that of a spokesman for
the community, an amanuensis for the illiterate, or, to put it more
precisely, for the inarticulate. It is impersonality of authorship,
not anonymity of authorship, that is a requisite of genuine folksong. "There own songs": the songs must be in the possession of
the folk, communally owned, so that any member of the folk may
feel that they are his to change if he wishes; they should not be
alien to the degree that the folk singer hesitates to change a word
or a phrase that needs alteration; they should be so completely
of the folk that any singer may convince himself that he is their
author.[11] "About there own lifes and there home folks that live
around them": the folksong should be concerned with the interests of the folk, whatever they may be. In the songs with which
this book is occupied, the interests are social, economic, occupa-
tional; their clichés are those of distressful bread rather than
sumptuous habiliments. The interests of the folk are, within their
own universe, infinite; and collectors must assiduously guard

[10] Most collectors cannot overcome their sophisticated repugnance to sentimen-
tality, but if the folk have not yet purged their newer songs of mawkish sympathy
for ravished working girls, abandoned wives, and frozen match girls, it is not within
the authority of collectors to impose such enlightenment upon them.

[11] Most collectors have had the amusing experience of meeting a singer who
vehemently claims authorship of a song that was popular years before his birth.

against disqualifying any because of preconceived personal judgments. If a folk composer wishes to make an imitative ballad about kings and queens and lords and ladies whom neither he nor his great-great-great-grandfather ever saw, he is free to do so; if he wishes to write a blues about a mean mistreatin' railroad daddy (about whom he has much more business writing), he is free to do so; but he may not write about esoteric or advanced concepts that the folk community as a whole is not familiar with. When the college boy changed the nonsense refrain of "Sweet Betsy from Pike" from "hoodle dang fol de di do, hoodle dang fol de day," to "Sing tangent cotangent cosecant cosine," he made an adaptation outside the folk domain. A folksong, therefore, is a song concerned with the interests of the folk, and in the complete possession of the folk. All other qualifications, such as the requirement of transmissional changes, are to be considered only as helpful tests in establishing either or both of the basic conditions of the definition.[12]

But who are the folk? is the inevitable question. Some writers contend that we no longer have a folk, but what really is meant is that their definition of "folk," like their definition of "folksong," is invalid. "Folk" in our culture is an economic term; when the milkmaid put down her pail and went down the river to the cotton mill, she did not necessarily cease to be a member of the folk. It is true that the infiltration of the radio, the automobile, television, and other blessings of modern civilization into former cultural pockets is educating the old agricultural folk out of existence, but a new folk, the industrial community, is taking its place. The modern folk is most often the unskilled worker, less often the skilled worker in industrial occupations. He is the CIO worker, not the AFL worker, who is labor's aristocrat. This new folk community is a precarious one, liable to be educated out of the folk culture almost overnight, but it is the only folk we have, and should be respected as such. The mine community as a whole is still folk; the textile community similarly; part of the farm com-

[12] This definition excludes from folksong many pieces included in this collection, such as most of the broadsides, the more turgid IWW songs, the productions of People's Songs composers, and songs of the more cultured unions. But since most of these are on the periphery of folksong, there is a possibility that some of them may yet be taken over by the folk. They are of interest also in establishing that amorphous line that separates folk material from conscious art.

munity is still folk; the seaman has almost left the folk culture. Individuals in these communities may have acquired sufficient acculturation to take them out of the folk, but their enlightenment has so far not leavened the entire group. If we do not accept people like Aunt Molly Jackson, Ella May Wiggins, and Woody Guthrie as the folk, then we have no folk, and we have no living folksong.

THE GENESIS OF THE PROTEST FOLKSONGS

These are the struggle songs of the people. They are outbursts of bitterness, of hatred for the oppressor, of determination to endure hardships together and to fight for a better life. Whether they are ballads composed and sung by an individual, or rousing songs improvised on the picket line, they are imbued with the feeling of communality, or togetherness. They are songs of unity, and therefore most are songs of the union. To understand the area of protest out of which they grew, they should be read and sung with a history of organized labor open beside them, preferably a history which shows that American unionism was idealistic as well as practical, that it was class conscious as well as job conscious, for economic protest is often synonymous with social protest. From the time of America's first strike—that of the Philadelphia journeymen printers in 1786—unions have fought not only for better wages but also for an improvement in the social status of their members. The introductory material which prefaces each group of songs in this collection is an integral part of the songs themselves, for it represents the area of protest which produced them, the conditions without which the songs would not have been made. Necessarily the groups are not closely coherent, for they are selections merely, representatives of a continuous utterance of protest. To perceive the continuity of American social and economic protest, one should bring to these songs a thorough familiarity with the social evolution of the United States, and particularly of the labor movement.

In his *Coal Dust on the Fiddle*, George Korson advances the thesis that in the bituminous industry the production of song paralleled the fortunes of the union.[13] In times of hardship, he

13 Philadelphia, 1943, p. 285.

contends, there is little activity among the balladeers; a feeling of apathy and depression settles on the bards, and they cease singing. This generalization may be true of labor minstrelsy as a whole, but it is not true of the struggle songs. Unions most prolific in songs and ballads of protest are those which are fighting for existence; tranquillity in the organization brings a corresponding lull in songs of discontent. The American Federation of Labor, a traditionally peaceful union, is virtually barren in songs which mark its path in the progress of unionism; on the other hand, the Industrial Workers of the World—the Wobblies—whose active life was comparatively short but turbulent, have contributed many songs to the history of militant labor organization. But even in the militant unions there is little singing except in time of conflict. Meetings normally are perfunctory, and if any singing is done it stops with adjournment, unless the last tune sung was a particularly catchy one. Walter Sassaman, regional director of the United Automobile Workers, an organization which has produced more songs in its comparatively brief existence than any other industrial union, said, "You have no idea of what meetings in our locals are like. Generally the men discuss shop news; every once in a while there are local issues to talk about—and that's the whole meeting. Most locals do not have even a phonograph to play records on."[14] But on the picket line the UAW has sung, in addition to the general union songs, nearly fifty vigorous songs of their own composition.

The evidence of outside influence, frequently of persons of some education if not sophistication, upon the folk-song makers has antagonized many folklorists who have had to make a decision about the authenticity of modern songs of protest. That there has been some influence is undoubted; that it has been necessary is at least probable. As Oscar Wilde said, "Misery and poverty are so absolutely degrading and exercise such a paralyzing effect over the nature of men that no class is ever really conscious of its own suffering. They have to be told of it by other people, and they often entirely disbelieve them." Most of the composers of these songs whose identity we know have been stimulated in their protest by some orienting influence. Aunt Molly Jackson got her social enlightenment not only from her "hard tough struggles"

[14] Quoted in *People's Songs*, April, 1946, p. 5.

but from her father, a preacher and union organizer. The Bible pointed up the inequalities of modern American society to John Handcox, another preacher and one of the most prolific composers among the Negro sharecroppers. Woody Guthrie gives us a first-hand account of his introduction to the larger perspective of social injustice:

> They [two Oklahoma organizers] made me see why I had to keep going around and around with my guitar making up songs and singing. I never did know that the human race was this big before. I never did really know that the fight had been going on so long and so bad. I never had been able to look out over and across the slum section nor a sharecropper farm and connect it up with the owner and the landlord and the guards and the police and the dicks and the bulls and the vigilante men with their black sedans and their sawed-off shotguns.[15]

The degree of outside influence can be estimated by reference to the object of protest. If it is the immediate purveyor of injustice, the Negro prisoner's captain or the miner's gun thug, there has been little outside stimulation; if the song contains lines like "I hate the capitalist system," as one does, there is a radical in the woodpile. But the injection of social enlightenment does not lift the singer out of the folk; an awareness of the degradation of one's environment is not culture. A textile worker can be hungry and know why without being educated. Agitators and organizers do no more than stimulate protest that has been simmering inarticulately in the singer.

THE STRUCTURE OF THE MODERN PROTEST SONG[16]

Making a union song in the rural South is a simple process of taking a gospel hymn, changing "I" to "We" and "God" to "CIO."[17] Orthodox clergymen may deplore the practice as a sign of modern degeneracy, and musicologists may interpret it as

---

[15] *American Folksong,* New York, 1947, p. 5.

[16] The generalizations in this section do not always apply to Negro songs.

[17] The union in the Southern folk community has become a sort of extension of the Church. Joe Glazer, a textile union organizer and composer, recalls a Georgia strike in which a picket line stand was called the "ministers' post" because there were four ministers on it.

an indication of immaturity in the union singing movement,[18] but labor has used established songs from the earliest times to carry its protest, and in so doing continues in a tradition that is as old as English folksong itself. William of Malmesbury, writing in the early twelfth century, tells of his ancient predecessor, Aldhelm, standing beside a bridge, singing secular ditties until he had gained the attention of passers-by, when he gradually began to introduce religious ideas into his songs. Twelve hundred years later Jack Walsh, who had never heard of Aldhelm or his biographer, posted his Wobbly band beside a highway and sang religious songs until he had gained the attention of passers-by, when he gradually began to introduce secular ideas into his songs.

Early American broadside collections abound with topical parodies of "Yankee Doodle"; the songster era shows a gradual widening of selection, with catchy tunes like that of "Villikins and His Dinah" predominating; in the modern period there is scarcely a folk or popular tune that has not been used as the base of a union song. Some are simple; a very effective picket-line vehicle of opprobrium was made by substituting "scabs" for "worms" in the children's favorite scare-chant:

> *The scabs crawl in*
> *The scabs crawl out*
> *The scabs crawl under and all about,*

repeated to distraction. Some are complicated, like this parody of a popular song, heard during the motion picture workers' strike in Hollywood in 1948:

SWINGIN' ON A SCAB

> *A scab is an animal that walks on his knees;*
> *He sniffs every time the bosses sneeze.*
> *His back is brawny but his brain is weak,*
> *He's just plain stupid with a yellow streak.*
> *But if you don't care whose back it is you stab,*
> *Go right ahead and be a scab.*

> REFRAIN: *Are you gonna stick on the line*
> *Till we force the bosses to sign?*

[18] An early critic of labor's songs of protest observed, "The significant thing about such of these 'songs of discontent' as are of native origin is that they are nearly all parodies [of gospel hymns]. American labor is just beginning to express itself."—Harry F. Ward, "Songs of Discontent." *Methodist Review,* September, 1913, p. 726.

This is your fight, brother, and mine,

—or would you rather be a goon?

A goon is an animal that's terribly shy;
He can't stand to look you in the eye.
He rides to work on the cops' coattails
And wears brass knuckles to protect his nails.
But if your head is like the hole in a spittoon,
Go right ahead and be a goon.

—or would you rather be a stool?

A stool is an animal with long hairy ears;
He runs back with everything he hears.
He's no bargain though he can be bought,
And though he's slippery he still gets caught.
But if your brain's like the rear end of a mule,
Go right ahead and be a stool.

And so on. But parodies of popular tunes are usually written by composers of some sophistication, and the impression they make on the workers who sing them is one of amused appreciation for the cleverness of the writer. The element of protest is secondary, if it is present at all. The genuine songs of protest which borrow melodies are written to the tunes of folksongs. Possibly because of the influence of the folk tune the protest song of unquestioned authenticity is written in the ballad stanza, riming abcb.[19] There are other striking signs of antiquity in the songs originating in rural areas. Meter is prevailingly accentual, and there is common use of anacrusis, though sometimes these initial extrametrical syllables exceed the norm of two. In Aunt Molly Jackson's "Poor Miners' Farewell," for example, the normal line reads,

They leave their dear wives and little ones too,

But one abnormal line reads,

They leave their wives and children to be thrown
out on the street.

This anacrusistic material is sung usually on a rising tone which builds up to the normal first melodic accent.

[19] Negro protest songs, like the Negro work songs, are usually in the short ballad stanza or long couplet form.

The Anglo-Saxon gleeman must have chanted *Beowulf* in much the same manner that the modern folk and hillbilly singer chants the *talking blues,* a rhythmical form which has been the basis for a great number of songs of discontent. Basically the stanza consists of a quatrain with four-accent lines, riming aabb, prevailingly iambic, which are chanted with exaggerated 2/4 rhythm to guitar chordings. An essential appendage to each stanza is an irregular passage of spoken phrases, incoherent and laconic. These may consist of from one to as many as a dozen phrases clarifying the preceding stanza and stating the singer's personal reaction to the thought it contains.

CHANTED: *Most men don't talk what's eating their minds*
About the different ways of dying down here in the mines;
But every morning we walk along and joke
About mines caving in and the dust and the smoke—
SPOKEN: *—One little wild spark of fire blowing us skyhigh and crooked—One little spark blowing us cross-eyed and crazy*
—Up to shake hands with all of the Lord's little angels.

Less often the stanza may be rimed abab:

I swung onto my old guitar;
Train come a-rumblin' down the track;
I got shoved into the wrong damn car
With three grass widows on my back.
—Two of them lookin' for home relief
—Other one just investigatin'.

Although some folk composers maintain that the words are made up first and then fitted to a tune, the reverse process is more usual. Often the resemblance is so close that the original is easily perceptible through a number of adaptations. Typical examples of this pervasive original are the self-commiserative songs derived from the popular nineteenth century sacred song, "Life is Like a Mountain Railroad":

Life is like a mountain railroad
With an engineer that's brave;
He must make the run successful
From the cradle to the grave.

Round the bend, and through the tunnel,
Never falter, never fail;
Keep your hand upon the throttle,
And your eye upon the rail.

CHORUS: *Blessed Saviour, thou wilt guide us*
Till we reach that blissful shore,
Where the angels wait to join us
In their peace forevermore.

Early in the present century the bituminous miners were singing:

A miner's life is like a sailor's
'Board a ship to cross the wave;
Every day his life's in danger,
Still he ventures being brave.
Watch the rocks, they're falling daily,
Careless miners always fail;
Keep your hand upon the dollar,
*And your eye upon the scales.**

Meanwhile, the textile workers were polygenetically adapting the hymn to their own purposes:

A weaver's life is like an engine,
Coming 'round the mountain steep;
We've had our ups and downs a-plenty
And at night we cannot sleep;
Very often flag your firer
When his head is bending low;
You may think that he is loafing,
But he's doing all he knows.

CHORUS: *Soon we'll end this life of weaving,*
Soon we'll reach a better shore,
Where we'll rest from filling batteries,
We won't have to weave no more.

Picket-line songs from the South are likely to be zippered adaptations of repetitive gospel hymns. The basic stanza line of "Roll the Chariot on" is "If the Devil gets in the way we'll roll it over him." Taken over by the picket-line marchers, the "chariot"

---

* A reference to the operators' frequent practice of underweighing the miners' coal cars before the unions succeeded in appointing a union checkweighman to relieve the miners of the necessity of keeping their "eye upon the scales."

becomes "union" and the "Devil," logically and metrically, becomes the boss, whatever his surname might be. There are scores of these zippered hymns that have attained some stability, of which the most popular are "Roll the Union on" and "We Shall Not Be Moved." For years the only adaptation of the latter was in the first line:

> Baldwin is a stinker,
> We shall not be moved;
> Baldwin is a stinker,
> We shall not be moved.
> Just like a tree that's planted by the water,
> We shall not be moved.

But recently the adaptation has become complete:

> Baldwin is a stinker,
> He should be removed;
> Baldwin is a stinker,
> He should be removed.
> Just like a fly that's sticking in the butter,
> He should be removed.

"We Shall Not Be Moved" may be used as an illustration of another type of song—the song-ballad. Basically a song, it tells a story by the accumulation of key stanza lines:

> Frank Keeny is our leader,
> We shall not be moved,
> etc.
> Mr. Lucas has his scabs and thugs . . .
> Keeny got our houses bonded . . .

Unfortunately it has not been possible to include in this book examples of a large class of protest songs, some of which are unapproached for bitterness, anger, vehemence, and sincerity, because they are unprintable. The conditions that lead to protest are never pleasant, and the reactions to such conditions are in kind. On the propriety of cursing to express protest, Woody Guthrie reflects:

The prophets cussed and they raved plenty, because they was out there in the hills and hollers yelling and echoing the Real Voice of the Real People, the poor working class, and the farmers, and the down and out. They tell me down in Oklahoma that the Indian language ain't got no cuss words in it. Well, wait till they get a little hungrier and raggedier. They'll work up some.

Some of these unprintable songs are concentrated venom. One apostrophe to a boss begins:

> *You low-life[20] trifling bastard,*
> *You low-life thieving snitch;*
> *You selfish, greedy, bastardly thief,*
> *You God-damned son of a bitch.*

And that's about as far as it can be carried.

Somewhat less offensive are the songs which substitute nonsense words for words that are not generally used in polite company. The bawdy version of "The Derby Ram" is familiar to most people conversant with folksong; this too has been taken up by the composers of protest songs:

> *When I went down to Frankfort town*
> *Many workers I did pass;*
> *'Twas there I saw the Governor*
> *And I kicked him in the Hocus Pocus Sonny Bocus.*
> *If you don't believe me*
> *And if you think I lie,*
> *Just go down to Frankfort town*
> *And you'll do the same as I.*

Except for the exclusion of certain offensive words, editing in this work has been limited to the correction of obvious misspellings, and to the arrangement in stanzaic form of some pieces which appeared in manuscript written as prose. In selecting from the two thousand English-language songs that formed the basis of this collection, I have sought first to choose songs typical of their immediate area of protest; when a further choice had to be made, I indulged in the exercise of literary evaluation, although to demand literary worth of folksongs is to deny them one characteristic of folk material—unsophistication. There are many inarticulate poets among the folk, but few are mute Miltons; to look for work

[20] "Low-life" is a euphemism substituted for the original adjectives.

on the Miltonic level in folksong is to bring it to the level of conscious art.

The temptation exerted upon every editor of folk material, to "fix up" corrupt lines and limping meter and to complete fragmentary songs, I have resisted by keeping before me Aunt Molly Jackson's criticism of folklorists she has known:

The reason most of thease calectors of folk songs changes an rearanges the songs is bacouse they colect a verce or 2 of a song then they try to compose something to add an what they compose there selfs is not true and it Just dont make sense.

1. An historical survey

Our songs are singing history

A history of America, vivid, dramatic, and personal, could be written with the songs of its people. Much of this history would be fittingly exultant, even glorious, in celebration of the birth of a nation founded on ideals of personal freedom; but much also would be pitched to a mournful tone, for the birth of American democracy was an agonizing travail for many people at the bottom of the economic and social pyramid. To write such a history would be a worthy undertaking for a scholar with the ability and temerity to attempt it; certainly it is a task beyond the comprehension of this study. The songs in this chapter and the incidents that produced them are samplings of the rich material that awaits further exploration; they are illustrations of but a few of the crises that the American people faced with the support of humble song.

None of the songs in this section makes any pretension to literature, and few could under the most liberal definition be considered as folksong. Most are broadsides, a category of literary marginalia that has been held in small esteem by scholars. One authority unequivocally called them "rubbish,"[1] and in a literary sense they are perhaps deserving of the oblivion from which they have been briefly resurrected, but they are valuable as evidence of an awareness of oppression among the people that must have been expressed in songs now lost. If we may judge by the analogy of contemporary folksongs which form the basis of succeeding chapters, there must have been a rich body of nontraditional folk protest material from the early periods of American history, but these meritless broadsides and hundreds like them are all that remain.

THE ARISTOCRACY AND LIMITED
TENURE OF OFFICE

Upon the shoulders of the framers of the Constitution fell the responsibility of putting it into effect; but many of these men, belonging to the upper classes, were distrustful of the common people and feared that the document they had chosen to guide the new nation was too dangerously democratic. In those days of uncertainty the wealthy merchants and the old colonial aristocracy sought methods of perpetuating their ascendency; consequently their party, the Federalists, aroused opposition among the less privileged classes, and though they held power during Washington's two administrations, the Federalists felt more and more the surging power of the people against them.

The French Revolution gave impetus to the fight against intrenched aristocracy, and when Washington retired after his second term as president, the Republicans (as the Anti-Federalists now called themselves) unstoppered their criticism and rebellion, confined before by their love and respect for Washington, and made John Adams' term of office a stormy one. Finally the Alien and Sedition Acts, enacted by the Federalists as a weapon against the Republicans, provided the new party with a political issue in the presidency campaign of 1800. Unanimously they chose Thomas

---

[1] George Lyman Kittredge, *English and Scottish Popular Ballads*, Boston and New York, 1904, p. xxviii.

Jefferson, the advocate of the common man, to be their candidate, and thus gave the United States one of its greatest presidents.

The composer of the following song must have rejoiced in the overthrow of the party whose spokesman, Alexander Hamilton, arguing in favor of a life term for senators during the Constitutional Convention, exclaimed, "All communities divide themselves into the few and the many. The first are rich and well-born and the other the mass of the people who seldom judge or determine right."[2] But the people had something else to say.

EVERY MAN HIS OWN POLITICIAN

Let every man of Adam's line
In social contact freely join
To extirpate monarchic power,
That kings may plague the earth no more.

As pow'r results from you alone,
Ne'er trust it on a single throne,
Kings oft betray their sacred trust,
And crush their subjects in the dust.

Nor yet confide in men of show,
Aristocrats reduce you low;
Nobles, at best, are fickle things,
And oft, far worse than cruel kings.

Nobles combine in secret fraud,
(Tho in pretence for public good)
To frame a law the most unjust,
And sink the people down to dust.

When laws are fram'd, the poor must lie,
Distrest beneath the nobles' eye;
Unpity'd there, to waste their breath,
In fruitless prayers 'till free'd by death.

A year is long enough to prove
A servant's wisdom, faith and love.
Release him from temptation then
And change the post to other men.

Now is the prime important hour
The people may improve their pow'r,
To stop aristocratic force,
And walk in reason's peaceful course.

[2] Charles A. and Mary R. Beard, *The Rise of American Civilization*, New York, 1945, Vol. I, p. 353.

Choose all your servants once a year,
With strict reserve and nicest care,
And if they once abuse their place,
Reward them with deserv'd disgrace.

—Broadside in American Antiquarian Society,
Worcester, Massachusetts. *ca.* 1801.

IMPRISONMENT FOR DEBT

An integral phase of the crusade against the establishment of a native aristocracy was the struggle of the working people to keep from being forced down into an American lower class. Economic servitude in the sweatshops created by the new factory system was leading inevitably to social enslavement as the workers, laboring for existence wages, began to sink from poverty into pauperism. But not only economic forces were crushing the working class into a separate social estate; judicial pressure was also exerted upon them. In 1830 five out of every six prisoners in New England and the Middle States jails were debtors, most of whom owed less than $20. Clearly, the law providing imprisonment for debt was a law of the poor, and was consequently an instrument for their debasement.

In 1817 Martin Van Buren, responding to the pressure from labor leaders who had made the grievance of debt imprisonment the principal issue in their pleas for reform, introduced in the New York legislature the first bill for complete repeal of the law. Five years later Colonel Richard M. Johnson, himself a former debtor, introduced a similar bill in the United States Senate, and persistently introduced it every year till in 1832, with the support of President Jackson, the abolition of imprisonment for debt in federal courts became law. The states quickly followed the lead of the government, and in a decade the working man was free of this humiliating debtors' law.

Johnson's part in their liberation was remembered by the laboring people. In 1830 he was widely supported for president in the forthcoming election by those who felt that Jackson had so far shown no particular concern for labor, and in 1836 he was elected vice-president in Van Buren's administration.

In 1815 freedom from this class law was still beyond the vision of one unfortunate whose note had been bought by a professional

creditor. Languishing in the Salem jail, he poured out his viru-
lence against the "Shark." Few broadsides retain so well the bitter
protest of this 138-year-old lament, which is interesting also for the
slang it contains—"hush money" for a bribe, and "jug" for a jail.

THE CHARLES TOWN LAND SHARK

The Charles Town Shark my Note he bought,
For to make money as he thought;
The debt must lose, the cost must pay,
Unless the Shark must run away.

He's like the Shark, amazing fierce,
Such land Sharks may they be more scarce,
A greater Shark may catch him too,
Then he will have what is his due.

Like the great Shark, seeks to devour
All that may fall within his power,
Austere, morose, and Savage too,
All you who know, is this not true?

His pay but once that will not do,
He wants it twice, they say 'tis true;
A viler wretch can there be found,
If you search the world around?

He likes hush money, as they say,
Give him enough and he will stay,
For a small sum he will not wait,
Because his avarice is too great.

He's avaricious as the grave,
In that a portion he will have,
I think no one will sigh or mourn
When to the grave this Shark is borne.

His unjust gain his soul will haunt,
No pleasure to him will it grant;
His guilty conscience will it sting,
Down to the grave Death will him bring.

On Negro Hill they say he goes,
Why is that for you may suppose.
Why doth this Shark these Blacks disgrace
A Blacker mind a frowning face.

'Tis said he once was very sick,
In consequence of a bad trick.
A certain Nurse of him took care,
And she let out the whole affair.

He boasts he's rich—most wretched too,
What is there bad he will not do?
A vagabond I think he'll be
The day will come when you shall see.

In human misery he delights,
He scarcely barks before he bites;
I sought compassion, none could find,
Because there was none in his mind.

In dirty business he is seen,
His conduct is amazing mean,
His wickedness to be portray'd,
Volumes before you must be laid.

To gratify his wicked mind,
Many in jail have been confin'd,
Vile wretched Shark, must pine away,
His debts must lose, the cost must pay.

Despis'd by all, where he is known,
Compassion he has never shown.
I hope the Shark will leave no seed,
For of Land Sharks there is no need.

Rejoice, poor man, this Shark must die,
And be as poor as you or I;
He lives despis'd, his name shall stink,
And into the lasting contempt sink.

I'm not discouraged nor dismay'd,
Although a Prisoner I was made;
My mind is tranquil and serene,
Though in the limits I am seen.

He said in jail I ought to stay,
Until my flesh did rot away;
The Laws thro' mercy are more just,
The Shark to me has done his worst.

No other business does he doe,
Than to buy notes and people sue;
Both men and women share the same,
Ah! Wretched Shark! Where is his shame.

If the Coat the Shark doth suit,
And that it will, none doth dispute,
Then he may wear it if he will,
At home or upon Negro Hill.

Compos'd on board the "Salem Jug,"
If once lock'd in 'twill hold you snug;
'Twill hold you fast till time shall say,
Now let the Prisoner go his way.

—Broadside in Harris Collection,
Brown University. 1815.

DISSOLUTION OF THE LANDED ARISTOCRACY

The manifest destiny of the United States as a symbol of democratic ideals is due to a fortuitous coincidence—the occurrence of the American Revolution in a brief period when the entire civilized world was imbued to a degree never before or since paralleled with an interest in personal freedom and the nobility of the common man. But the excesses of the French Revolution (which displaced the American rebellion as the great representation of democratic principles) convinced many liberals that the investment of government in hereditary aristocrats had been indeed divinely inspired, and world opinion turned again toward the right. In America the trend was noticeable; sentiment among many prominent people favored the establishment of a titled nobility, though most conceded the inexpediency of endangering the new nation by seeking to legalize such an aristocracy. The people who would have formed this projected American upper class, however, almost managed to perpetuate their ascendancy by control over the land through which the franchise had been traditionally limited; but little by little the crusaders against the restrictions imposed by landholders began to realize the ideals for which the Revolution was fought.

The emergence of American democracy was not a continuous process, but a series of localized movements, impelled by oppressed groups who saw their own situation incompatible with the principles of democracy. And as always, when discontent was crystallized into action, songs of protest began to emanate from the people. Two such struggles to realize the innate rights of man were the Dorr Rebellion and the New York Anti-Rent War.

The anti-rent war

No event in American history illustrates more vividly the amazing stubbornness with which aristocracy in the United States died than the New York rent war that flared with intermittent violence through nearly forty years of the mid-nineteenth century. The oppression that the Down-Renters fought against was not merely the superficial ill-treatment that is usually associated with the landlord-tenant relationship, but feudalism — feudalism with all its medieval ramifications, devoid only of its traditional nomenclature. It is even more significant that the issue was never completely resolved, for "Today some upstate farmers still pay in cash the equivalent of the old reservations of wheat, fowls, and a day's service." [3]

The foundations of American feudalism were laid in 1639 when Kiliaen Van Rensselaer, a shrewd Dutch merchant, privateer, and speculator, obtained from the Dutch West India Company a charter giving him not only possession of large tracts of land in southeastern New York, but also baronial titles, authority to exercise full governmental control, and power to require fealty from the colonists in the form of labor and military servitude. When the Dutch possessions in the New World fell into the hands of the British, the patroon system was changed very little beyond the Anglicization of titles and the extension of the landed aristocracy through additional millions of acres in the Hudson River area. Even the American Revolution failed to disturb the serenity of the patroons' control beyond the deprivation of their baronial titles and a few of the privileges pertaining thereto.

The most important provisions of the colonial charter were perpetuated in a bill of sale drawn up for Stephen Van Rensselaer III by his brother-in-law, Alexander Hamilton. This contract, which became a model for other patroon leases, was only nominally a bill of sale, since it sold not the land but only its agricultural usufruct, reserving wood, mineral, and water rights, and privilege of free entry to the patroon. The "purchaser" (who had been enticed into settling the land by a seven-year free occupation) paid a yearly rent of a dozen bushels of wheat, several fowls, and a day's labor with horse and cart; and, furthermore, had to assume

---

[3] Henry Christman, *Tin Horns and Calico*, New York, 1945, p. 30.

all legal obligations such as taxes and road building. He was discouraged from selling the lease by a clause giving the landlord a transaction fee of one-quarter of the purchase price.

Despite these intolerable restrictions, there was little protest on the part of the tenants, since Rensselaer recognized the precariousness of his legal position and hesitated to jeopardize his ownership by forcing collection of unpaid rents. His heirs were not endowed with similar wisdom, however, and after Stephen's death in 1839 they began to dun recalcitrant tenants for the back rents. They met with immediate and violent opposition. The farmers dressed in outlandish costumes to prevent identification, painted their faces, gave themselves Indian names, and resisted almost every expedition of sheriff's deputies into the farm countries with violence.

The history of the next decade recounts a gradual extension of the passive rebellion through southern New York, and the emergence of educated leadership in the persons of such men as George Evans, Lawrence Van Deusen, Dr. Smith Boughton, and Thomas Devyr, who directed the protest into political channels. The controversy reached its zenith in the fall of 1845 when the "American Jeffreys," Judge Amasa Parker, engineered wholesale imprisonments of Anti-Rent leaders. The jails overflowed into log stockades, built especially to accommodate anticipated convictions of Down-Renters. Public opinion, outraged by the injustice of the convictions and the exceptionally severe sentences meted out by Parker, suddenly turned so sharply in favor of the Down-Renters that in 1845 Governor Silas Wright, who had been an implacable foe of the Anti-Rent forces, was coerced into directing the state legislature to end the leasehold system. In the same year a new state constitution was framed which presented the issue of new feudal leases and relaxed the worst provisions of the existing contracts. With this partial victory the solidarity of the Anti-Renters began to crumble and the tenants were lured into allowing their cause to become a political football which was promptly kicked to pieces between the Whigs and the Democrats. Although most of the landlords had capitulated after 1850, a few of the more obstinate ones sought refuge in the traditional bastions of reaction—the courts—and found there sufficient legal technicalities to keep the lease system alive, if not kicking. Sale of the properties to speculators who were more experienced in ruthlessness than the decadent aristocrats carried the war on a much smaller scale into the 1880's.

The three decades and more of violence produced a store of songs and ballads rich in quantity, if not in literary quality, which have been preserved in contemporary newspapers, journals, broadsides, and the memory of old farmers who remember the struggles and songs of their parents.

"THE END OF BIG BILL SNYDER," the most popular of the Anti-Rent songs sung throughout the period of violence, was written by a sympathizer named S. H. Foster, and celebrates the discomfiture of Bill Bill Snyder, a universally despised deputy sheriff who was imported by the landholders in 1841 to serve writs. While on one such foray into the hills he was captured by a band of "Indians" and soundly thrashed. In recording Snyder's death the song is faithful to poetic rather than factual truth.

THE END OF BIG BILL SNYDER

(Tune: "Old Dan Tucker")

The moon was shining silver bright;
The sheriff came in the dead of night;
High on a hill sat an Indian true,
And on his horn, this blast he blew—

REFRAIN: *Keep out of the way—big Bill Snyder—*
We'll tar your coat and feather your hide, Sir!

The Indians gathered at the sound,
Bill cocked his pistol—looked around—
Their painted faces, by the moon,
He saw, and heard that same old tune—

Says Bill, "This music's not so sweet
As I have heard—I think my feet
Had better be used;" and he started to run,
But the tin horn still kept sounding on,

"Legs! do your duty now," says Bill,
"There's a thousand Indians on the hill—
When they catch tories they tar their coats,
And feather their hides, and I hear the notes"—

And he thought that he heard the sound of a gun,
And he cried, in his fright, "Oh! my race is run!
Better had it been, had I never been born,
Than to come within the sound of that tin horn;"

And the news flew around, and gained belief,
That Bill was murdered by an Indian chief;
And no one mourned that Bill was slain,
But the horn sounded on, again and again—

Next day the body of Bill was found,
His writs were scattered on the ground,
And by his side a jug of rum,
Told how he to his end had come.

—From a handbill by S. H. Foster in Henry Christman,
Tins Horns and Calico, New York, 1945, p. 326.

The Dorr rebellion

One of the last strongholds of the limited franchise was
Rhode Island, where a small group of hereditary landholders
exercised almost a feudal control over the state under an old
charter issued by Charles II in 1663. This colonial charter, which
represented the state's constitution through the first half of the
nineteenth century, vested the sole right of government in the
original grantees, who extended the franchise over the years to
other owners of landed estates. By 1840 this antiquated system had
denied the right to participation in civil government to more than
half the adult male population of Rhode Island, and even the
small electorate remaining was so controlled by the residents of
the older communities that it was possible for the civil life of the
state to be determined by about one-tenth of its population.

From the last years of the eighteenth century progressive groups
had fought through legislative channels for a new charter, but the
government officials, representing exclusively the interests of the
landholders, ignored their efforts. Finally, extended-suffrage agitators decided that only direct, extra-legal action could remedy
the intolerable situation, and in 1840 the Rhode Island Suffrage
Association was formed, projecting itself into a "People's Party,"
which in 1842 elected its own legislature, with Thomas Wilson
Dorr as governor.

Like Franklin D. Roosevelt, Dorr (1805-54) was a patrician
who cast his lot with the plebeians. His father was a prosperous
manufacturer, and his family was firmly established in the higher
stratum of Rhode Island society. Again like Roosevelt, Dorr
graduated from Harvard and practiced law until his election to

the state legislature. Nominally a Whig, Dorr soon allied himself with the Democrats.

His election by the People's Party was met with resolute opposition by Samuel W. King, the landholders' governor-elect. Fortified by federal benediction, King declared martial law, imprisoned under his notorious "Algerine" edict large numbers of Dorr's followers, branded Dorr a traitor, and offered a large reward for his apprehension. After the defection of many of his intimidated supporters, Dorr surrendered to the landholders' government, was convicted of treason, and was sentenced to life imprisonment on June 27, 1844.

But public opinion was seething, and Dorr's release was forced the following year. The surrender of the government on the charter issue followed, and a constitutional charter, granting the people a practical suffrage law, was instituted. Dorr's civil rights were restored in 1851, but the year he spent in prison had broken his health, and he died in retirement in 1854.

The facetious "Rhode Island Algerines' Appeal to John Davis," ostensibly issuing from King's followers but in reality written by the suffragists, anticipated that Governor John Davis of Massachusetts would support Governor King's requisition to return Dorr should he flee to Massachusetts. The suffragists had the satisfaction of seeing Davis turned out of office at the next election in favor of Governor Morton, who upheld the principles on which the People's Party was founded. The contemptuous term "Algerine" derived from the Algerian pirates, whose enslavement of Americans early in the century had made them the object of national despite.

RHODE ISLAND ALGERINES' APPEAL TO JOHN DAVIS

(Tune: "Tippecanoe")

Prepare your forces, honest John—
Each man his sabre draw,
For oh! we fear a third attack
Of Thomas W. Dorr.

REFRAIN: *O dear! that dreadful Dorr!*
The traitor, Thomas Dorr—
We fear he'll take Rhode Island yet,
In spite of "Martial Law."

Another thing we greatly fear,
From what we've heard and saw—
That certain States would lend their aid
To help T. W. Dorr.

John Tyler too, once promised troops
To help us through the war;
But now we fear if called upon,
He'd prove a friend to Dorr.

Should Congress strictly scan our claims
We fear they'd find a flaw
That would displace our government,
And yield the reins to Dorr.

We'll own to you deeds have been done
Licensed by "martial law"
That would have hung the followers
Of Thomas W. Dorr.

We've tried by art and stratagem
To rule with "order and law"
Yet there are those who boldly talk
About their Governor Dorr.

The ladies too, have swelled his ranks
And threatened swords to draw,
They'll curse the Charterists to the face
For what they've done to Dorr.

Clambakes and meetings they appoint
Regardless of the law
And resolutions boldly pass
To favor Thomas Dorr.

Though Algerines have threaten'd them
Inflictions of the law,
They do not fear the cannon's mouth
When advocating Dorr.

Read o'er our troubles, honest John
And some conclusion draw
Pray tell us what we have to fear
From women, clams, and Dorr.

—Broadside in the Harris Collection,
Brown University.

"Landholders' Victory" chronicles one of the clashes which ensued between forces of the rival governors, Dorr and King.

LANDHOLDERS' VICTORY

Brave suffrage men, assist while I sing
The signal victory of Rhode Island's King:
No earthly record can be found to tell
How many fled,[4] who might have staid and fell!

On Tuesday night[5] the Charter leaders saw
Mysterious movements made by Gov. Dorr;
Their cheeks turned pale, their breathing shorter grew
To hear what King and burgess meant to do.

They looked, then listened and began to quiver,
A steamboat went like lightning down the river
To gather troops to aid their righteous fight,
In killing men who asked for equal rights!

The Mayor's call for help was quick obeyed,
The boys aside their bats and yard-sticks laid;
And to the place appointed quickly run,
Tickled, like other boys, to bear a gun.

The boat returned and brought the promised aid,
Each one appeared, for battle all arrayed;
When a dead pause ensued, they stood aghast,
And found their hired courage failing fast.

They knew the suffrage men would never yield,
Though they might be induced to quit the field;
Therefore they said, "Perhaps it may be wise,
To make them think we wish to compromise."

No sooner said than done. Up heralds went,
To tell the people if they'd be content,
And each one to his home in peace retire,
That King would grant them all that they require.

Three cheers for King were given, long and loud,
And peace and quiet reigned throughout the crowd;
The suffrage men dispersed, with feelings kind,
Till twenty men, perhaps, were left behind.

When lo, the false deceptive Charter band,
Whose only merit is a bank of sand,
With impudence unparalleled, in face of heaven,
Marched up and broke the promise they had given!

[4] Landholders' Party.
[5] May 17, 1842.

But here an honest, fearless few they found,
Who meant to hold possession of the ground,
Though troops and beardless, brainless striplings too,
Appeared thrice in front and back review.

These 20 suffrage men they dare not face,
Though told that Gov. Dorr had quit the place
But stood a moment trembling near the plain,
And then retraced their footsteps back again.

When these important movements all were done,
A memorable victory they had won;
Low falsehood had been used for to deceive
And thus the suffrage men induced to leave.

Ye charter men, your valor should be told,
And written down in characters of gold;
The guns not fire, the blood you did not spill,
Should cause the pilgrim State to blush for Bunker Hill.

Such sights on battle-ground before were never seen;
There, trembling, stood, wise Daniel's Billy Green,
While Charter men and leaders, by the score,
Sneaked to their homes and sought the ground no more.

Say, reader, dost thou know these sages wise,
Whose deeds the Journal lauds up to the skies
Many (let it be told to their disgrace)
Possess no ground for their last resting place!

Others there are, landholders to the bone,
They keep the land of others as their own,
The Bankrupt law enables such great men
To creep out through a hole and start again.

These are the men who love to rule the State
And have their laws decide the poor man's fate;
Yes, and would have the poor their offerings bring,
And pour them in the lap of Sammy King.

But this can never be. Spirits have risen
Fired by the memory of their sires in heaven
They ask their rights, 'tis all the boon they crave
Determined not to be the rich man's slave.

—Broadside in Harris Collection, Brown University.

After the suppression of the rebellion and the flight of Dorr, the levity disappeared from the Chartists' songs.

SUFFRAGE PLEDGE

Here on this sacred spot,
United heart and hand,
We pledge to liberty,
A consecrated band.

Too long, alas! we've bow'd
Beneath a tyrant's laws;
The voice of justice cries—
Maintain your righteous cause.

Although our chosen guide
Is exiled from his home,
The day approaches near,
When he'll no longer roam.

That glorious morn will break,
When freedom's sun shall rise,
And roll in majesty
Through bright, unclouded skies.

The anthems of the free
On every breeze shall float,
And ransomed prisoners join
To swell the joyful note.

The aged and the young
Their thankful offerings bring,
And chant the requiem o'er
The usurped power of King.

Hail! happy day; thrice hail!
Farewell to "martial law";
The conquering hero comes!
Hail! Thomas Wilson Dorr.

—Broadside in Harris Collection,
Brown University.

THE MOVEMENT FOR A SHORTER WORKING DAY

Agitation against the traditional sunup-to-sundown working day began in 1791, when Philadelphia carpenters struck for shorter hours. During the decade of 1825-35 the movement for a ten-hour day spread like fire through labor's ranks and resulted in numerous strikes. The mechanics and artisans, who were well organized in trade unions, first succeeded in gaining the ten-hour day, but for the textile operatives and other industrial workers, the working day remained twelve hours or more. As late as 1929 one of the bloodiest clashes in labor history, the textile strike at Marion, North Carolina, grew out of workers' demands for a reduction of the twelve-hour, twenty-minute shift.

Following the Civil War, labor began campaigning for an eight-hour day. Foremost in the battle was Ira Steward, Boston machinist and union leader, who organized the Grand Eight Hour League of Massachusetts. Eagerly following his example, similar leagues sprang up all over the country. The national government and six states were induced to make eight hours the legal working day, but since such laws were subject to the restrictions imposed by "yellow dog" contracts which forced workers to relinquish their rights, the victory proved hollow. Faced by this obstacle the movement lost its support, and labor fell back once again on strikes to exact the eight-hour day. Eventually the states adopted unrestricted maximum-hour laws, and in 1930 the Federal Government approved comparable legislation.

SIX TO SIX [6]

(Tune: "Adam and Eve")

In days now gone the working men begun, sires,
To work with the sun, and keep on till he was done, sires,
The bosses were as bad as the overseers of blackees,
Because they wished the working men to be no more than lackies.
The niggers have their tasks, and when done they may spree it,
But the Jers they were asked to stick to work as long as they could
see it.
The blackees they had friends of all varieties;
But the workies made themselves their own abolition societies
O dear! oh dear! why didn't they fix
The hours of labor from SIX to SIX.

Old Time, as on his swift wing, he ranges
Brings round about as many great changes.

[6] A ten-hour day with one hour off for breakfast and one hour off for dinner.

Houses are built high, and church steeples higher,
And patent chests invented that get colder in the fire;
Pills are manufactured that cure all diseases;
Rocking chairs in which the sitter at his ease is;
Monied corporations, and institutions old, sires,
The people discover are not good as gold, sires,
As a notion new, the workies thought they'd fix,
The hours of labor from SIX to SIX.

By this the bosses were all made to stare, sires,
And to a man, each one did declare, sires,
The measure was violent—wicked—agrarian;
But they only said this 'cause the measure was a rare 'un,
Meetings were held in old Independence square, sires,
'Twas the second declaration that had been made there, sires,
And while the Bosses were coming to their senses,
Six to six was painted and chalked on all the fences!
O dear, oh dear, we had to fix,
The hours of labor from SIX to SIX.

—Broadside in Harris Collection, Brown University

JAMES BROWN

(Tune: "John Brown's Body")

James Brown's body toils along the rocky road,
James Brown's body bends beneath a crushing load,
James Brown's body feels the point of hunger's goad,
His soul cries out for help.

REFRAIN: *Come, O bearer of Glad Tidings,*
Bringing joy from out her hidings,
Come, O bearer of Glad Tidings,
O come, O come, Eight Hours!

James Brown's wife is worn and pale with many cares,
James Brown's wife so weak can scarce get up the stairs,
James Brown's wife is dying 'neath the load she bears,
Her soul cries out for help.

James Brown's children go a-shivering in the cold,
James Brown's children young, with work are growing old,
James Brown's lambs are torn by wolves outside the fold,
O, save, O, save the lambs!

James Brown feels oppression's iron within his breast,
James Brown broods and ponders, he is not at rest.
James Brown swears he will with wrong and power contest,
His own right arm shall help.

James Brown may sometime become a desp'rate man,
James Brown may sometime go join the tramper's clan,
James Brown then may say, "I'll do the worst I can,"
Oh, blame not him alone.

James Brown hears the call, his soul is up in arms,
James Brown grasps the shield, his soul with ardor warms,
James Brown marches forth to fight the thickening harms,
Now dauntless, strong and free.

—Broadside in Harris Collection,
Brown University. By E. R. Place.

THE IRISH IMMIGRANT

Hardships in Europe sent streams of miserable people to the United States in search of a better life, but often what they found was the same misery Americanized.

Until the potato blight spread to Germany and the political pogroms that followed the abortive mid-nineteenth century revolutions blasted the German lower classes, the bulk of American immigration came from Ireland. That unfortunate land suffered many oppressions from man and nature. In 1798 a revolution was brutally suppressed, and after the Napoleonic Wars the collapse of British wheat prices resulted in the eviction of thousands of Irish peasants, but the worst blow was the potato famine of 1846. People died like flies in Ireland; "travelers along the highways reported that unburied dead lay where they fell, with their mouths stained green by weeds and thistles eaten for nourishment in their last extremity."[7] Over half the working class of Ireland streamed into America, forming the largest national group among the 4,300,000 immigrants who arrived between 1840 and 1860.

When these waves of unhappy people crashed in upon the shores of the United States, they piled up into a surging, be-

[7] Charles A. and Mary Beard, *The Rise of American Civilization*, New York, 1945, I, 641.

wildered mass, whose only common emotion was no longer aspira-
tion but fear. Desperate for survival, they fought like beasts with
each other for man-killing jobs at wages as low as fifty cents a day.
They were reckoned as the earth's expendables by employers, and
in the South were assigned to labor too dangerous or debilitating
for the slaves. As a cotton transport master explained to a passenger
who inquired why there were so many Irish roustabouts, "The
niggers are worth too much to be risked here. If the paddies
are knocked overboard or get their backs broken, nobody loses
anything." [8]

American native labor was at first violently antipathetic to
these ignorant peasants who, unaccustomed to a decent standard
of living, eagerly accepted what pittance employers deigned to
throw them and thus threatened to demolish the wage scales that
had been built up through years of painful struggle by American
workers. Craft unions never accepted the immigrants, but more
enlightened workers and their leaders eventually recognized that
the Irish responded heartily to union agitation, just as the Slavs
were to do fifty years later in the coal fields, and became the most
militant unionists. Unscrupulous employers found that the Frank-
enstein's monster they had nurtured while it aided them against
native labor was now turning against them. "When they receive
employment," complained one disgruntled capitalist, "are they
not the first to insist on higher wages [and] to strike?" [9]

Employers began to discriminate against Irish laborers, and the
"No Irish Need Apply" notation which accompanied many job
advertisements became the source of bitter resentment among the
Irish. Dozens of broadsides incorporating the phrase were printed,
expressing all gradations of protest. Some indignantly recited the
accomplishment of Irishmen:

> *They insult an Irishman and think nought of what they say;*
> *They'll call him green, an Irish bull, it happens every day.*
> *Now to these folks I say a word, to sing a song I'll try,*
> *And answer to these dirty words, "No Irish Need Apply."*
> *So if you'll give attention, I'll sing my song to you,*
> *And the subject of my song shall be, What Irish Boys Can Do.*

[8] Ulrich B. Phillips, *American Negro Slavery*, New York, 1918, p. 302.
[9] Jesse Chickering, *Immigration into the United States*, Boston, 1848, p. 64.

Others chronicled the traditional Irish retaliation against oppression:

NO IRISH NEED APPLY

I'm a decent boy just landed
From the town of Ballyfad;
I want a situation, yes,
And want it very bad.
I have seen employment advertised,
"It's just the thing," says I,
But the dirty spalpeen ended with
"No Irish Need Apply."

"Whoa," says I, "that's an insult,
But to get the place I'll try,"
So I went to see the blackguard
With his "No Irish Need Apply."
Some do count it a misfortune
To be christened Pat or Dan,
But to me it is an honor
To be born an Irishman.

I started out to find the house,
I got it mighty soon;
There I found the old chap seated,
He was reading the Tribune.

I told him what I came for,
When he in a rage did fly,
"No!" he says, "You are a Paddy,
And no Irish need apply."

Then I gets my dander rising
And I'd like to black his eye
To tell an Irish gentleman
"No Irish Need Apply."
Some do count it a misfortune
To be christened Pat or Dan,
But to me it is an honor
To be born an Irishman.

I couldn't stand it longer
So a hold of him I took,
And gave him such a welting
As he'd get at Donnybrook.
He hollered "Milia murther,"
And to get away did try,
And swore he'd never write again
"No Irish Need Apply."

Well, he made a big apology,
I told him then goodbye,
Saying, "When next you want a beating,
Write 'No Irish Need Apply'."
Some do count it a misfortune
To be christened Pat or Dan,
But to me it is an honor
To be born an Irishman.
—Collected by Pete Seeger.

Much of the surplus labor among the Eastern Irish immigrants was siphoned off into Western railroad building.

PAT WORKS ON THE RAILWAY

In eighteen hundred and forty-one
I put me corduroy breeches on,
I put me corduroy breeches on,
To work upon the railway.

REFRAIN: *Fi-li-me-oo-re-oo-re-ay,*
Fi-li-me-oo-re-oo-re-ay,
Fi-li-me-oo-re-oo-re-ay,
To work upon the railway.

In eighteen hundred and forty-two
I left the old world for the new;
Bad cess to the luck that brought me through,
To work upon the railway.

Our contractor's name it was Tom King,
He kept a store to rob the men;
A Yankee clerk with ink and pen
To cheat Pat on the railway.

THE TARRIERS' SONG

REFRAIN

Every morning at seven o'clock
There's twenty tarriers working at the rock.
And the boss comes along, and he says, "Kape still,
And come down heavy on the cast-iron drill."

REFRAIN: *And drill, ye tarriers, drill,*
Drill, ye tarriers, drill!
It's work all day for the sugar in your tay,
Down behind the railway.
And drill ye tarriers, drill,
And blast! And fire!

Now our new foreman was Jean McCann,
By God, he was a blame mean man;
Last week a premature blast went off,
And a mile in the air went big Jim Goff.

Next time payday comes around
Jim Goff a dollar short was found;
When he asked "What for?" Came this reply,
"Yer docked for the time you was up in the sky."

THE KNIGHTS OF LABOR

The most incredible organization in the history of the American labor movement was also the first great union, the Noble and Holy Order of the Knights of Labor, or, as it was known officially during its first ten years, the * * * * *. From a meeting of nine somewhat fatuous garment cutters in 1869 it grew in two decades to an organization of more than 700,000 members.

The founder of the Knights of Labor and the creator of its guiding principles was a tailor named Uriah Stephens. As a member of the abortive Garment Cutters Association which had been organized in Philadelphia in 1862, Stephens became convinced that the first essential for a successful labor union was absolute secrecy, and in setting up his own little union he modeled it after ritualistic fraternal organizations. He was elected its presiding officer, or Master Workman, and the other organizers divided among them the grandiloquent titles of Venerable Sage, Worthy Foreman, and Unknown Knight, as well as more mundane appellations like Recording Secretary, Financial Secretary, and Treasurer. New members were admitted by invitation only, and subjected to a fraternalistic initiation before being told the name of the union or its purposes.

Stephens was surrounded by an adolescent fringe and was himself some distance from the attainment of intellectual maturity, but he had a vision—the foundation of a new social order based on coöperation, which would first encompass the world's laborers and then spread out to include everyone. There were to be no barriers of race, creed, or skill in this first One Big Union; everyone who at any time had worked for wages could become a member. This broad requirement technically permitted capitalists to join, and indeed the Knights of Labor were not averse to drawing membership from the manufacturing class. The Knights held that there was no antipathy between labor and capital, and in a social system built on coöperation both could thrive.

Stephens believed that the aims of the union could be achieved only through the exercise of three principles: secrecy, education, and coöperation. Secrecy and the elaborate ritualism which attended it were necessary to prevent the infiltration of employers' spies and other ill-wishers, but eventually it had to be discarded because the opposition of the Catholic Church to secret societies kept many sympathetic workers from joining the association.

The other precepts were nebulous. Education was a laudable goal to be striven for, but education in what, and how it was to be administered, was never clearly explained. The fundamental principle of the Order—coöperation—was similarly ill defined. Both Stephens and Terence V. Powderly, who succeeded him as Grand Master Workman in 1879, spoke of the new social order and its achievement in such idealistic generalities that the organizers felt free to promise prospective members anything. When the promises were not fulfilled, many disillusioned members dropped out.

The chief source of contention between the militant worker and the Knights of Labor was its attitude toward immediate industrial relations. Strikes were discouraged, not because of any benevolence on the part of the Knights of Labor leaders, but because they were not considered an efficient means of achieving the end for which the organization was founded—the establishment of a kind of socialistic commonwealth in the United States in which the wage system and other blights of capitalism would be abolished. No practical substitute for strikes was offered. Political activity was recommended as a substitute for direct clashes with employers, but despite support of liberal candidates, the Knights of Labor's participation in politics was half-hearted.

Aside from its uncertain way of action, the chief weakness of the Knights of Labor was its heterogeneity. All workers sympathetic to the purposes of the union were welcomed into the fold, regardless of the nature of their trade or profession, or whether they had any skill at all, and in time the organization resembled less a labor union than a social fraternity. Of course the idea behind this cutting-through of trade distinctions was the basis on which the industrial union, now recognized as the most powerful combination of labor, was to be founded, but in 1880 this idea was palpably impracticable. Other barriers than trade distinctions prevented the stable organization of the unskilled worker. Differences of race, religion, and language had to be overcome before unionization could take place. Labor had to creep before it could walk, and had to pass through the phase of horizontal organization before it could achieve vertical organization. And guiding labor along this tortuous path of development required a sensible plan of action and sensible leaders to carry it through. The Knights of Labor had neither a sensible plan nor sensible leaders. Powderly, the inheritor of Stephens' precepts, and the union's head through its period of greatest expansion, once remarked that he believed temperance was the main issue in the liberation of the workingman.

During the entire life of the Knights of Labor its leaders condemned strikes, but at the same time found themselves forced to support strikes which arose through their inability to control impetuous branch leaders. The collapse of the Knights of Labor grew directly from such a local dispute which began on Jay Gould's Wabash line in 1885. Through the militancy of the local Knights of Labor assembly the strike spread rapidly through the entire Southwest system until Jay Gould, unprepared to combat the stoppage, assented to the workers' demands.

This victory resulted in an immediate upsurge in the Knights of Labor's prestige, and tens of thousands of workers swarmed to join the powerful champion of labor. But during the year Gould built up strength, baited the Knights of Labor into another strike in 1886, and crushed the uprising, breaking the back of the Knights of Labor in the process. Another unfortunate strike in the Chicago stockyards in the same year sealed the downfall of the organization. By 1893 the membership had fallen from the peak of 700,000 to 7,500, and even this remnant soon drifted away.

The general assembly of the Knights of Labor "always ceased its labors" at the close of each session by singing "If We Will, We Can Be Free."

IF WE WILL, WE CAN BE FREE

Base oppressors, cease your slumbers,
Listen to a people's cry,
Hark! uncounted, countless numbers
Swell the peal of agony;
Lo from Labor's sons and daughters,
In the depths of misery
Like the rush of many waters,
Comes the cry "We will be free!"
Comes the cry "We will be free!"

By our own, our children's charter,
By the fire within our veins,
By each truth-attesting martyr,
By our own tears, our groans, our pains,
By our rights, by Nature given,
By the laws of liberty,
We declare before high heaven
That we must, we will be free,
That we must, we will be free.

Tyrants quail! the dawn is breaking,
Dawn of freedom's glorious day,
Despots on their thrones are shaking,
Iron hands are giving way—
Kingcraft, statecraft, base oppression,
Cannot bear our scrutiny—
We have learned the startling lesson,
If we will, we can be free,
If we will, we can be free.

Winds and waves the tidings carry;
Electra in your fiery car,
Winged by lightning, do not tarry,
Bear the news to lands afar;
Bid them tell the thrilling story
Louder than the thunder's glee
That a people ripe for glory,
Are determined to be free,
Are determined to be free.

—Elizabeth Balch, "Songs for Labor," *The Survey*,
Vol. 31 (January 3, 1914), p. 411.

KNIGHTS OF LABOR

I'll sing of an order that lately has done
Some wonderful things in our land;
Together they pull and great battles have won
A popular hard working band.

Their numbers are legion, great strength they possess,
They strike good and strong for their rights;
From the North to the South, from the East to the West,
God speed each assembly of Knights.

REFRAIN: *Then conquer we must,*
Our cause it is just,
What power the uplifted hand;
Let each Labor Knight
Be brave in the fight,
Remember, united we stand.

They ask nothing wrong, you plainly can see,
All that they demand is but fair;
A lesson they'll teach, with me you'll agree,
And every purse-proud millionaire.
Fair wages they want, fair wages they'll get,
Good tempered they wage all their fights;
Success to the cause, may the sun never set
On each brave assembly of Knights.

Then fight on undaunted, you brave working men,
Down the vampires who oppress the poor;
You use noble weapons, the tongue and the pen,
Successful you'll be, I am sure.
With hope for your watchword and truth for your shield,
Prosperity for your pathway lights,
Then let labor make proud capital yield,
God speed each assembly of Knights.

—Broadside in American Antiquarian Society.

NOBLE KNIGHTS OF LABOR

In the year of '69 they commenced to fall in line,
The great Knights, the noble Knights of Labor,
Now in numbers mighty strong, gaining fast they march along,
The great Knights, the noble Knights of Labor.
They are men of brains and will, education, pluck and skill,
And in time they'll change the workingman's situation.
East and West, where'er we go, from the North to Mexico,
They're as thick as flies, and soon they'll rule the Nation.

REFRAIN: *Oh, the great Knights, the noble Knights of Labor,*
The true Knights, the honest Knights of Labor,
Like the good old Knights of old, they cannot be
bought or sold,
The great Knights, the noble Knights of Labor.

—Broadside in American Antiquarian Society.

THE GENERAL STRIKE

A general strike of the extent imagined by the composer of this song never happened, but a series of general strikes of lesser compass broke out in the two decades following the Civil War. The depression of the 1870's heightened the violence as wages were cut. The workers received no consideration for their plight, and the noted clergyman and orator, Henry Ward Beecher, summed up this attitude in his statement:

God intended the great to be great and the little to be little. . . . I do not say that a dollar a day is enough to support a working man. But it is enough to support a man! Not enough to support a man and five children if a man insists on smoking and drinking beer. . . . But the man who cannot live on bread and water is not fit to live.

THE GENERAL STRIKE

The labor sensation spread fast over this nation,
While men in high station do just as they like;
They'll find out their mistake when it will be too late,
When they see the results of a general strike.
The butchers, the whalers, the tinkers, the tailors,
Mechanics and sailors will surely agree,
To strike and stand still, let the rich run the mill,
While I sing of the sights that I fancy we'll see.
REFRAIN: *We'll see Italians knocked sprawling,*
        Policemen help calling, capital crawling from
            labor's attack;
        We'll see washwomen giving blarney to the
            famed Denis Kearney,[10]
        For hanging the Chinamen up by the neck.

We'll see men and women run through the streets screaming
At the sight of each other all naked and bare;
We'll see Henry Ward Beecher the Plymouth Church preacher,
Giving up his fine robes for the fair sex to wear.
We will see men of fashion get into a passion,
At their coachmen and footmen doing just as they like;
You will see Kate O'Connor with a women's rights' banner,
Leading our working girls into the strike.
                    *   *   *
(Three more stanzas in this vein)
                        —Broadside in Harris Collection, Brown University.

[10] Denis Kearney, an unscrupulous opportunist who was repudiated by discerning labor organizations, founded a spurious union in California in 1878 whose chief purpose was to fight Chinese immigration.

THE SINGLE TAX MOVEMENT

From the time when the worker first became articulate, his struggle for a better life has been based on the thesis that an individual has the right to the fruits of his labor. What else accrued to him through forces over which he had no direct control, such as the augmentation of land values through the movement of population, he was content to accept as the gift of a beneficent God. To Henry George this philosophy contained the fallacy on which poverty was founded. As a journalist in San Francisco during the booming seventies, he watched the structure of civilization and its attendant wealth growing about him, yet in its shadow he saw poverty becoming conversely more widespread and more degrading. Like the Wobblies, who were later to declare, "For every dollar the parasite has and didn't work for, there's a slave who worked for a dollar he didn't get," George was convinced that there was an inescapable ratio between vast wealth and abysmal poverty, and he determined to trace the devious line of relationship between the two. In 1879 he published the results of his analysis in an impassioned treatise entitled *Progress and Poverty*.

In *Progress and Poverty* George came independently to a conclusion which had been probed earlier by men like Thomas Paine and John Stuart Mill, that land is the basic factor in the equation. It was for George a comparatively easy decision to arrive at, for the West was being founded on land speculation rather than the exploitation of land for mineral resources. Absentee speculators invested in vast areas of cheap, undeveloped land which they knew, either by shrewdly anticipating the movement of population or by directing the movement by influencing the extension of railroad lines, would expand in value. The unearned profits thus derived could be plowed back into more land. George concluded from his observations that

In allowing one man to own the land on which and from which other men live, we have made them his bondsmen in a degree which increases as material progress goes on. . . . It is this that turns the blessings of material progress into a curse. . . . Civilization so based cannot continue.

His solution was extraordinarily direct. The value that land derives from society should accrue to society; since "Private property in land has no warrant in justice," it should be abollished. He was willing to allow landholders to retain the fiction of ownership, but economic rent of the land—that difference between buying price (initial outlay and cost of improvements) and selling price—was to be considered surplus income to which the landholder was not entitled. George argued that a tax on this economic rent would be sufficient to maintain all functions of government, and that taxes upon the products of labor would not be necessary. From this contention the movement received the name "single tax."

Henry George's plan was impracticable, despite the soundness of the principle behind it, but it offered a possibility for social reform that instantly captured the imagination of the thousands who felt themselves unable to cope with the existing system. This inarticulate mass of people found in *Progress and Poverty* a brilliant expression of what they had not been able to put into words, and in twenty-five years *Progress and Poverty* went through more than a hundred editions. George's eloquent condemnation of the land monopolists left little for the people to say, but a few amateur composers tried to show the relation of progress to poverty in a less abstract way.

MARY'S LITTLE LOT

Mary had a little lot,
The soil was very poor;
But still she kept it all the same
And struggled to get more.

She kept the lot until one day
The people settled down;
And where the wilderness had been
Grew up a thriving town.

Then Mary rented out her lot
(She would not sell, you know),
And waited patiently about
For prices still to grow.

They grew, as population came,
And Mary raised the rent;
With common food and raiment now
She could not be content.

She built her up a mansion fine
Had bric-a-brac galore;
And every time the prices rose,
She raised the rent some more.

"What makes the lot keep Mary so?"
The starving people cry;
"Why, Mary keeps the lot, you know,"
The wealthy would reply.

And so each one of you might be
Wealthy, refined, and wise,
If you had only hogged some land
And held it for the rise.

—From WPA Collections, Library of Congress
Archive of American Folk Song.

THE FREIGHT HANDLERS' STRIKE

In the summer of 1882 the unorganized freight handlers of the New York Central & Hudson River and the New York
Lake Erie & Western railroads struck for an increase of pay from
17 cents to 20 cents an hour. Freight rates for merchandise moving
West had recently advanced, so the public sympathized with the
strikers' cause. At first railroad officials—Gould, Vanderbilt, and
Field—brought in inexperienced strikebreakers who were unable
to keep freight from piling up, and the shippers appealed to the
courts to compel the railroads to keep the freight moving. Later
the railroads hired experienced strikebreakers, freight began to
move westward, and the strike was broken.

THE FREIGHT HANDLERS' STRIKE

(Tune: "Rambling Rake of Poverty")

It was at Cooper's Institute, Jack Burke and I chanced to meet;
It's years since last we parted, leaving school on Hudson Street.
He introduced me to his friends, the Doyles, the O's, the Macs,
And the subject of the evening was about the railroad strike.

REFRAIN: *We're on the strike and we won't go back,*
Our claims are just and right;
Trade unions and the public press
Will help us with all their might.

There's Field, Jay Gould, and Vanderbilt, their millions they did save
By paying starvation wages and working men like slaves;
They hum round honest labor as the bee does round the flower,
And suck the sweetness of your toil for 17 cents an hour.

They advertised in English, French, Irish, and Dutch,
They got a sample of all nations to work in place of us;
They marched them to the depot and told them not to fear,
And to shake their courage up in them, they gave them lager beer.

The lager beer and sandwiches with them did not agree;
In place of handling merchandise they all got on the spree.
The Russian Jews soon spread the news about their jolly times,
And all the bums from Baxter Street rushed for the railroad lines.

The Italians made themselves at home and soon began to call
For William H., the railroad king, to pass the beer along;
Jay Gould was making sandwiches and Field began to cry
Because he couldn't snatch the man that blew up his English spy.

Those mean monopolizers had the cheek to take the stand
And ask to get protection from the honest working man
Who tries to sell his labor in a manly upright way,
And will not handle railroad freight for less than two a day.

Does the devil makes those fools believe that they are smart and
clever—
Does he tell them wealth will bring them health and make them live
for ever;
Does he lead them from their gambling dens and to some shady bower,
To make them fix a workman's pay at 17 cents an hour?

—From broadside in Harris Collection, Brown University.

THE PULLMAN STRIKE

The bitter labor disputes of the seventies and eighties were founded on very solid grievances. The tremendous prosperity that was indicated by the expansion of American industry after the Civil War was not passed on to the workers whose efforts helped create it; in fact, real wages actually declined. This situation could lead nowhere but to organized industrial revolt, whose portents were everywhere visible.

The capitalists recognized these warning signs, but attempted to circumvent the inevitable consequences of their policies by the most extreme methods short of raising wages. The most fantastic of these experiments toward achieving artificial stability in industrial relations was the paternalistic venture of resourceful, cunning, ruthless, and unlovable George Mortimer Pullman, founder and president of the Pullman Palace Car Company.

Pullman's invention and development of the sleeping car and his destruction of competition built up the company's original capitalization of $10,000,000 to a worth of $62,000,000 in twenty-five years, affording him sufficient funds to execute his schemes. He moved the Pullman shops from Elmira, Detroit, St. Louis, and Wilmington to one gigantic factory near Chicago as the first step in his plan; next he built a truly beautiful city in the middle of four thousand company-owned acres on the open prairie twelve miles south of Chicago. The town, with its houses, streets, and public buildings, was planned by outstanding architects and landscape engineers, and was built of the best materials, nearly all of which, incidentally, were manufactured by the company. All utilities, including gas, were also company-built and company-maintained. And all was for his workers.

At the peak of its prosperity before the panic of 1893 the town provided, in 1800 buildings, shelter for 12,500 people. Fine public buildings had been erected, including a very well-appointed library, a beautiful theatre, and a magnificent edifice called the Green Stone Church. The homes were roomy, well designed, and provided with the most modern conveniences. As a company press agent stated, Pullman was "a town in a word, where all that is ugly and discordant and demoralizing is eliminated and all that which inspires self-respect is generously provided." Unspoken but implied was the conclusion that George M. Pullman was the very embodiment of beneficence, a selfless philanthropist.

But there were shadows in Pullman's aureola. The model town had been constructed for other purposes than to create a contented and docile force of employees; it was also a business proposition built to return a profit of 6 per cent. Besides the utilities which returned a 6 per cent profit, there was a steam-heat plant returning 6 per cent; a huge dairy farm returning 6 per cent; ice houses, lumberyards, hotel, livery stables, the church, the bank, and the library, all designed to return 6 per cent. Even the town's sewage was used as fertilizer for the company truck farm, and the resulting vegetables sold in Chicago. Thus George Mortimer Pullman squeezed the last 6 per cent out of his employees.

There were even less admirable features about Pullman. Neither houses nor land could be purchased; leases could be terminated in ten days; no improvements or adaptations could be made on company property; plays at the theatre were censored; "undesirable" orators were excluded from its stage; pernicious influences like liquor were prohibited; and the government of the town was completely in the hands of Pullman through the town agent. For these services and disservices, Pullman's employees (who were coerced into living in Pullman) paid exorbitant rents, often 25 per cent higher than in adjoining communities, and even more exorbitant utility rates (gas was almost twice as expensive as in Chicago). The Green Stone Church went unused for several years because of the $3,600 rent demanded. Clergymen resented Pullman's restriction of religious freedom. Father John Waldron, the local Catholic priest, who was forced to resign his pastorate, denounced Pullman as a "capitalistic czar; a man who ruled, crushed, and oppressed by the force of money."

The financial panic of 1893 occasioned a drastic retrenchment in Pullman activities. The wholesale dismissals cut the town's population to eight thousand, and the wages of those workers still retained were cut by as much as 40 per cent. But while Pullman's right hand slashed wages, his left continued to collect the high rents without reduction. In defiance of law, rent was withheld from salaries, and one employee framed a weekly pay check of two cents.

In May of 1894 the employees asked Pullman to consider their grievances, but he unequivocally refused to talk about wages or rents, and promptly fired three members of the grievance committee. Meanwhile the American Railway Union, founded by Eugene V. Debs in 1893 but already claiming a membership of 150,000, had been unionizing Pullman employees. Debs applied to Pullman for arbitration, but Pullman's paternalism forbade him to allow the corruption of his employees by unions, and the ARU's appeals were ignored. Against his own better judgment, Debs risked the life of his union in a strike of Pullman workers on June 21, 1894, but warned the men to conduct a peaceable campaign. As the strike spread, the railroad association forced the workers' hand by importing Canadian strikebreakers, and by pleading danger of violence had 3,400 special deputies appointed to keep the trains rolling. Their next effective move was their appeal to President Cleveland to safeguard the mails. Cleveland, against Governor Altgeld's protest, promptly dispatched four companies of infantry to Chicago. But the most successful coup perpetrated by the railroads was their application for a blanket injunction from the Federal District Court against the strike. The injunction was granted, and when it was ignored by Debs he was imprisoned. Deprived of leadership, the strikers capitulated and returned to work, only to find that union members had been blacklisted by the General Managers Association. Never again was a known ARU member to find work on an American railway.

This most important of strikes had ominous aftermaths. Thereafter the practice of government by injunction became widespread in labor disputes; and Debs's imprisonment resulted in his espousal of Socialism, which in turn led to the formation of the IWW, which in turn led to the birth of American Communism.[11]

THE PULLMAN STRIKE
(Tune: "The Widow's Plea For Her Son")

Near the City of Chicago, where riot holds full sway,
The workingmen of Pullman are battling for fair play;
But the Boss he would not listen to the workingmen's appeal,
And scorned their mute advances, no sympathy did feel.
The railroad men refused to move even a single car,
Till suddenly from Washington they heard the White House Czar
Proclaim them all lawbreakers, and then in mournful tone
To their countrymen they sent their cry with sad and dismal moan:

REFRAIN: Remember we are workmen, and we want honest pay,
And gentlemen, remember, we work hard day by day;
Let Pullman remember, too, no matter where he roams,
We built up his capital, and we're pleading for our homes.

The troops are ordered from the East and from the Western shore,
The firebrands of anarchy are brought to every door;
Honest workmen repudiate the work of thugs and tramps,
And think it is an outrage to be reckoned with these scamps.
Arbitration is what they asked, but the Boss he quick refused,
"Your fight is with the railroads," was the answer they perused;
But Pullman will regret the day he gave this harsh reply;
And workingmen throughout the land will heed our pleading cry.

—"The Pullman Strike Songster" in
Harris Collection, Brown University.

11 Ralph Chaplin, *Wobbly*, Chicago, 1948, p. 14

A.R.U.

Been on the hummer since ninety-four,
Last job I had was on the Lake Shore.
Lost my office in the A.R.U.,
And I won't get it back till nineteen-two.
And I'm still on the hog train flagging my meals,
Riding the brake beams close to the wheels.

—Carl Sandburg, *The American Songbag,* New York,
Harcourt, Brace, and Co., 1927, p. 191.

THE PEOPLE'S PARTY

The Populist movement of the last quarter of the nineteenth century was only by necessity a political movement, and
in a way it was actually anti-political, for it sought to combat the
forces of plunder that had been fostered by the two major parties.
Idealistically, it was an uprising of the common people to recover
the political control that had passed into the hands of urban
capitalists. In the South this exploitation manifested itself in the
expanding tobacco trust which controlled the tobacco growers of
Virginia and North Carolina, and in the usurious system of merchant capitalism that enmeshed the land-poor farmers. In the
Midwest analogous complaints beset the farmer in the form of
the currency question. The powerful minority whose wealth was
based on financial speculation and industrial expansion favored
the gold standard; the midwestern farmer, heavily in debt for his
newly acquired lands, stood to lose through the continued appreciation of the dollar.

In all sections a principal grievance was the railroads. Far from
being the unqualified blessing commonly supposed, the railroad
to the farmer was the embodiment of the forces of greed, a vicious
process of creating dependency and then exploiting it. When the
railroads probed deeper and deeper into the West, the farmers
could no longer independently haul their grain by horse and
wagon; they were forced to ship by rail. The railroads, virtually
unregulated, then adjusted their rates by what the traffic would
bear. Increasingly the middleman drove his wedge deeper and
deeper between the farmer and consumer, and engorged profit
from both ends of the process of food supply. The situation,
aggravated by other factors, soon became intolerable for the

farmers, and spontaneous protest groups sprang up all over the country. The forerunners of the People's Party tried to dissociate their agitation from mere political activity. As one such group pledged in 1873, "The organization, when consummated, shall not, so far as in our power to prevent, ever deteriorate into a political party." But the leaders of these organizations soon recognized that the only practical way to effect social or economic reform was through the legislatures, and this meant the building of political power strong enough to force through laws favorable to agrarian interests. The culmination of these groups, social, educational, and political, which spread like a network over rural America, was the People's Party, founded in 1892.

To strengthen its cause the Populists solicited the adherence of labor, and in their platforms denounced the oppressors of labor who denied the workingman the right to organize and by ruthless practices endeavored to keep him in economic slavery. The Knights of Labor offered their support, but the AFL was reluctant to endorse the middle-class issues of "employing farmers."

After six years of influential activity, the People's Party disintegrated. The basic reason for its collapse was its instability; at no time were the various factions which made it up in complete solidarity concerning the nation's problems, and very often there was open dissension, with one faction dickering with the Republicans while another courted the Democrats. In 1896, the year which marked the collapse of the People's Party as a practical force in national politics, the Populists were forced into supporting for vice-president Arthur M. Sewell, a bank president and railway director.

But other weaknesses assured the downfall of the People's Party; its espousal of labor's cause was only rhetorical, a fact that many labor leaders soon perceived; race hatred weakened a large faction of the Southern branch, and condemnation of unrestricted immigration deprived the party of the support of millions. The party's choice of leaders was also unfortunate. The spokesman for the Populists, the influential framer of many of their principles, and at one time their candidate for the presidency, was Ignatius Donnelly, a man of dubious intellectual stability known to Shakespearean scholars as the author of *The Great Cryptogram,* a monument of misguided ingenuity.

While the People's Party was a prominent force in American politics, its militant defense of the principle that wealth belonged to those who produced it was commemorated by a body of song unequaled by parties whose purposes were fundamentally political.

PEOPLE'S PARTY SONG

What portentous sounds are these,
That are borne upon the breeze?
What means this agitation deep and grand?
Whence comes this discontent?
Why are parties torn and rent
That before in solid phalanx used to stand?

REFRAIN: *Hark! See the people are advancing,*
In solid columns to the fight;
We will let the bosses see
We're determined to be free,
And for bullets we'll use ballots in the fight.

Let the demagogue and knave
Storm and bluster, fret and rave,
And assail with filth our leader's honored name.
All that malice can devise
Of scurrility and lies,
Only adds a brighter luster to his fame.

Then arise, ye workingmen,
In support of gallant Ben[12]
Who is trying to unravel right from wrong.
Don't be lured by party pride,
Tell the bosses, "Stand Aside!"
And swell up your ranks at least three million strong.[13]

—From broadside in Harris Collection, Brown University.

THE WORKINGMEN'S ARMY

(Tune: "Marching Through Georgia")

When rebel shot and rebel shell burst open Sumter's wall,
When honest Abraham Lincoln's voice aroused the people all,
General Butler was the first who answered Lincoln's call,
To lead on the great Union army.

[12] General Benjamin F. Butler, presidential candidate on the Greenback-Labor and Anti-Monopoly ticket in 1884.
[13] Butler received 130,000 votes.

REFRAIN: *Hurrah, hurrah, hurrah for liberty!*
Hurrah, hurrah, we workingmen are free!
We've burst the bonds of party like those of slavery,
And joined the great workingmen's army.

And there's now another army, fighting for another cause.
Striving to get fair and just and equitable laws;
And Butler, tried and true, is now again, as then he was,
Commanding the workingmen's army.

He'll push aside from power and place, with strong, avenging hand,
The sordid politician who would desecrate the land;
He'll burst the rings, and make this nation pure and free and grand,
With his brave, fearless, workingmen's army.

—From broadside in Harris Collection, Brown University.

A HAYSEED LIKE ME

I was once a tool of oppression
And as green as a sucker could be;
And monopolies banded together
To beat a poor bum like me.

The railroads and party bosses
Together did sweetly agree;
And they thought there would be little trouble
In working a hayseed like me.

But now I've roused up a little
And their greed and corruption I see;
And the ticket we vote next November
Will be made up of hayseeds like me.

—Anna Rochester, *The Populist Movement in
the United States*, New York, 1943, p. 2.

KEEP STEADY

Come now, boys, keep steady, the day is at hand
When every true patriot all through the land
Will go to the polls, and their suffrages throw,
And strike at oppression one desperate blow.
The people have been humbugged now long enough
Befooled and cajoled by nonsensical stuff
But their temper is up, and they're ugly clean through,
On the fourth of November, you'll see what they'll do.

REFRAIN: *Keep sober and steady, and mind what you're at;*
Don't be turned from your purpose by this one or that;
Our motives are pure, and our motto is grand;
Self-protection's the war-cry all over the land.

* * *

—From broadside in Harris Collection, Brown University.

THE PEOPLE'S RALLY CRY

(Tune: "Battle Cry of Freedom")

We will rally round the flag, boys, we'll rally till we gain
For every workingman his freedom;
We will rally from the workshop, from city, hill, and plain,
To give the workingman his freedom.

REFRAIN: *Our Union, forever! Press on, boys, press on!*
We'll down with the money, and up with the man;
While we rally round the flag, boys, and rally till we gain
For every workingman his freedom.

We are joining hands to conquer the wrongs that gall us sore,
That all may work and live in freedom;
And we'll fill the Union up with a million votes or more
To give the workingman his freedom.

We will welcome to our numbers all who are true and brave,
Who'll give to toil the fullest freedom;
Right to all that's earned by labor, t'unchain the wages slave
And raise him up to manhood's freedom.

So we're forming everywhere—North and South, and East and West
To give the slave of wage his freedom;
And we'll hurl the Idol GOLD from the land we love the best
And give to every soul his freedom.

COXEY'S ARMY

Few of the Populist leaders recognized that the wheels which carried our economy were moving in a continuous cycle of expansion, prosperity, crisis, depression, and recovery, and fewer still saw that at the same time the entire machine was rolling smoothly down hill. So when the financial crisis of 1893 moved into the paralyzing depression of 1894, the normalcy of the situation was not perceived; and it was thought that only drastic action would save the country. The Populists therefore planned and sponsored an army of protest—the "Commonweal Army"—which gathered recruits in various parts of the country in 1894 for a march on Washington. The only division which actually reached its objective was a force of five thousand men led from Massillon, Ohio, by a wealthy Ohio Populist, "General" Jacob Sechler Coxey. He brought with him a speech which he planned to deliver in support of a $500,000,000 federal works project bill for unemployment relief introduced by Senator Peffer of Kansas.

President Cleveland's administration, more familiar with the apparent vagaries of the American economic system than the naïve Populists, ignored the proposals and took notice of the Army only to have its leaders arrested for treading on the Capitol grass. On the fiftieth anniversary of his march on Washington, Coxey delivered from the Capitol steps the address he had prepared for May 1, 1894.

ON TO WASHINGTON

(Tune: "John Brown's Body")

We're headed straight for Washington with leaders brave and true,
The foremost men, the mighty men, who fight the Wall Street crew;
They lead the People's Army forth, injustice to undo,
And truth goes marching on.

REFRAIN: *Glory, glory, hallelujah!*
Glory, glory, hallelujah!
Glory, glory, hallelujah!
And truth goes marching on.

—Broadside in Harris Collection, Brown University.

COXEY ARMY

(Tune: "Marching Through Georgia")

Bring the good old bugle, boys, we want to tell in song
The Coxey Army's marching from the town of Massillon;
Soon they'll meet old Grover, a good four million strong
Marching in the Coxey Army.

REFRAIN: *Hurrah! Hurrah! We want the jubilee!*
Hurrah! Hurrah! Hard working men are we!
We only want a chance to live in this land of the free
Marching in the Coxey Army.

Coxey is our leader, from the state of Ohio.
When we get to Washington, he'll let the legislators know
That we are all working men, and not tramps "on the go,"
Marching in the Coxey Army.

—Broadside in Harris Collection, Brown University.

THE NATIONAL GRASS PLOT

(Tune: "Star Spangled Banner")

O say, can you see, by the dawn's early light,
That grass plot so dear to the hearts of us all?
Is it green yet and fair, in well-nurtured plight,
Unpolluted by the Coxeyites' hated foot-fall?
Midst the yells of police, and swish of clubs through the air,
We could hardly tell if our grass was still there.
But the green growing grass doth in triumph yet wave,
And the gallant police with their buttons of brass
Will sure make the Coxeyites keep off the grass.

—Broadside in Harris Collection, Brown University.

HARD TIMES

Depression years tend not only to paralyze industry, but also to induce debility in the people who live through them. But the people have staffs to support them in time of crisis; one of these is song. When hard times come, songs become more plaintive, but even this expression acts as a catharsis for the singer, and purges him of despondency. Songs of protest are rarely despair songs; there is always that feeling of anger that eventually leads the singer and the cause for which he is fighting out of the darkness.

All depressions produced songs of lament, and songs of laughter in the depths of misery; the depression of 1932 brought forth scores of songs with titles like "CWA Blues," "Workin' for the PWA," "Depression Blues," "Unemployment Stomp," "One Dime Blues," "Don't Take Away My PWA," "CCC Blues," "NRA Blues," and "Welfare Blues"; but the most famous perhaps is "Beans, Bacon, and Gravy." There are at least three well-documented claims for the authorship of this song, but all that can be said with certainty of its origin is that it was born of hard times.

BEANS, BACON, AND GRAVY

I was born long ago, in 1894,
And I've seen many a panic, I will own;
I've been hungry, I've been cold,
And now I'm growing old,
But the worst I've seen is 1932.

REFRAIN: *Oh, those beans, bacon, and gravy,*
            They almost drive me crazy,
            I eat them till I see them in my dreams,
                        In my dreams;
            When I wake up in the morning,
            And another day is dawning,
            Yes, I know I'll have another mess of beans.

We congregate each morning
At the county barn at dawning,
And everyone is happy, so it seems;
But when our work is done
We file in one by one,
And thank the Lord for one more mess of beans.

We have Hooverized on butter,
For milk we've only water,
And I haven't seen a steak in many a day;
As for pies, cakes, and jellies,
We substitute sow-bellies,
For which we work the county road each day.

If there ever comes a time
When I have more than a dime
They will have to put me under lock and key;
For they've had me broke so long
I can only sing this song,
Of the workers and their misery.

THE URGE TO COMPLACENCY

Many semireligious songs perpetuate the beatitude "Blessed are the poor in spirit, for theirs is the kingdom of heaven," which modern protestors against the inequalities of wealth reject so vociferously. The phrase "Six feet of earth makes us all of one size" is a popular one among these songs of terrestrial complacency. The following broadside is a nineteenth-century expression of the theme; a late example is the rural jukebox favorite "They Can Only Fill One Grave," composed by Roy Acuff, popular hillbilly entertainer and unsuccessful candidate for the governorship of Tennessee.

SIX FEET OF EARTH

I will sing you a song of this world and its ways,
And of the many strange people we meet,
From the rich man who rolls in his carriage and four,
To the poor starving man on the street.
There is many a man, in tatters and rags,
We should never attempt to despise,
For think of the adage and remember, kind friends,
That six feet of earth makes us all of one size.

There is the rich man with thousands to spare if he choose,
Though he haughtily holds up his head,
And he thinks he's above the mechanic who toils,
And is honestly earning his bread;
Though his gold and his jewels he can't take away,
To that land up above when he dies,
For death levels all and conclusively shows,
That six feet of earth makes us all of one size.

There is many a coat that is tattered and torn,
Yet covers a brave manly heart,
But although he's not dressed like his neighbor in silk,
Society keeps them apart.
On one fortune smiles, while on the other it frowns,

No matter what venture he tries,
But death calls them to the grave in the end,
And six feet of earth makes them all of one size.

* * *

—Broadside in Harris Collection, Brown University.

2. Negro songs of protest

Look down dat lonesome road!
Look down!
De way are dark an' col'
Dey makes me weep, dey makes me moan,
All cause my love are sold.

THE SOCIAL BACKGROUND

"A nigger sings about two things—what he eats and his woman."[1] Euphemistically rephrased and with some extension of definite bounds made to include spirituals, this critical dictum of a Southern plantation overseer represents the opinion of most people today in regard to the nature and extent of Negro folksong. Even scholars who believe that there are other motivations for the composition of folksong than the satisfaction of the need for entertainment and diversion, are not agreed on explanations for the comparative paucity of songs embodying protest and discontent from an ethnic group whose history in America for the past three hundred years has been a story of almost continuous oppression

[1] John A. Lomax, "Self-Pity in Negro Folk Songs," *The Nation*, vol. 105 (August 9, 1917), p. 141.

by the dominant majority. Hundreds of abolitionist songs expressing all gradations of protest from empty rhetoric to bitterness have been preserved from a group to whom slavery was at worst a vicarious grievance, but from the Negro himself very few songs other than his spirituals remain. Opinions differ as to how much expression of hatred, revenge, and protest is to be found in the spirituals. One scholar said of these, "Nowhere in these songs can we trace any suggestion of hatred or revenge, two qualities usually developed under slavery."[2] Other observers, like Sterling Brown and John Lovell, Jr., are convinced that the spirituals are symbolic expressions of conscious protest; some, represented by Lawrence Gellert, believe that the Negro has concealed his songs of discontent from white listeners whom he distrusts; a few, like Alan Lomax, maintain that all Negro song is protest—not the superficial "You-hurt-me-I-hate-you-I-fight-you" sort of thing, but a deeper, more profound manifestation of discontent whose meaning is often hidden from the singer himself, so that it becomes almost subconscious. And of course there remains on the other hand a considerable body of opinion which holds that there is very little genuine protest in Negro song—spirituals and secular pieces—except that which has been stimulated by the catalytic agent of white agitation.

On the basis of the insufficient evidence that remains from the early periods of American Negro history, it is probably impossible to find where in this morass of conflicting theories the truth lies. The best that may be hoped for is a syncretism of the more logical contentions; but even this goal may not be achieved without a reëxamination of the acculturation of the Negro during slavery times. There can be no social or economic protest without awareness of imposed oppression; sometimes this awareness comes from without, sometimes—and this process is much slower—it grows spontaneously out of innate understanding. Whether the Negro under slavery had attained the level of cultural orientation necessary before protest can become articulate must be determined before the search for songs of protest can be justified. Traditionally it has been supposed that the enslaved Negro was congenitally submissive, and therefore he willingly accepted economic security

[2] Wilson R. Howe, "The Negro and His Songs," *Southern Workman*, vol. 51 (August, 1922), p. 382.

and paternalistic solicitude in exchange for personal liberty. Too often, however, the statement of this belief emanates from authors who tacitly concur with the Southerner who told Lawrence Gellert, "Niggers are a happy and contented lot. Find me one that ain't and I'll give you a ten-dollar bill, suh. Worth it to string up the biggity black so-and-so." Life among the magnolias was for the slave far from being an idyllic existence. Economic security was assured only to the best workers (whose skill, strength, and willingness increased the expected optimum work-production unit and conversely decreased the food and clothing allotment for the weaker hands, women, and children); for the others, bare subsistence was often so uncertain that extra-legal appropriation of food and clothing—"taking" to the slaves, "stealing" to the masters —became so general that it was considered by the slaveholders to be a racial trait of the Negro. When Mr. Bones answered "Nobody in here but us chickens, boss," his joke had for many in his audience social implications too deep for laughter.

> Ol' massa's chicken
> Live in the tree;
> Chicken never roost
> Too high fo' me.
>
> Went out strollin'
> See what I can see;
> Chicken never roost
> Too high fo' me.[3]

With every fluctuation in the national or international business index, the suffering of the Negro slave increased. In time of depression or panic he was the first to feel deprivation; in time of prosperity his productivity was forced higher so that the master could take advantage of favorable business conditions. The oft-repeated statement that it was economically unwise for the slaveholder to mistreat his slaves just as it would be economically unwise for him to destroy farm equipment or mistreat domestic animals appeals only to superficial logic, for the analogy is invalid. The slave was neither a plow nor a mule; he was a rational being, and like his fellow intelligent human beings, he was in a state of constant dissatisfaction with his immediate condition. Kind

[3] Howard W. Odum and Guy B. Johnson, *Negro Workaday Songs*, Chapel Hill, 1929.

treatment by his master would progressively raise the standard of his expectation until eventually the structure of the Southern social system would be undermined; consequently the preservation of the slavocracy depended on the slaveholders' ability to keep the slaves' expected share of the common good—the Carlyleian Common Denominator—as small as possible. In still another way the difference between the Negro and the mule made deliberate mistreatment an expediency: Punishment by deprivation or curtailment of food or clothing allotments, separation of families, and unusual corporal punishment became for the slaves direct incentives for increased production and more abject obedience; a mule similarly treated would not react. The psychological effects of frustrating the natural rebelliousness of the human animal by systematized cruelty were of no concern to the slaveholder.

The fact that the Negro, in many cases, responded as expected has been interpreted as proof of submissiveness as a Negro racial characteristic. This belief is supported also by the fact that the Negro, rather than the Indian, became the American slave.[4] But what has been taken for submissiveness might have been an intelligence more highly developed than the Indian's; intelligence to understand that a tree must bend in a gale, or break. The Indian refused to bend, and thereby nearly succeeded in exterminating himself. The West African Negro at the time of his exploitation had attained a relatively high degree of civilization, and was too far advanced culturally to accept without complaint enslavement as his divinely ordained status among men.

The necessity of keeping the incipient rebelliousness of a subjugated intelligent people under constant control was recognized by the slavocrats, who, blind as they may have been to the inherent rights of man, were not blind to economic and social expediency. Free assembly and communication among slaves, which would have led to the exchange of ideas and dissemination of the seeds of revolt, above all else had to be prevented, and so a number of regulations were instituted which made the slave a prisoner on his master's plantation. Not only was he forbidden to buy or sell without his master's permission, to carry arms, to vote, or to testify

---

[4] Early attempts to enslave the Indian failed because of his total lack of submissiveness. Not only did the Indian prefer to die rather than work in slavery, but he frequently escaped, and unlike the escaped Negro, returned in strength to kill his former master.

in any case involving a white man, but he was not allowed to meet with his fellow slaves unless a white man were present. Movement beyond plantation limits without a pass, signed by his master, stating the slave's reason for being abroad and the time when he had to return, guaranteed for the offending slave a lashing from the armed bands of patrollers who rode circuit regularly throughout the South. These prohibitions and others were extended to curtail the activities of free Negroes (who were a constant source of uneasiness to the slavocrats), and had provisions also to punish whites who were in any way responsible for incitement to unrest among the slaves.[5] In 1852 Louisiana passed a law stating:

> Whosoever shall write, print, publish, or distribute any thing having a tendency to produce discontent among the free coloured population of the state, shall, upon conviction, be sentenced to imprisonment at hard labor for life, or suffer death, at the discretion of the court.[6]

"Incitement" was capable of the widest interpretation: to teach a slave to read and write, for example, in many parts of the South visited the betrayer of his class with severe punishment.[7] Even religion, which the slaveholders encouraged for its efficacy in sublimating protest and discontent, was censored; preachers were enjoined to deliver but one text, *Be obedient,* and to relate it to temporal life by illustrating the godliness of loyalty to the master.

Not only sublimation of protest was consciously striven for by the slaveholders, but misdirection of protest also. The discontent of the slaves, which simmered ominously despite the many controls set upon it by the masters, was turned in upon itself by the building up of an artificial caste system in which domestic workers (invariably the most tractable of the slaves) were favored with better food, clothing, and shelter, and placed in semiofficial as-

[5] The general laws, regulations, and restrictions cited here are a conflation of slave laws, which varied from state to state. In some states no provisions were made prohibiting some phases of slave activity, but usually local ordinances made up the lack. In any case, it is certain that "The dominant race in the South depended more upon expediency than upon fine-spun legal enactments in their dealings with the inferior."—H. M. Henry, *The Police Control of the Slave in South Carolina,* Emory, Va., 1914, p. 134.

[6] George M. Stroud, *A Sketch of the Laws Relating to Slavery in the Several States of the United States of America,* Philadelphia, 1856, p. 249.

[7] Slave narratives offer evidence that persons who taught reading to Negroes were in danger of losing their lives. E.g., see B. A. Botkin, *Lay My Burden Down,* Chicago, 1945, p. 50.

cendency over the common (and less pliant) field workers. A further hint of the instability of slavery is evident in the fact that the slavocrats went so far as to channel the slaves' discontent against other whites—poor whites, to be sure, but whites neverthe-less. It was more than mere economic expediency that drew recruits for the hated "paterollers" from the poor whites, or "white trash," as many of this class are known even today by the Negroes. This particular channel of protest misdirection was eminently success-ful; Negro folklore and folksong abound with expressions like

> *Little nigger baby, black face an' shinin' eye,*
> *Jes' as good as de po' white trash in de sweet bye an' bye.*

It is perhaps indicative of the number of protest songs that have been lost through white suppression that there is a consid-erable stock of Negro songs still current directing insult against the poor white, songs that were more likely to have been tolerated than proscribed by the slavocrats. Throughout the South at the present time considerate Negroes will not sing "Oh, My God, Them 'Taters" in the presence of poor whites for fear of hurting their feelings:

"OH, MY GOD, THEM 'TATERS"

Paw didn't raise no corn this year;
Paw didn't raise no 'maters;
Had bad luck with the cabbage crop,
But Oh, my God! them 'taters!

Sixty cent pertaters!
Nigh six-bit pertaters!
Had bad luck with the cabbage crop,
But Oh, my God! them 'taters!

The significance of this song, not immediately apparent, is that the Negro, though frequently in a worse economic plight, could ridicule the poor white who had to pour his energies into a worn-out farm which could produce nothing but potatoes.[8] The hypocrisy of the poor whites, who expressed contempt for the Negro while pursuing his women, is reflected in song also:

Lookin' for my wife this mornin'
Where do you think I found her?
Down in the middle of the cotton field
With the white boys all around her.

There can be no doubt that the Negro ante-bellum South was never without unrest, not all of which could be sublimated into religion or misdirected into internecine class hatred and despite for outcasts of the dominant race. Of the numerous outlets for the great body of residual discontent the most overt were sabotage, escape, and revolt, all of which required a higher degree of understanding than is necessary for the singing of songs of protest. Sabotage was extremely common, and manifested itself in various ways, from simple hoe-breaking to self-mutilation, infanticide, and suicide.[9] No accurate figures exist to show how many slaves succeeded in escaping, but certainly the number exceeded one hun-

[8] Concerning Negro songs of ridicule, Professor Guy B. Johnson suggests the possibility of tangential development of American Negro protest songs from a carry-over of African songs of ridicule, which had attained a definite pattern in native folk culture. There does not appear to be any unquestionable survival of this genre in Negro songs of protest, however.

[9] A folk-memory of slavery sabotage was discovered by Lawrence Gellert a few years ago in Atlanta, Georgia. Seeing two large Negro boys handling a third rather roughly, he intervened, only to be told by the boy on the bottom, "That's all right, mister, we's jes' playin' 'spoilin' de 'gyptians.'" "Despoiling the Egyptians" was slave-lingo for destroying the masters' property.

dred thousand. Herbert Aptheker, in his *Negro Slave Revolts in the United States*, records more than 250 reported slave insurrections, some of which attained astounding magnitude. Gabriel's Conspiracy in 1800, for example, involved, according to one observer, an estimated fifty thousand slaves. Some historians have disparaged the Negro slave revolts because they were in most cases minor and in all cases unsuccessful. But the amazing thing about these revolts, in view of the restrictions imposed on the slaves by the masters, is not that they occurred extensively, but that they occurred at all. One wonders how the awareness of oppression, which is prerequisite to this kind of violent protest, became so widespread. There is no question that the restrictions and mistreatments inflicted by the slaveholders did much to engender active unrest where only passive discontent existed, but it is equally certain that agitation came from outside—from Southern white antislavists, from the quarter-million free Negroes in the South, from Northern abolitionists, white and Negro.[10]

Despite this evidence of seething unrest, it is not to be supposed that all the slaves were in a state of incipient revolt. Just as the labor force of the United States today abounds in "scissorbills,"[11] so the ante-bellum South abounded in what the discrimination-conscious Negro derisively calls "handkerchief-heads."[12] Published slave narratives show that there was at least as much complacency as discontent among the slaves.[13] And it should be remembered that almost every slave revolt was suppressed through the aid of a treacherous slave who betrayed his fellows. Perhaps the slave culture in the early part of the nineteenth century could be compared to fourteenth-century England, with part of the population consciously or unconsciously resigned to hardship and misery on earth as a trial to prove their worthiness for heaven, and a smaller, more militant group, better oriented to the wider aspects of human relationships, disseminating the revolutionary ideas of *Piers Plowman* and the Lollards. No all-inclusive generalizations can be made

10 More than a score of Negro journals and papers were published before the Emancipation Proclamation.
11 Complacent workers who refuse to join the union, or who become "popsickle men," members of company unions.
12 Negroes obsequious to whites.
13 See B. A. Botkin, *Lay My Burden Down;* Bernard Robb, *Welcum Hinges;* Orland Kay Armstrong, *Old Massa's People.*

concerning the extent of unrest among the slaves; all that can be advanced with any confidence is a theory of acculturation which finds the ante-bellum Negro protest movement neither invariable nor continuous, but only representative of the controlling majority. With the exceptions that this conclusion implies in mind, it may safely be concluded that the prevailing reaction to slavery among the Negroes was one of discontent, unrest, and protest.

Where then are the songs that in other cultures, and in other phases of our culture, chronicle the discontent of the oppressed group? Such violent upheavals as the slave revolts should have produced many songs and ballads,[14] yet next to nothing remains. The song about Nat Turner, unlike the other songs in this study, is not a typical representative of a large group, but is virtually anomalous.

THE SPIRITUALS

The most obvious place to begin searching for Negro songs of protest is in the spirituals, the largest and most stable body of Negro song preserved from slavery days; but of the approximately one thousand spirituals extant, only a handful—and these from the Civil War period—contain any unequivocal overt protest against the system of slavery or the oppressors who administered it.

It has been mentioned that some students of Negro folksong maintain that the spirituals were full of deliberately hidden double meanings, consciously inserted by their composers, and recognized by all the Negroes who sang them. This theory was first advanced by Sterling Brown[15] who buttressed his arguments with quotations from the writings of Frederick Douglass and Harriet Tubman who, it should be noted, were hardly typical slaves. John Lovell, Jr., has been perhaps the most outspoken proponent of this interpretation of the spiritual, and has offered the best evidence to support it, though his arguments are not always impregnable. Few readers, for instance, will see in "nearly every spiritual" the three *leitmotifs* which he finds there: "the Negro's obsession for freedom, . . . the slaves' desire for justice in the judgment upon his betrayers which

[14] Although it must be admitted that the Negro talent for folksong composition lies in other directions than the ballad.
[15] Sterling Brown, *The Negro Poetry and Drama*, Washington, 1937.

some might call revenge," and "the slaves' tactic of battle, the strategy by which he expected to gain an eminent future."[16] Lovell offers this as a typical interpretation of a spiritual, in this case, "I Got Shoes":

"When I get to heav'm" means when I get free. It is a Walt Whitman "I," meaning any slave, present or future. If I personally don't, my children or grandchildren or my friend on the other side of the plantation will. What a glorious sigh these people breathed when one of their group slipped through to freedom! What a tragic intensity they felt when one was shot down trying to escape! So, the group speaks in the group way, all for one, one for all. "When I get to heav'm, gonna put on my shoes," that means he has talents, abilities, programs manufactured, ready to wear. On Douglass' plantation the slaves bossed, directed, charted everything—horse-shoeing, cart-mending, plow-repairing, coopering, grinding, weaving, "all completely done by slaves." But he has much finer shoes than that which he has no choice to wear. He does not mean that he will outgrow work, but simply that he will make his work count for something, which slavery prevents. When he gets a chance, he says, he is going to "shout all over God's heav'm"—make every section of his community feel his power. He knows he can do it.[17]

This is certainly a plausible interpretation of the spiritual, undeniably stimulating, and just possibly valid, but there is a good deal of speciousness in it too. The first sentence is plain enough in significance—"When I get to heav'm" means when I get free—and not too difficult to apprehend. But to continue probing for hidden meanings like this excerpt was utterly beyond the capacity of most slaves. To comprehend such symbolism as is contained in the last four sentences of Lovell's interpretation even after the meaning had been explained would impute to the slave an understanding of literary symbolism possessed by few people today who are trained to recognize such buried meanings. It makes of Uncle Tom an enigmatist as skillful as Dylan Thomas. If Lovell's conclusions are accepted, a theme of symbolic protest could be found in every spiritual, but too many spirituals and Negro religious songs are transparent conflations of biblical text and temporal application to make this theory tenable. Even the story of

[16] John Lovell, Jr., "The Social Implications of the Negro Spiritual," *Journal of Negro Education*, vol. 8 (October, 1939), p. 640.
[17] *Ibid.*, p. 641.

Dives and Lazarus—made to order for social implication—ends
with this stanza:

> Now sinners I have sung to you
> This awful dreadful story;
> Believe, believe, this record true,
> And strive to get to glory.
> Tormenting Divers warns us all
> And Jesus now is calling.
> Oh! hasten to the gospel call
> And thus be save from ruin.[18]

Of course the white influence in this song is obvious, but as
Pullen Jackson has conclusively shown, the Negro spiritual, instead
of being purely of Negro origin as formerly believed, is a selective
adaptation of white spirituals, which in turn derive from earlier
and more conscious religious art. Since this adaptation seems in
most cases to have consisted mainly of simplification of rime—

> If you get there before I do
> You may tell them I am coming

of the white spiritual becomes in the Negro adaptation,

> If you get there before I do
> Tell all my friends I'm coming too

the fact of their white origin would preclude the possibility of
any extensive and deliberate imbedding of symbolic meaning.

But it is just as rash to conclude that there is no symbolism in
the spirituals as to state that they are all symbolic. The spirituals
were all things to all men; of three Negroes singing "I Got Shoes,"
one Negro might interpret the shoes as his latent abilities, mordant
in a slave society; another might see himself literally strolling
through heaven in golden footwear; for the third singer the word
"shoes" might not arouse any image in the extensional world
whatever. As observers from a distance of a century or more, we
are in no position to make arbitrary interpretations; we are just
as likely, from this distance, to be as wrong as the Northerner who

[18] Reprinted by permission of Dodd, Mead, & Co., from *More Mellows*, by
R. Emmet Kennedy, copyright 1931 by R. Emmet Kennedy.

without any knowledge of the economic condition the song reflects, tries to find the hidden implication in "Oh my God Them 'Taters."

In favor of the theory of hidden meaning in the spirituals, it must be said that the Southern slavocrats thought that some of them at least carried a message which had to be suppressed. Of the evidently innocuous spiritual "We Shall Be Free" (also titled "My Father, How Long?") Thomas Higginson, one of the early collectors of spirituals, wrote:

> For singing this the negroes had been put in jail in Georgetown, S. C. at the outbreak of the Rebellion. "We'll soon be free" was too dangerous an assertion, and though the chant was an old one, it was no doubt sung with redoubled emphasis during the new events. "De Lord will call us home" was evidently thought to be a symbolic verse; for, as a little drummer boy explained it to me, showing all his white teeth as he sat in the moonlight by the door of my tent, "Dey tink *de Lord* mean for say de Yankees."[19]

Even this statement cannot be taken unreservedly as evidence of conscious symbolism, for Allen, commenting on the same spiritual and the significance which its words had for the citizens of Georgetown, says, "In this case the suspicion was unfounded."[20] The whites in this case may have been frightened by a phantom, like the army censors who in the last war prohibited the mailing of chess-game moves because they thought that the apparently esoteric symbols were secret messages of a spy ring.

Nevertheless it is probable that the Negroes at the time of the Civil War, when freedom at last seemed to be within the range of hope, reëxamined the old spirituals and songs with a view to finding symbolic application behind words that probably had only their obvious meaning when first written. In any event, it is safer to conclude that symbolism, where it is to be found in the early spirituals, is *ex post facto*. The composition of spirituals in which the symbolism is obvious, or in which the protest becomes explicit, can usually be attributed to the Civil War era when manumission was imminent, and the slaves were therefore less fearful of intimi-

19 Thomas Wentworth Higginson, "Negro Spirituals," *Atlantic Monthly*, vol. 19 (June, 1867), p. 691.
20 William Francis Allen, *Slave Songs of the United States*, New York, 1867.

dation. In his note to "Many Thousands Go" ("No More Auction Block for Me") Allen says:

A song to which the rebellion had actually given rise. This was composed by nobody knows whom—though it was the most recent doubtless of all the spirituals—and had been sung in secret to avoid detection. It is certainly plaintive enough. The peck of corn and pint of salt were slavery's rations.

Many spirituals suggest themselves as likely vehicles for symbolism: "Go Down, Moses," and "The Lord Delivered Daniel," among the better-known examples; among the less familiar are a number of spirituals like "Good News, Member," which may well have been used to report the success of an escaped slave's flight via the Underground Railroad:

> *Good news, member, good news, member;*
> *Don't you mind what Satan say.*
> *Good news, member, good news, member—*
> *I heard from heaven today.*

> *My brudder have a seat and I am glad,*
> *My brudder have a seat and I am glad,*
> *Good news, member, good news.*

> *My Hawley have a home in Paradise,*
> *My Hawley have a home in Paradise,*
> *Good news, member, good news.*

Similarly, the hope to escape might be understood by spirituals of which "I Want to Join the Band" and "Oh, Brothers, Don't Get Weary" are typical:

> *What is that up yonder I see?*
> *Two little angels comin' a'ter me.*
> *I want to join the band,*
> *I want to join the band,*
> *I want to join the band.*

> *Oh, brothers, don't get weary,*
> *Oh, brothers, don't get weary,*
> *Oh, brothers, don't get weary,*
> *We're waiting for the Lord.*

We'll land on Canaan's shore,
We'll land on Canaan's shore,
We'll land on Canaan's shore,
We'll rest forever more.[21]

Though there may be some question concerning the extent of symbolism in the spirituals, there can be no doubt that the suggestiveness of the words and mood was limited only by the imagination and emotional receptivity of the listener. "Run to Jesus" impresses the modern white reader as having no special distinction either in words or feeling, yet it was the song which first suggested to Frederick Douglass the thought of escaping from slavery.[22]

The question whether the spirituals were pregnant with suggestiveness of symbolism is actually too slight an aspect of the function of the spiritual as an outlet for Negro sorrow and discontent to warrant the attention that has been given it. The real value of the spiritual as a vehicle for emotional relief lay in its mood and tone rather than in its words. Du Bois calls them the Sorrow Songs: "They are the music of an unhappy people, of the children of disappointment; they tell of death and suffering and unvoiced longing toward a truer world, of misty wanderings and hidden ways." [23]

Significantly, the dominant tone of the music is sorrow, with overtones of hope; in such a setting, the words mean little. The lyrics of "I'm Troubled in Mind" are in a biblical way adequate for the situation, but the tremendous empathic response which the contributor of this spiritual said it evoked doubtless was elicited by the music.[24]

[21] There are a number of Going-to-Canaan songs and spirituals (see end of this chapter for one which has crossed the line into white hillbilly song). Brown and Lovell interpret Canaan as meaning Canada, but until the Act of 1850 which consolidated and enforced the fugitive slave laws, the goal of the Negro was the other side of the Ohio. Canada was utterly beyond the comprehension of the majority of escaped slaves. In his *History of the Underground Railroad in Chester and the Neighboring Counties of Pennsylvania*, R. C. Smedley observes, "The idea prevailed to a considerable extent among the slaves that when they crossed the Susquehanna they were on free ground, and were safe" (p. 48).

[22] J. B. T. Marsh, *The Story of the Jubilee Singers*, Boston, 1880, p. 188.

[23] W. E. B. Du Bois, *The Souls of Black Folk*, Chicago, 1924, p. 253.

[24] It has been suggested that improvised religious songs such as the ring shouts have been vehicles for protest. But for the ring shout, at least, there does not seem to be any possibility of secular protest finding a way into the frenzied religious fervor. The Negro in the throes of a ring shout is not thinking of temporal woes.

SECULAR SONGS

Very few Negro secular songs of protest have been preserved from before the Civil War, certainly too few to justify any
generalizations except those which may be based on songs of
later origin which seem to derive from similar ancestry. It is not
surprising that ante-bellum secular protest songs—which must have
existed in appreciable number—have vanished. The traditional
ephemerality of Negro secular song, the restricted communication
among the slaves (and the expediency of utilizing the few opportunities of communication for messages of more importance), the
severity of punishment should any Negro be caught singing songs
objectionable to the whites, the inability of most slaves to read
and write—all combined to obviate the possibility of these songs
being disseminated to an extent in ante-bellum days sufficient for
them to have become traditional. That some songs of protest
existed in the pre-Civil War era is indicated by the imbedded—
petrified—protest found in many of the minstrel songs which,
though debasements, derived ultimately from Negro secular songs.

WALK IN JOE

Black my boots in de kitchen
Sebenty-five cents to de quarter,
Black 'em wid Day & Martin, make 'em shine,
    an' dat for sartin
Massa sue me for de treason, 'kase he couldn't
    dat's de reason.

   Walk in Joe, walk in Joe,
   Walk in Joe, now I'll be your friend, John;
   A long way to go and no money for to spend.

Sheep's meat is too good for colored people;
Sheep's meat is too good for niggers;
When I went into de house, no one dar 'cept a mouse
Sittin' by de fireplace, dar was a rat eatin' grease.
                                    —Broadside in Library of Congress.

NIGGER BE A NIGGER

Nigger be a nigger whatever you do;
Ties red rag round de toe of his shoe,
Jerk his vest on over his coat,
Snatch his britches up round his throat.
God make a nigger, make 'im in de night;
Make 'im in a hurry an' forgot to paint 'im white.

The process of imbedding Negro protest into blackface minstrel ridicule is seen in the two versions of a song whose refrain, beginning with "Oh, it's hard to be a nigger," is the nucleus around which a ring of maverick stanzas revolve. The first is obviously far from the original, but still further from the second, a minstrel song become a children's rime (submitted by a Pennsylvania white informant):

> White man goes to college,
> Nigger goes to fiel';
> White man learns to read an' write,
> Nigger learns to steal.

> REFRAIN: Oh, it's hard to be a nigger!
> Oh, it's hard to be a nigger!
> 'Cause a nigger don't get no show.

> I went walking one fine day;
> I met Mis' Chickie upon my way.
> Oh, her tail was long and her feathers were blue—
> Caw, caw, Missis Chickie, I'm on to you.

> REFRAIN: Oh, it's hard to be a niggie, niggie, niggie;
> Oh, it's hard to be—
> And you can't get your money when it's due.

The decade immediately following the Civil War made many contributions to the Negro songbag, but most of these are lamentably the product of white ventriloquism. I have included a few as illustrations of the type because, though most are palpably far from the folk, some have had their bar sinister obscured if not removed by their subsequent adoption by more cultured Negro singers. More authenticity may be detected in songs like "Slavery Chain Done Broke at Last," and "You Are Free."

Another large class of early Negro secular songs of discontent was undoubtedly metamorphosed into the blues, a category of Negro expression so well known that little illustration or discussion is necessary here. Richard Wright's definition of the blues, however, is worth recording:

The form of the blues is simple and direct; there is usually one line that repeats and rimes, followed by a longer line that rimes with the preceding two and expresses a judgment, clarification, or resolution, as

> *I woke up this morning, rain water in my bed;*
> *I woke up this morning, rain water in my bed;*
> *You know my roof is leaking, Lord, leaking on my head.*

The form of the blues can be expressed figuratively: A man encounters a strange object; he walks around it twice, noting all of its features, then he renders a statement as to its meaning and relationship to him.[25]

The years following emancipation may best be described as the era of disillusionment—the time when the Negro discovered that freedom meant a continuance of the old restrictions but now carried on beyond the law, with a cessation only of such security as the master had afforded him—and as such may be extended to the present day. It is a period teeming in productiveness of songs of protest, but how many of the extant songs derive from the postbellum years is impossible to tell. There are no internal evidence, allusions, or written texts to determine the date of composition by; virtually the only guide available for establishing the age of a Negro song is to see how widespread certain phrases were at the time of collection. Fragments like

> *Nigger and white man*
> *Playin' seven-up;*
> *Nigger win de money,*
> *Skeered to pick it up.*
>
> *Aught for aught*
> *And figger for figger;*
> *All for de white man,*
> *Nothin' for de nigger.*
>
> *Went down to (N)*
> *Never been there before;*
> *White folk on the feather bed,*
> *Nigger on the floor.*
>
> *Nigger plow de cotton,*
> *Nigger pick it out;*
> *White man pockets money,*
> *Niggers does without.*

[25] From "Notes on Jim Crow Blues," the preface to Keynote album 107, *Southern Exposure.* Copyright Mercury Records Corp. Used by permission.

are found everywhere in the South. Some have crept into white
hillbilly music.[26] The antiquity of these phrases is established not
only by their wide diffusion, but also by the sometimes intangible
insincerity of the context in which they are found, so that whatever genuine protest the fragment once had has been lost, leaving
only a shell of rhetorical protest:

> *Niggers get the turpentine,*
> *Niggers pick it out;*
> *White man pockets the money,*
> *Niggers does without.*
> *White man thinks he's smart,*
> *Niggers knows he's dumb;*
> *White man sits and thinks,*
> *Us niggers eats and drinks.*
> *Come now and do your number,*
> *Don't do de big apple, but do de cucumber.*[27]

Even the last two lines of the refrain of "Me and My Captain,"
title song of Lawrence Gellert's collection of chain-gang songs,
seem to have been preserved for the felicity of phrase rather than
for the sincerity of protest:

> *Me and my captain*
> *We don't agree;*
> *He don't know*
> *'Cause he don't ask me.*
>
> *He don't know,*
> *He don't know my mind;*
> *When he see me laughing*
> *Just to keep from crying.*

[26] If the Negro borrowed his religious song from the white man, as the consensus
of recent scholarship indicates, the debt was more than repaid by his contribution of
much secular song to the white man. Jimmie Rodgers, the man who put the yodel
into hillbilly song and whom the rural South knows perhaps better than any other
singer, rode to the top of the Victor Record Company's popularity list in the early
1930's with a repertoire made up almost entirely of conflate fragments of Negro
song. Constantly his compositions are collected by folklorists and accepted as genuine
folksong—which of course is as it should be. See Vance Randolph's *Ozark Folksongs*,
vol. IV, for "The Soldier's Sweetheart"; Mellinger Henry's *Songs Sung in the Southern Appalachians* for *Blue Yodel No. 1* (listed as "T for Texas," p. 71); MacEdward
Leach and Horace P. Beck, "Songs from Rappahannock County, Virginia," JAFL,
vol. 63, p. 280, for *Blue Yodel No. 8* (listed as "Mule Skinner Blues").

[27] Collected from Negro workers at a turpentine still near Bristow, Florida.

Protest, to be genuine, must have a hint at least of bitterness in it; any feeling of good-naturedness (not humor) drains all the meaning from a song of nominal protest and leaves only words.

The ephemerality of Negro secular song, the prevailing slightness of content, the ease with which expression is uttered, the flexibility of form, the absence of stanza continuity, the simplicity of statement, the lack of originality, the undoubted fact that much of it is communally composed—in short, nearly every characteristic of Negro song foredooms it to quick oblivion. That is why, although coöperative Negro informants seem to be bottomless wells of song, few songs, as such, have become traditional. The bulk of Negro song consists of perhaps a few hundred phrases which have long since become mavericks; after these basic stanzas have been deleted what is left is seldom on a higher literary plane than mere conversation—often not as high—and has as little chance of being preserved, even by the composer. Particularly this is true of chain-gang songs. A new prisoner was usually not allowed to talk, so he put his story into the song the gang happened to be singing:

> Little boy, little boy,
> How did you get so long?
>> Oh my Lord, believe I'll go to rolling;
>> Oh my Lord, believe I'll go to rolling;
>> Oh my Lord.
>
> They accused me of murder,
> I ain't harmed a thing.
>> Oh my Lord . . . .
>
> Little Willie, little Willie,
> Where did you come from?
>> Oh my Lord . . . .
>
> I came from Houston,
> The murderers' home.
>> Oh my Lord . . . .

And so on.

The largest group of Negro secular songs other than the blues (a category daily getting further and further from the folk) is work songs, which in turn are comprised—so far as collected songs are concerned—of chain-gang songs. Chain-gang songs form the bulk of Lawrence Gellert's published collection, and an imposing percentage of his unpublished collection of two thousand Negro songs of protest—a number which he resolves into about 150 basic song patterns. The theme is nearly always the same—complaint against the callousness and brutality of the captain or walker, the weight of the hammer, the wretchedness of living conditions. The same themes, with but slight variations growing out of the nominal freedom of the Negro imprisoned only by the economic and social strictures of the South, appear in the remainder of Gellert's songs which were collected on plantations, sharecroppers' farms, and lumber and turpentine work camps.

Gellert's finds have been questioned by other collectors, who have been unable to duplicate them. A few only are to be found in Odum and Johnson's studies, and a few more in unpublished recordings in the Library of Congress Archive of American Folk Song, but for the majority Gellert seems to have been uniquely successful as a song catcher.

He attributes this success to the unparalleled intimacy which he as a white collector attained with his informants. A collector, he says, who lives for weeks with the Negro, sleeping on "dirty floor pallets in miserable ghetto hovels" and sharing their pitiable fare, is likely to be far more successful in eliciting songs of protest than one who approaches his Negro informants through a white guard who summons them by bawling "Line up, niggers, and sing for the white gentleman."

The last two decades have seen a great production of songs of discontent, written by Negro "composers" of all cultural levels. The best of these, judging from an aspect of sincerity and genuine folk content, are those emanating from Negro sharecroppers, miners, textile workers, and other manual laborers of the less desirable trades. Evaluated as literature, few reach so high a level of accomplishment as *Strange Fruit*. As in many labor songs, the line that divides conscious art from folksay is often obfuscated, and consequently identification of folk material is difficult. Many of the late songs are manifestly products of political agitation—a perfectly valid and perhaps even laudable purpose in song writing, but one which raises again the obstacle of cultural orientation to folk acceptance.

WHITE ABOLITIONISTS

The Hutchinsons, probably America's most famous singing family, toured through the country for twenty years during the first half of the nineteenth century singing what were then topical songs. They allied themselves with reform movements of "every kind, sight, and smell," as Woody Guthrie would say. Some of these movements were undeniably twaddle, but their abolitionist activities made up for the other idealistic but abortive causes with which they were affiliated. Establishing a precedent for many of the songs being written today on topical subjects, they borrowed folk tunes for their propaganda.

GET OFF THE TRACK

(Tune: "Old Dan Tucker")

Ho the car Emancipation,
Rides majestic thro' our Nation
Bearing on its train the story,
Liberty, a Nation's glory.

REFRAIN: *Roll it along, roll it along,*
Roll it along through the Nation;
Roll it along through the Nation,
Freedom's Car, Emancipation.

Men of various predilections,
Frightened, run in all directions,
Merchants, Editors, Physicians,
Lawyers, Priests, and Politicians.

Get out the way, every station,
Clear the track, Emancipation.
Roll it along thro' the Nation,
Freedom's Car, Emancipation.

With slight adaptations, this basic song was used in the fight for industrial emancipation.

THE WORKINGMAN'S TRAIN

(Tune: "Old Dan Tucker")

Ho, the car Emancipation
Leaves, today, Industrial Station,
Bearing on its train of treasures
Labor's hopes in labor measures.

REFRAIN: *Get all aboard,*
Get all aboard,
Get all aboard, leave your plunder,
Get off the track or you'll fall under.

Tracks of scheming politician
Are but railroads to perdition;
Civil Service not our freight, sir.
Banks and tariffs, let them wait, sir.

Hark ye, Dives, Dick and Harry,
Come and view the freight we carry,
Blessings in all forms and guises,
Life, with all its joyful prizes.

—From broadside in Harris Collection,
Brown University.

SLAVES APPEAL

Is there no balm in christian lands,
No kind physician there,
To heal a broken heart and save
A brother from despair?

Is there no love in christian hearts,
To pity griefs like mine,
No tender sympathetic art
Sweet mercy to enshrine?

Must vile oppression's reckless form
Still beat upon my soul,
No sun of freedom ever dawn,
To make my spirit whole?

Just God, behold the negro's woe;
The white man's sins forgive;
Open his heart thy Love to Know,
To bid his brother live.

—Broadside, 1834. Harris Collection,
Brown University.

MY COUNTRY

(Tune: "America")

My country, 'tis for thee,
Dark land of slavery,
For thee I weep;
Land where the slave has sighed,
And where he toiled and died,
To serve a tyrant's pride—
For thee I weep.

From every mountain side,
Upon the ocean's tide,
They call on thee;
Amid thy rocks and rills,
Thy woods and templed hills,
I hear a voice which trills—
Let all go free.

Our fathers' God! to thee,
Author of liberty,
To thee we pray,
Soon may our land be pure,
Let freedom's light endure,
And liberty secure,
Beneath thy sway.

—Sung at Harmony Grove, Framingham,
Massachusetts, July 4, 1866.
—Broadside in Harris Collection, Brown University.

NEGRO ABOLITIONISTS

Frederick Douglass, the escaped slave who, like Harriet
Tubman, became a leading Negro abolitionist, gave this song to
the Jubilee Singers with the comment that it first suggested to him
the thought of escaping from slavery.

RUN TO JESUS

REFRAIN: *Run to Jesus, shun the danger,*
I don't expect to stay much longer here.

He will be our dearest friend,
And will help us to the end.
I don't expect to stay much longer here.

Oh, I thought I heard them say,
There were lions in the way.
I don't expect to stay much longer here.

Many mansions there will be,
One for you and one for me.
I don't expect to stay much longer here.

—J. B. T. Marsh, *The Story of the Jubilee Singers,*
Boston, 1880, p. 188.

Woody Guthrie made this "Ballad of Harriet Tubman." So unerringly does he strike at the heart of the matter in composing his song-stories, that annotations are an impertinence. It is perhaps excusable, however, to add that Harriet Tubman, whom John Brown called "the most of a man, naturally, that I ever met with," personally assisted over three hundred slaves to freedom, journeying time and time again into the South despite the danger to her life. She died on March 10, 1913, in Auburn, New York.

BALLAD OF HARRIET TUBMAN

(Tune: "Kansas Boys")

I was 5 years old in Bucktown, Maryland,
When into slavery I was sent;
I'll tell you of the beatings and of the fighting
In my 93 years I spent.

I helped a field hand make a run for freedom
When my 15th year was rolling around.
The guard he caught him in a little store
In a little slavery village town.

The boss made a grab to catch the field hand,
I jumped in and blocked the door;
The boss then hit me with a 2 pound iron scale
And I went black down on the floor.

On a bundle of rags in our log cabin
My mother she minstered to my needs.
It was here I swore I'd give my life blood
Just to fight to turn my people free.

In '44 I married John Tubman,
I loved him well till '49
But he would not come and fight beside me,
So I left him there behind.

I left Bucktown with my two brothers
But they got scared and went back home.
I followed my Northern star of freedom
And walked in the grass and trees alone.

I slept in a bar loft and in a haystack,
I stayed with my people in slavery's shacks
They said I'd die by the boss man's bullets
But I told them, I can't turn back.

The sun was shining in the early morning,
When I finally come to my free State Line,
I pinched myself to see if I was dreaming—
I just could not believe my eyes.

I went back home and got my parents
I loaded them into a buckboard hack;
We crossed 6 states and other slaves followed,
And up to Canada we made our tracks.

One slave got scared and tried to turn backward
And I pulled my pistol in front of his eyes;
I said, get up and walk to your freedom,
Or by this fireball you will die.

When John Brown hit them at Harper's Ferry,
My men were fighting right at his side,
When John Brown swung upon his gallows,
It was then I hung my head and cried.

Give the black man guns and powder,
To Abe Lincoln this I said.
You've just crippled the Snake of Slavery
We've got to fight to kill it dead!

When we faced the guns of lightning
And the thunders broke our sleep,
After we faced the bloody rainstorms
It was dead men that we reaped.

Yes, we faced the zigzag lightning
But was worth the price we paid;
When our thunder rumbled over
We'd laid slavery in its grave.

Come and stand around my deathbed,
I will sing some spirit songs;
I'm on my way to my greater Union
Now my 93 years are gone.

—Composed by Woody Guthrie, September 18, 1944.

SLAVERY DAYS

On Sunday, August 21, 1831, after a series of portents which convinced him of the divine inspiration for his rebellion, Nat Turner gathered a half-dozen fellow slaves and set out with the zeal of John Brown to free the South from slavery. Turner was a man whose natural gifts gained him some influence as a preacher among the slaves of Southampton County, Virginia, but whose innate intelligence was stultified by superstition. Five years before his final rebellion he had successfully escaped from his master, but returned after a month of freedom because he felt that flight from a lawful owner was irreconcilable with his religion. The ridicule heaped upon him by the other slaves stimulated a period of reconsideration which culminated in his revolt. Turner and his five companions began by killing their master and his family, and set out toward the county seat, killing every white they met. When Turner's force (which had grown to seventy slaves) was overwhelmed by regular and volunteer troops, about 150 persons, of whom 51 were white, had been killed. Turner himself eluded his pursuers for nine days, when he was captured and summarily hanged. The revolt meant the end of Southern abolitionist societies, but a more important result was that the slavocracy never again was free of the terror of incipient rebellion.

NAT TURNER

You mought be rich as cream,
And drive you a coach and four horse team;
But you can't keep the world from moving around,
And Nat Turner from the gaining ground.

You mought be reader and writer too,
And wiser than old Solomon the Jew;
But you can't keep the world from moving around,
And Nat Turner from the gaining ground.

And your name it mought be Caesar sure,
And got you cannon can shoot a mile or more;
But you can't keep the world from moving around,
And Nat Turner from the gaining ground.

—From Lawrence Gellert's unpublished collection.

One of the most unusual methods of escape was employed in 1848 by Henry Brown, a slave who had himself shipped in an unmarked wooden box, three feet one inch long, two feet wide, and two feet six inches deep, from Richmond, Virginia, to Philadelphia by the Adams Express Company. His accomplishment caught the public imagination, and Henry—thereafter "Box"—Brown journeyed through Northern cities recounting his escape before large audiences.

ESCAPE FROM SLAVERY OF HENRY BOX BROWN

(Tune: "Uncle Ned")

Here you see a man by the name of Henry Brown,
Ran away from the South to the North;
Which he would not have done but they stole all his rights,
But they'll never do the like again.

REFRAIN: *Brown laid down the shovel and the hoe,*
Down in the box he did go;
No more Slave work for Henry Box Brown,
In the box by express he did go.

The orders they were given and the cars they did start,
Roll along—roll along—roll along—
Down to the landing where the steamboat met,
To bear the baggage off to the North.

When they packed the baggage on they turned him on his head,
There poor Brown liked to have died;
There were passengers on board who wished to set down,
And they turned the box on its side.

When they got to the cars they throwed the box off,
And down upon his head he did fall,
Then he heard his neck crack, and he thought he was dead,
But they never throwed him off any more.

When he got to Philadelphia they said he was in port,
And Brown he began to feel glad,
And he was taken on the wagon and carried to the place,
And left "this side up with care."

The friends gathered round and asked if all was right,
As down on the box they did rap,
Brown answered them saying "yes, all is right,"
And he was then set free from his pain.

—Broadside in American Antiquarian Society,
Worcester, Massachusetts.

As hard and as hateful as life on the plantation must have been for most slaves, it was at least bearable in the companionship of one's family and friends, and immensely to be preferred to the prospect of being sold to the deep South, to the unknown region of nameless horror. "All [escaped slaves] who were interrogated as to why they left their homes, gave nearly related answers. In the majority of cases it was the fear of being sold to go further South. . . . Being 'sold to Georgia' was the terror of plantation life." [28]

JOHNNY COME DOWN DE HOLLOW

Johnny come down de hollow—
    Oh, hollow.
De nigger trader got he—
    Oh, hollow.
De speculator bought me—
    Oh, hollow.
I'm sold for silver dollars—
    Oh, hollow.
Boys, go catch de pony—
    Oh, hollow.
Bring him round de corner—
    Oh, hollow.
I'm goin' way to Georgia—
    Oh, hollow.
Boys, good-bye forever—
    Oh, hollow.

—H. M. Henry, *The Police Control of the
Slave in South Carolina,* p. 56.

HILO! HILO!

William Rino sold Henry Silvers—
    Hilo! Hilo!
Sold him to de Georgy trader—
    Hilo! Hilo!

[28] R. C. Smedley, *History of the Underground Railroad* . . . , p. 270.

His wife she cried, and children bawled—
Hilo! Hilo!
Sold him to de Georgy trader—
Hilo! Hilo!

—J. D. Long, *Pictures of Slavery*,
Philadelphia, 1857, p. 198.

I AM SOLD AND GOING TO GEORGIA

This song is usually sung by the chained gangs of slaves who are on their way, being driven from Maryland, Virginia, and Kentucky, to the more southern states for sale. The last line of each verse is the chorus, and gives a most impressive effect when sung—as it often is— by 60 or 150 voices echoing the plaintive grief of their hearts. This last line is intended as an appeal to all who have it in their power to aid in bringing about the jubilee of emancipation.

—J. W. C. Pennington, D.D.

Despite Dr. Pennington's contemporary affidavit that this is a Negro song, most observers will agree that its white origin is transparent; but it is worth including, if only for Dr. Pennington's intriguing phrase, "sung . . . by 60 or 150 voices."

O! When shall we poor souls be free?
When shall these slavery chains be broke?
I am sold and going to Georgia,
Will you go along with me?
I am sold and going to Georgia,
Go sound the jubilee.

I left my wife and child behind,
They'll never see my face again;
I am sold and going to Georgia,
Will you go along with me?
I am sold and going to Georgia,
Go sound the jubilee.

I am bound to yonder great rice swamp,
Where my poor bones will find a grave;
I am sold and going to Georgia,
Will you go along with me?
I am sold and going to Georgia,
Go sound the jubilee.

> Farewell, my friends, I leave you all,
> I am sold, but I have done no fault;
> I am sold and going to Georgia,
> Will you go along with me?
> I am sold and going to Georgia,
> Go sound the jubilee.

—Library of Congress, Archive of American Folk Song, WPA Collection.

JOHNNIE, WONTCHA RAMBLE

I looked up on the hill and spied old Master ridin'   (2)
Johnnie, wontcha ramble, hoe, hoe, hoe.

Had a bull whip in one hand, cowhide in the other,   (2)
Johnnie, wontcha ramble, hoe, hoe, hoe.

Pocket full of leather strings to tie your hands together,   (2)
Johnnie, wontcha ramble, hoe, hoe, hoe.

Ole Mastah, don't you whip me, I'll give you half a dollar,   (2)
Johnnie, wontcha ramble, hoe, hoe, hoe.

Oh, no, Bully Boy, I'd rather hear you holler.   (2)
Johnnie, wontcha ramble, hoe, hoe, hoe.

—From Library of Congress, Archive of American Folk Song.

MISSUS IN DE BIG HOUSE

> Missus in de big house,
> Mammy in de yard.
> Missus holdin' her white hands,
> Mammy workin' hard.
> Mammy workin' hard,
> Mammy workin' hard,
> Missus holdin' her white hands,
> Mammy workin' hard.
>
> Ol' marse ridin' all time,
> Niggers workin' 'roun'.
> Marse sleepin' day time,
> Niggers diggin' in de groun'.
> Niggers diggin' in de groun',
> Niggers diggin' in de groun',
> Marse sleepin' day time,
> Niggers diggin' in de groun'.

—Odum and Johnson, op. cit., p. 117.

NOBODY KNOWS

This song was a favorite in the Sea Islands. Once when there had been a good deal of ill feeling excited and trouble was apprehended, owing to the uncertain action of the government in regard to the confiscated lands on the Sea Islands, General Howard was called upon to address the colored people earnestly. To prepare them to listen, he asked them to sing. Immediately an old woman on the outskirts of the meeting began "Nobody Knows the Trouble I've Seen" and the whole audience joined in. The General was so affected by the plaintive melody that he found it difficult to maintain his official dignity.

—Thos. P. C. Fenner, "Cabin and Plantation Songs," in Mrs. M. F. Armstrong and Helen Ludlow, *Hampton and Its Students*, New York, 1874.

This song was for the Negro what "John Brown's Body" was for the whites.

Oh, nobody knows de trouble I've seen
Nobody knows but Jesus.
Nobody knows de trouble I've seen
Glory hallelujah.

Sometimes I'm up, sometimes I'm down,
Oh, yes, Lord.
Sometimes I'm almost to de groun',
Oh, yes, Lord.

Although you see me goin' 'long so,
Oh, yes, Lord.
I have my trials here below,
Oh, yes, Lord.

One day when I was walkin' 'long,
Oh, yes, Lord.
De el'ment open'd an' Love came down,
Oh, yes, Lord.

I never shall forget that day,
Oh, yes, Lord.
When Jesus washed my sins away,
Oh, yes, Lord.

FATHER HOW LONG

See note on this song on page 78 above.

My father how long*   (3)
Poor sinner suffer here?

* *Mother, etc.*

And it won't be long (3)
Fore de Lord will call us home.

We'll soon be free (3)
De Lord will call us home.

We'll walk de mercy road (3)
Where pleasure never dies.

We'll walk de golden streets (3)
Of de new Jerusalem.

My brudder do sing (3)
De praises of de Lord.

We'll fight for liberty (3)
When de Lord will call us home.

—Thos. W. Higginson, "Negro Spirituals,"
Atlantic Monthly, vol. 19 (June 1867).

I'M TROUBLED IN MIND

The person who furnished this song (Mrs. Brown of Nashville, formerly a slave) stated that she first heard it from her old father when she was a child. After he had been whipped he always went and sat upon a certain log near his cabin, and with the tears streaming down his cheeks, sang this song with so much pathos that few could listen without weeping from sympathy; and even his cruel oppressors were not wholly unmoved.

—J. B. T. Marsh, The Story of the Jubilee Singers,
Boston, 1880, p. 173.

This song was in the repertoire of the Jubilee Singers, a group of young Negro singers who in 1871 carried their old spirituals through the world hoping to raise $20,000 for the impoverished school which was to grow into Fisk University. Despite harassing discrimination, the concert tour was successful above all expectations, and the eight young singers returned to their school with more than $100,000.

I'm troubled, I'm troubled, I'm troubled in mind,
If Jesus don't help me, I surely will die.

O Jesus, my Saviour, on thee I'll depend.
When troubles are near me, you'll be my true friend.

When ladened with trouble and burdened with grief,
To Jesus in secret I'll go for relief.

In dark days of bondage to Jesus I prayed,
To help me to bear it, and he gave me his aid.

UNDERGROUND RAILROAD

A slave song with undoubted hidden meaning is "The Drinking Gourd." It is an audible map of the local branch line of the Underground Railroad. The "Drinking Gourd" is, of course, the Big Dipper—north. "Peg foot" refers to an old white man with a wooden leg who led the Negroes north.

THE DRINKING GOURD

When the sun comes back and the first quail calls,
Follow the drinking gourd,
For the old man is waiting for to carry you to freedom
If you follow the drinking gourd.

REFRAIN: *Follow the drinking gourd,*
Follow the drinking gourd,
For the old man is waiting for to carry
you to freedom
If you follow the drinking gourd.

The river bank will make a very good road,
The dead trees show you the way,
Left foot, peg foot travelling on,
Following the drinking gourd.

The river ends between two hills,
Follow the drinking gourd.
There's another river on the other side,
Follow the drinking gourd.

Where the great big river meets the little river,
Follow the drinking gourd.
The old man is a-waiting for to carry you to freedom,
If you follow the drinking gourd.

I'M ON MY WAY

A typical "going-to-Canaan" song; possibly an Underground Railroad song. The Carter Family, famous white hillbilly singers, have made a record of a version of this song utterly without slavery significance.

I'm on my way, and I won't turn back!   *(3)*
I'm on my way, great God, I'm on my way.

I'm on my way to Canaan's land   *(3)*
I'm on my way, great God, I'm on my way.

I ask my sister to come go with me   *(3)*
I'm on my way, great God, I'm on my way.

If she says no, I'll go alone   *(3)*
I'm on my way, great God, I'm on my way.

I ask my boss to let me go   *(3)*
I'm on my way, great God, I'm on my way.

If he says no, I'll go anyhow   *(3)*
I'm on my way, Great God, I'm on my way!

JUBILEE SONGS—NEGRO

Compare "A-goin' Shout" with a more literate version "No More Mourning" sung by Carl Sandburg on Musicraft record 209.

A-GOIN' SHOUT

Ummmmmmmmph, Ummmmmmmmmph, heaven   (3)
Over thee, over thee
I got de glory in my soul
And de witness in my breast
I'm goin' whar Jesus is.

Ummmmmmmmmph, Ummmmmmmmmph, heaven   (3)
Over thee, over thee,
Befo' I'd be a slave
I'd be buried in my grave
An' go home to my Lawd and be free.

Ummmmmmmmmmph, Ummmmmmmmmmph, Ummmmmmmmmmph   (3)
Ummmmmmmmmmph, Ummmmmmmmmmph, prayer a movin' man
    O' God!
De Lawd has been my dwellin' place
I mought had a been a slave
An' go home to my Lawd and be save.

—Collected by Rev. John Brown, from Petersburg, Virginia, 1938. In Library of Congress, Archive of American Folk Song, WPA Collection.

MANY THOUSAND GONE

No more auction block for me,
No more, no more;
No more auction block for me,
Many thousand gone.

No more peck o' corn for me . . .

No more driver's lash for me . . .

No more pint o' salt for me . . .

No more hundred lash for me . . .

No more mistress' call for me . . .

SLAVERY CHAIN

(Tune: "Joshua Fit de Battle of Jerico")

REFRAIN: *Slav'ry chain done broke at last*
Broke at last, broke at last,
Slavery chain done broke at last,
Goin' to stand up proud and free.

O mah Lord, how ah did suffer
In de dungeon and de chain
An' de days I went wit' head bowed down,
An' my broken flesh an' pain,
But brethren . . .

I done 'point a mighty captain
For to marshal all my hosts,
An' to bring my bleeding ones to me,
An' not one shall be lost,
For brethren . . .

Now no more weary travelin'
Since mah brethren said to me,
"Dere's no more auction block for you,
For you too shall be free,"
For brethren . . .

ABE LINCOLN FREED THE NIGGER

Abe Lincoln freed the nigger
With the gun and the trigger;
And I ain't going to get whipped any more.
I got my ticket,
Leaving the thicket,
And I'm a-heading for the golden shore!

—B. A. Botkin, *Lay My Burden Down*, p. 223.

YOU ARE FREE

"You Are Free" is probably the most exuberant of all jubilee songs.

> Mammy, don't you cook no more,
> You are free, you are free!
> Rooster, don't you crow no more,
> You are free, you are free!
> Old hen, don't you lay no more eggs,
> You are free, you are free!

—Botkin, *op. cit.*

JUBILEE SONGS—WHITE VENTRILOQUISM

BABYLON IS FALLEN

> Don't you see de black clouds risin' ober yonder,
> Whar de massa's ole plantation am?
> Neber you be frightened, dem is only darkeys,
> Come to jine and fight for Uncle Sam.

> REFRAIN: *Look out dar, we's a gwine to shoot!*
> *Look out dar, don't you understand?*
> *Babylon is fallen, Babylon is fallen,*
> *And we is gwine to occupy the land.*

> Don't you see de lightnin' flashin' in de cane brake,
> Like as if we gwine to hab a storm?
> No, you is mistaken, 'tis de darkey's bayonets,
> And de buttons on dar uniform.

> Way up in de corn-field, whar you hear de t'under,
> Dat is our ole forty-pounder gun;
> When de shells are missin' den we load wit' punkins,
> All de same to make de cowards run.

> Massa was de Kernel in de rebel army,
> Eber sence he went an' run away;
> But his lubly darkeys, dey has been a watchin'
> An' dey take him pris'ner tudder day.

> We will be de massa, he will be de servant,
> Try him how he like it for a spell;
> So we crack de butt'nutts, so we take de Kernel,
> So de cannon carry back de shell.

—Broadside in American Antiquarian Society,
Worcester, Massachusetts.

THE YEAR OF JUBALO

Has anybody seen my massa
With the moustache on his face?
Go long the road some time this mornin'
Like he gwine to leab de place.

REFRAIN: *De massa run, ha! ha!*
De darky stay, ho! ho!
It must be now dat de kingdom am a comin'
And de year of jubalo.

He seed a smoke way up de ribber
Where de Linkum gunboats lay;
He took his hat and he left mighty sudden,
And I speck dat he runned away.

He six feet one way, two feet todder,
And he weigh three hundred pound;
His coat so big dat he can't pay de tailor,
An' it won't go half-way around.

De oberseer he gib us trubble
And he dribe us round a spell,
Den we lock him up in the smoke house cellar,
Wid de key throwed in de well.

De whip am lost and de handcuff broken,
An' mass'll get him pay.
He old enough, big enough, ought to know better,
Dan to take an' runned away.

—Informant: Merton Knowles, WPA Project Worker:
"Heard it from my mother, it was brought back by
returning Union soldiers, and became a part of our
folklore." (Indiana) In Library of Congress, Archive
of American Folk Song.

OLD MASSA HE COME DANCIN' OUT

Old massa he come dancin' out
An' he call de blackuns round.
He pleased so well dat he couldn't stand
Wid both feet on de ground.

You, Pomp and Pete and Dinah, too,
You'll catch it now, I swear.
I'll whip you good for mixin' wid
De Yanks when dey was here.

Say, don't you hear dem 'tillery guns,
You niggers, don't you hear?
Ole General Bragg is a mowin' 'em down,
Dem Yankees ober here.

Dar comes our troops in crowds and crowds,
I knows dat red and gray,
But oh! What makes dem hurry so
And trow dere guns away?

Ole massa now keep both feet still
And stare with bofe his eyes.
Till he see de blue coats jest behind
Dat take him wid surprise.

Ole massa busy wadin' round
In swamps up to his knees,
While Dinah, Pomp, and Pete dey look
As if dey mighty pleased.

—Library of Congress, Archive of American Folk
Song, WPA Collection. Collected by Merton
Knowles of Indiana from his mother, who
learned and sang the song after the Civil War.

DISILLUSION

It is a little-known fact that approximately two hundred thousand Negroes fought for the North against their former masters during the Civil War, but usually their place was behind the man behind the gun. Their status as soldiers did not change in nearly a century. The first song, which was recorded by John Jacob Niles during the first World War, is parallel in theme to the following, which chronicles a complaint voiced often among Negro soldiers in the second great conflict.

LORDY, TURN YOUR FACE

Black man fights wid de shovel and de pick,
Lordy, turn your face on me.
Never gits no rest 'cause he never gits sick,
Lordy, turn your face on me.

Jined de army fur to git free clothes,
Lordy, turn your face on me.
What we're fightin' 'bout, nobody knows
Lordy, turn your face on me.

Never goin' to ride dat ocean no more,
Lordy, turn your face on me.
Goin' to walk right home to my cabin door
Lordy, turn your face on me.

—John Jacob Niles, *Singing Soldiers,*
New York, Scribners, 1927, p. 48.

UNCLE SAM SAYS

Airplanes flying cross the land and sea;
Everybody flying 'cept a Negro like me—
Uncle Sam says, "Your place is on the ground;
When I fly my airplanes, don't want no Negroes around."

Same thing for the Navy, the ships goes to sea;
All they got is a mess boy's job for me—
Uncle Sam says, "Keep on your apron, son;
You know I ain't gonna let you shoot my big Navy guns."

If you ask me, I think democracy's fine;
I mean democracy without a color line—
Uncle Sam says, "We'll live the American way;
Let's get together, and kill Jim Crow today."

—Words by Josh White and Warren Cuney.
Keynote Album 107. Copyright Mercury
Records Corp. Used by permission.

I WENT TO ATLANTA

I went to Atlanta,
Never been there befo'
White folks eat de apple,
Nigger wait fo co'

REFRAIN: *Catch dat Suth'n*
Grab dat train,
Won't come back no' mo'

I went to Charleston,
Never been dere a-fo'
White folks sleep on feather bed,
Nigger on de flo'

I went to Raleigh,
Never been dere a-fo'
White folks wear de fancy suit,
Nigger over-o'

—Library of Congress, Archive of American
Folk Song, unpublished collection.

The best-known (and best) Negro ballad, the best-known Negro work song, the best song of protest against imminent technological unemployment, "John Henry" has all the stature of the man whose memory it immortalizes. Undoubtedly the Negro saw John Henry as the apotheosis of his own unrealized potentialities, for here was a Negro who beat the white man at his own game. These stanzas are admittedly too few to be at all representative of the tremendous number of variations that have been recorded, but then John Henry was a mighty big man—too big to fit comfortably on one page.

JOHN HENRY

When John Henry was 'bout 3 days old
Sittin' on his mammy's knee;
He gave a whoop and a holler and a lonesome cry—
Said that hammer be the death of me,
That hammer be the death of me.

Now John Henry said to the Captain one day
A man ain't nothin' but a man;
Before I'll be bothered with an old steam drill
I'll die with my hammer in my hand,
I'll die with my hammer in my hand.

When they brought that new steam drill
They thought it was mighty fine;
John Henry made his 14 feet
While the steam drill only made 9,
While the steam drill only made 9.

Now John Henry swung his hammer around his head,
He brought the hammer down on the ground;
Man in Chattanooga 300 miles away
Heard an awful rumblin' sound,
He heard an awful rumblin' sound.

Now John Henry had a pretty little wife,
Name was Polly Ann;
When John Henry was a-sick and lyin' in his bed
His Polly drove steel like a man,
His Polly drove steel like a man.

When John Henry died they hadn't no box
Big enough to hold his bones,
So they buried him in a box car deep in the ground,
And let two mountains be his gravestones,
And let two mountains be his gravestones.

Numerous attempts to recolonize Africa with freed slaves were made both before and after the Civil War. All these projects were failures, including the one sponsored by the American Colonization Society which resulted in the founding of Liberia, for in 1930 Liberia, ironically enough, was stigmatized by the League of Nations for being itself a slavocracy.

The most pretentious scheme in the history of Africanism was that of Marcus Manasseth Garvey, who carried on his "Back to Africa" movement in a grandiose way. He organized an African government, established a nobility, founded an African Legion, Black Cross Nurse society, and an African Motor Corps, and even bought a steamship line to transport the four million persons who joined his "nation." But his plan was abortive, and in 1923 he was imprisoned for using the mails to defraud.

ARISE YE GARVEY NATION

Arise, ye Garvey nation, home abroad, go forth;
Go forth across the seven seas, proclaim,
Proclaim a future year of freedom
When home across the sea shall meet at home sweet home.

REFRAIN: *On and on swell the chorus,*
On and on, Marcus Garvey, on before us,
On and on swell the chorus,
Our Marcus Garvey, lead the way.
Glory, glory, hear the everlasting song,
Shout hosanna as we boldly march along.
Faithful soldiers, here we know Marcus Garvey's
on before
Saying, "We want freedom over the world we go."

We must have ships to sail across the seven seas,
They must be strong enough to stand the storms;
Then give material for them to make the ships for us,
That we may sail across the sea for home, sweet home.

Legions arise protecting millions of your race,
Arise, arise, be not afraid to fight;
Be strong, be brave, until you know the victory's won,
Be brave enough to stand your ground where'er you go.

Black Cross nurses prepare yourselves for future days,
When all shall march upon the battlefields;
You must be filled with Garvey spirit to win the fight,
The motor corps arise, take up the wounded, dead.

—Composed by Bishop I. E. Guinn; broadside
in Brown Collection, Brown University.

CHAIN GANG SONGS

"Anvils laugh at broken hammers." This is the theme
of "Grey Goose," the story of an indestructible *anserina* who symbolizes the road prisoner, whose worth was measured by his ability
to "make his time." The "Grey Goose," which dates to the period
immediately preceding 1914 (the black years of chain-gang oppression) has been found nowhere but in prison camps, yet it is strikingly analogical to the fourteenth-century English "Cutty Wren,"
in which the wren symbolizes the oppressed but indomitable
peasant. This is a remarkable example of polygenesis in folk song.

GREY GOOSE

Last Sunday morning, Lawd, Lawd, Lawd,
Last Sunday morning, Lawd, Lawd, Lawd,
My daddy went a-huntin', Lawd, Lawd, Lawd,
My daddy went a-huntin', Lawd, Lawd, Lawd.
Well, along came a grey goose, Lawd, Lawd, Lawd,
Along came a grey goose, Lawd, Lawd, Lawd.
Well up to his shoulder, Lawd, Lawd, Lawd,
It's up to his shoulder, Lawd, Lawd, Lawd.
And ram back the hammer, Lawd, Lawd, Lawd,
It's ram back the hammer, Lawd, Lawd, Lawd.
Well, the gun went off aboola, Lawd, Lawd, Lawd.
The gun went off aboola, Lawd, Lawd, Lawd.
And down he came a-fallin', Lawd, Lawd, Lawd,
It's down he came a-fallin', Lawd, Lawd, Lawd.
He was 6 weeks a-fallin', Lawd, Lawd, Lawd,
He was 6 weeks a-fallin', Lawd, Lawd, Lawd.
He was 6 weeks a-haulin', Lawd, Lawd, Lawd,
6 weeks a-haulin', Lawd, Lawd, Lawd.
The wimmen was a-twitterin', Lawd, Lawd, Lawd,
The wimmen was a-twitterin', Lawd, Lawd, Lawd.
Yes, your wife and my wife, Lawd, Lawd, Lawd,
They all was a-twitterin', Lawd, Lawd, Lawd.
They gave a feather pickin', Lawd, Lawd, Lawd,
They gave a feather pickin', Lawd, Lawd, Lawd.

He was 6 weeks a-pickin', Lawd, Lawd, Lawd,
6 weeks a-pickin', Lawd, Lawd, Lawd.
Well, they put him on a-cookin', Lawd, Lawd, Lawd,
They put him on a-cookin', Lawd, Lawd, Lawd.
He was 6 weeks a-cookin', Lawd, Lawd, Lawd,
6 weeks a-cookin', Lawd, Lawd, Lawd.
They put him on to parboil, Lawd, Lawd, Lawd,
They put him on to parboil, Lawd, Lawd, Lawd.
He was 6 weeks a-parboilin', Lawd, Lawd, Lawd,
6 weeks a-parboilin', Lawd, Lawd, Lawd.
Well, they put him on the table, Lawd, Lawd, Lawd,
They put him on the table, Lawd, Lawd, Lawd.
The fork couldn't stick him, Lawd, Lawd, Lawd,
The fork couldn't stick him, Lawd, Lawd, Lawd.
And the knife couldn't cut him, Lawd, Lawd, Lawd,
The knife couldn't cut him neither, Lawd, Lawd, Lawd.
They throwed him in the hog pen, Lawd, Lawd, Lawd,
They throwed him in the hog pen, Lawd, Lawd, Lawd.
He broke old Jerry's jaw bone, Lawd, Lawd, Lawd,
Broke old Jerry's jaw bone, Lawd, Lawd, Lawd.
So they took him to the sawmill, Lawd, Lawd, Lawd,
They took him to the sawmill, Lawd, Lawd, Lawd.
He broke the saw's teeth out, Lawd, Lawd, Lawd,
He broke the saw's teeth out, Lawd, Lawd, Lawd.
Well, the last time I seed him, Lawd, Lawd, Lawd,
The last time I seed him, Lawd, Lawd, Lawd.
He was flyin' over the ocean, Lawd, Lawd, Lawd,
Flyin' over the ocean, Lawd, Lawd, Lawd.
With a long string of goslins, Lawd, Lawd, Lawd,
A long string of goslins, Lawd, Lawd, Lawd.
They was all goin' quink-quank, Lawd, Lawd, Lawd,
All goin' quink-quank, Lawd, Lawd, Lawd.

—Unpublished manuscript in the Library of
Congress, Archive of American Folk Music.

THE CUTTY WREN

O where are you going? said Milder to Malder,
O we may not tell you, said Festle to Fose.
We're off to the woods, said John the Red Nose,
We're off to the woods, said John the Red Nose.
What will you do there? said Milder to Malder,
O we may not tell you, said Festle to Fose.
We'll shoot the Cutty Wren, said John the Red Nose,
We'll shoot the Cutty Wren, said John the Red Nose.
How will you shoot her? said Milder to Malder,

O we may not tell you, said Festle to Fose.
With bows and with arrows, said John the Red Nose,
With bows and with arrows, said John the Red Nose.
That will not do, said Milder to Malder,
O what will do then? said Festle to Fose.
Big guns and big cannons, said John the Red Nose,
Big guns and big cannons, said John the Red Nose.
How will you bring her home? said Milder to Malder,
O we may not tell you, said Festle to Fose.
On four strong men's shoulders, said John the Red Nose,
On four strong men's shoulders, said John the Red Nose.
That will not do, said Milder to Malder,
O what will do then? said Festle to Fose.
Big carts and big waggons, said John the Red Nose,
Big carts and big waggons, said John the Red Nose.
How will you cut her up? said Milder to Malder,
O we may not tell you, said Festle to Fose.
With knives and with forks, said John the Red Nose,
With knives and with forks, said John the Red Nose.
That will not do, said Milder to Malder,
O what will do then? said Festle to Fose.
Big hatchets and cleavers, said John the Red Nose,
Big hatchets and cleavers, said John the Red Nose.
Who'll get the spare ribs? said Milder to Malder,
O we may not tell you, said Festle to Fose.
We'll give it all to the poor, said John the Red Nose,
We'll give it all to the poor, said John the Red Nose.

—A. L. Lloyd, *The Singing Englishman*, London, n.d., p. 7.

CORN PONE

Corn pone, fat meat,
All I ever gets to eat
Better, better
Than I ever gets at home,
Far better than I ever gets at home.

Cotton socks, striped overall,
No Sunday rags at all
Finer, finer
Than I ever gets at home,
Far better than I ever gets at home.

Iron bunk for my bed,
Straw beneath my head
Softer, softer
Than the sort I gets at home,
Far softer than I ever gets at home.

Heavy ring on my arm,
And my feet got bracelet 'round,
Stronger, stronger
Than I got to wear at home,
Far stronger than I got to wear at home.

Baby, baby, let me be,
Chain gang good enough for me,
Better, better
Than I ever gets at home,
Far better than I ever gets at home.

—Lawrence Gellert: *Me and My Captain*
p. 10, copyright 1939.

I'M SO DEEP IN TROUBLE

I'm so deep in trouble,
White folks can't get me straight;
Stoled a hog and charge me for murdering case.

Carry me to the courthouse,
And give me my trial;
Got forty year on hard rock pile.

Wearing double shackles,
From my head right down to my knees;
Eating nothing 'cept slop of corn, bread and peas.

Went to the walker,
And head Boss man too;
Please, all you big white folks, see what you can do.

Say, all right, you black man,
Won't forget you nohow;
Come around to see me 'bout forty year from now.

—Lawrence Gellert: *Me and My Captain*,
p. 10, copyright 1939.

IF YOU CATCH ME STEALIN'

If you catch me stealin'
Don't blame me none.
If you catch me stealin'
Don't blame me none.
You put a mark on mah people,
An' it must be carried on.

Trouble, trouble, had it all mah day.
Trouble, trouble, had it all mah day.
An' it seem like trouble,
Gonna follow me to my grave.

Can't pawn no diamonds,
Can't pawn no clo'
Can't pawn no diamonds,
Can't pawn no clo'
An' boss man told me,
Can't use me no mo'.

Rather get me a job, like white folks do.
Rather get me a job, like white folks do.
Trampin' 'round all day,
Say, "Nigger, nothin' fo' you."

Try one mo' time,
Won't try no mo'.
Try one mo' time,
Won't try no mo'.
Gonna load me a box of balls
Fo' my fohty foh.

I'm tellin' you, white folks, like de Chinaman tell de Jew.
I'm tellin' you, white folks, like de Chinaman tell de Jew.
If you care nothin' 'bout Nigger,
Cinch I care nothin' 'bout you.

—Lawrence Gellert, *Negro Songs of Protest*,
New York, 1936, copyright 1936.

ONE DAY OLD AND NO DAMN GOOD

Hush, my babe, don't be forlorn
'Cause you were lynched 'fore you were born;
Your skin is black and they'd like it understood
Though you're one day old you're no damn good.

Don't hush, my babe, you're right to squawk
Your skin will creep, 'fore you can walk;
You live as long as some people think you should,
When you're one day old and no damn good.

Some day you may be president
And have a white house for a residence,
So dry your tears, and don't you frown,
'Cause the whip and the rope can't keep you down.

This nightmare, babe, can't last the night.
We'll end it soon, both black and white;
We'll mark the grave, with a rotten slab of wood,
Signed, "one day old and no damn good."

—By N. Kalin; in People's Songs Library, unpublished.

"I saw Jeff Buckner lynched in Texas when I was about eight years old. I wrote this song to express my grief and my feeling of helplessness. . . . It is to be sung very slowly and mournfully."— Frank Beddo.

JEFF BUCKNER

They hanged Jeff Buckner from a sycamore tree,
And I was there, and I was there.
He went to his death so silently,
And I was there, but I never said a word.

They put him in a wagon with a rope around his neck,
And I was there, and I was there.
They pulled away the wagon and his neck it did break,
And I was there, but I never said a word.

Jeff Buckner's face was as black as coal,
And I was there, and I was there.
But white as snow alongside of my soul,
For I was there, but I never said a word.

They nailed King Jesus to an iron-bolted tree,
And I was there, and you were there.
And meek as a lamb to the slaughter went he,
And we were there, but we never said a word.

—From People's Songs Library.

Huddie Ledbetter—Leadbelly—the great Negro folk singer whom the Lomaxes brought up from the Deep South, where he had served several terms in work farms, can be taken as a typical example of how articulate protest develops. In their book *Negro Folk Songs as Sung by Leadbelly* (p. 184) the Lomaxes remark, "Note the 'Farmer tol' de merchant' stanza ("Boll Weevil") which is, so far as we can tell, the only class conscious sentiment in Leadbelly's songbag." After he had settled in New York and had become acquainted with people who were protesting against racial discrimination, Leadbelly added a number of class-conscious songs like "The Bourgeois Blues" to his repertoire.

THE BOURGEOIS BLUES

Me and my wife run all over town,
Everywhere's we'd go people would turn us down.

REFRAIN: *Lawd, in the bourgeois town, hoo!*
The bourgeois town.
I got the bourgeois blues,
Gonna spread the news all around.

Me and Margie we was standing upstairs,
I heard a white man say, "I don't want no niggers up there."

Home of the brave, land of the free,
I don't want to be mistreated by no bourgeoisie.

Me and my wife we went all over town,
Everywhere we go the colored people turn us down.

White folks in Washington, they know how
Chuck a colored man a nickel just to see him bow.

Tell all the colored folks, listen to me,
Don't try to buy no home in Washington, D. C.

"God Made Us All" is one of the recent but large production of calypso songs on topical matters, written by well-known West Indian calypsonians as Lord Invader, Sir Lancelot, Macbeth the Great, and the Duke of Iron. The protest in the calypso is undisguised, partly because of the greater freedom from censorship today, and partly because the calypso is primarily a medium for expressing an interpretation of observed facts.

GOD MADE US ALL

If you are a Negro it is plain to see
You are bound to suffer misery and tyranny.
If you are a Negro it is plain to see
You are bound to suffer misery and tyranny.
But we should be race conscious and always be
Living in unity and tranquillity
For God made us all, and in him we trust,
Nobody in this world is better than us.

Listen what I am outlining to you,
Negroes fought in World Wars One and Two.
Some lose their lives, others lose a hand,
We fought gallantly for United Nations.
So if we Negroes are good enough to fight,
I don't see why we can't have our equal right.
For God made us all, and in him we trust,
Nobody in this world is better than us.

We ought to unite with one another,
As the scripture say, to love thy brother;
If you are a Jew or an Italian,
A Negro or a subject of Great Britain,
This is what I want you to realize,
Six feet of earth make us all of one size.
For God made us all, and in him we trust,
Nobody in this world is better than us.

I heard this speaking of democracy,
That is only diplomacy and hypocrisy,
It is about time this should be cut out,
The way the Negroes are treated down South.
In my opinion it's a burning shame,
Like they want to bring back slavery again.
For God made us all, and in him we trust,
Nobody in this world is better than us.

—By Rupert Grant ("Lord Invader") copyright 1946

THE NEW "BAD MAN" BALLADS

The victim of the legal manifestations of racial discrimination can take what solace he can find in the certainty that he will be memorialized in song. The range of this type of Negro song is illustrated by the following three ballads. The first is of Negro origin; the other two were composed by a white man,

Woody Guthrie, but he would be offended were anyone to point
out the distinction, which is to him somewhat less than academic.
"Buoy Bells for Trenton" tells the story of the "Trenton Six,"
whose fate at this writing is still in the process of being determined.

SCOTTSBORO

Paper come out—Done strewed de news
Seven po' chillun moan Deat' house blues
Seven po' chillun moanin' Deat' house blues.
Seven nappy heads wit' big shiny eye
All boun' in jail and framed to die
All boun' in jail and framed to die.

Messin' white woman—Snake lyin' tale
Hang and burn and jail wit' no bail.
Dat hang and burn and jail wit' no bail.
Worse ol' crime in white folks' lan'
Black skin coverin' po' workin' man
Black skin coverin' po' workin' man.

Judge and jury—All in de stan'
Lawd, biggety name for same lynchin' ban'
Lawd, biggety name for same lynchin' ban'
White folks and nigger in great Co't house
Like cat down cellar wit' nohole mouse.
Like cat down cellar wit' nohole mouse.

—Lawrence Gellert, *Negro Songs of Protest,*
New York, 1936, p. 44.

THE FERGUSON BROTHERS' KILLING

Let's stop here and drink us a hot cup of coffee
That Long Island bus was an awful long ride;
But we've got to keep your blood warm, our young brother,
*   Charles,*
Because you've reenlisted for quite a long time.

You've been over the ocean and won your good record
A Private First Class needs hot coffee the same
As Alonzo or Joseph or just plain old Richard
We'll all drink a hot cup to each brother's name.

It's nice of the Bus Terminal to have a good Tea Room
Mr. Scholakis is the owner, there's his card on the wall.
Let's sit over here and wash down our troubles,
And if you know a tall story, my brother, tell them all.

The waiter shakes his head, wipes his hands on his apron,
He says there's no coffee in all that big urn;
In that glass gauge there it looks like several inches,
It looks like this Tea Room's got coffee to burn.

We made him a speech in a quiet friendly manner
We didn't want to scare you ladies over there;
He calls for a cop on his fone on the sly,
And the cop come and marched us out in the night's air.

The cop said that we had insulted the Joint man.
He made us line up with our faces to the wall;
We laughed to ourselves as we stood there and listened
To the man of law and order putting in his riot call.

The cop turned around and walked back to young Charlie
Kicked him in the groin and then shot him to the ground;
This same bullet went through the brain of Alonzo
And the next bullet laid my brother Joseph down.

My fourth brother Richard got hauled to the station
Bawled out and lectured by the judge on his bench.
The judge said us Fergusons was looking for trouble;
They lugged Richard off for a hundred day stretch.

This morning two hearses roll out toward the graveyard
One hearse had Alonzo and the other took Charles.
Charles' wife, Minnie, brings her three boy children
And friends and relatives in some old borrowed cars.

Nobody has told these three little boys yet,
Everybody rides crying and shaking their heads.
Nobody knows quite how to make these three boys know
That Jim Crow killed Alonzo, that Charles too is dead.

The town that we ride through is not Rankin, Mississippi,
Nor Bilbo's Jim Crow town of Washington, D. C.
But it's greater New York, our most fair minded city
In all this big land here and streets of the brave.

Who'll tell these three boys that their Daddy is gone?
(He helped whip the Fascists and Nazis to death)
Who'll tell these three sons that Jim Crow coffee
Has killed several thousand the same as their dad?

—Composed by Woody Guthrie, March 5, 1946.

BUOY BELLS FOR TRENTON

Well, the buoy bells are ringing
I can hear them on the wind
Ringing loud to bring the ships and sailors home.
They should sound like bells of freedom
But they ring like bells of death
For six in Trenton's death house marked to die.

REFRAIN: *Bling, Blang, Blong, I can hear them*
Louder as the stormy waters rise;
Bling, Blang, Blong, you can hear them
Ringing for the boys framed up to die.

I shipped thru these same waters
And I heard these channel bells
Guide our ships to beat that super race.
I sail home past my warning bells
And find you marked to die
Just for having dark skin on your hands and face.

Now my bells ring o'er the rooftops
And they ring on every tree
They take me to that civil war we fought to set you free
If that Trenton Court can take you
Six for one and one a day,
The race hate Fascists are at work, my bells are telling me.

Yes, my buoy bells in Boston
Rang in blood that hateful night
When old Judge Thayer sat
And let Sacco and Vanzetti die;
He called them Wops and radical rats,
That same old race hate
That ruled the judge and jury's heart when your death
line they signed.

—Composed by Woody Guthrie, June 1, 1949.

One of a number of topical songs on the political proponents of Jim Crow philosophy, but unlike "Listen Mr. Bilbo" and "The Rankin Tree," this is of genuine folk origin, having been written by a Negro sharecropper. Of the tune he says, "Make it up yourself; that's what we all do." Note the maverick sixth stanza, found most often toward the end of "Frankie and Albert."

BALLAD OF TALMADGE

It's sunny again in Georgia,
No finer breathing place.
Since the undertaker
Throwed dirt in Talmadge face.
Now he's gone, poor man, he's gone.

He split his guts wide open,
Wore his tonsils sore
With mean and hateful cussin;
Now he can't cuss no more.
He's gone, poor man, he's gone.

He promise when he Governor
Us colored good as dead.
Sure God I ain' agrievin'
Cause he shoo'd off hisself instead.
He's gone, poor man, he's gone.

I got thinkin' maybe Jesus
Done left us in the lurch;
Then Devil he take Talmadge,
I flew right back to Church.
He's gone, poor man, he's gone.

He weren't so good lookin'
He don't dress him so nice,
But prettiest sight I ever see
When they ship him home on ice.
He's gone, poor man, he's gone.

Rubber tire buggy,
Soft down cushion hack,
Drag him to the cemetery,
Forget to bring him back.
He's gone, poor man, he's gone.

Old iron is iron,
But tin it never last;
So we come to the end of our story,
Cause that's all that I has.
He's gone, poor man, he's gone.

—Collected by Lawrence Gellert.

3. The songs of the textile workers

It's hard times in the mills, my love,
It's hard times in the mills.

With the single exception of the miners, no organized labor group has produced more songs of social and economic protest than the textile workers. Their songs are plentiful from the earliest period of American labor history, and at the present time are richer in sincerity, quality, genuine folk content, and protest, than those emanating from any other industry. Reasons for this prolificacy are not hard to find.

The principal reason is an historical one, for the American factory system started with the industrialization of yarn-making shortly after the Revolution. British manufacturers at that time had a half-century advantage over American mechanization, a monopoly they sought frantically to preserve by keeping machines, experience, and even skilled workers in England. But this kind of communicative blockade collapses with the emigration of one man who can build a machine, and so the history of American industrialization began with the building in 1798 of a yarn-making mill in Pawtucket by an immigrant English mechanic, Samuel Slater, who was financed by American capitalists. At first the American textile industry was limited to the production of yarn only, but in 1815 all the processes of cotton-cloth manufacture were mechanized by Francis C. Lowell, who had spent several years in England studying methods of textile manufacture. Following this start of American industry, textile plants spread rapidly through New England, with sporadic and usually ineffectual labor organizations trailing close behind.

If Samuel Slater was the father of the American textile industry, he was also the father of the thoughtless exploitation of its operatives that has been the blight of textile manufacture, for his first workers were nine children, all under twelve years of age. In 1820 half of the textile operatives were boys and girls of ten or younger, who earned from thirty-three to sixty-seven cents for a seventy-five-hour week. It must be admitted that certain observers deplored the ill-treatment of children by mill owners; one group of Massachusetts reformers "berated Rhode Island mill owners for using the strap instead of sprinkling water on the children to keep them awake during their eleven- to fourteen-hour shifts."[1]

The other half of the textile labor force, composed principally of young women from nearby farms, possessed the understanding that the children lacked, and therefore protested against the conditions in the factories—by organizing and striking, by going back to the farm, and by singing.

One of their early songs expresses the feeling which predominated in the mills during the early decades of the nineteenth century.

THE LOWELL FACTORY GIRL

When I set out for Lowell,
Some factory for to find,
I left my native country,
And all my friends behind.

REFRAIN: *Then sing hit-re-i-re-a-re-o*
Then sing hit-re-i-re-a.

[1] Herbert Harris, *American Labor*, New Haven, 1940, p. 310 n.

But now I am in Lowell,
And summon'd by the bell,
I think less of the factory
Than of my native dell.

The factory bell begins to ring,
And we must all obey,
And to our old employment go,
Or else be turned away.

Come all ye weary factory girls,
I'll have you understand,
I'm going to leave the factory
And return to my native land.

No more I'll put my bonnet on
And hasten to the mill,
While all the girls are working hard,
Here I'll be lying still.

No more I'll lay my bobbins up,
No more I'll take them down;
No more I'll clean my dirty work,
For I'm going out of town.

No more I'll take my piece of soap,
No more I'll go to wash,
No more my overseer shall say,
"Your frames are stopped to doff."

Come all you little doffers
That work in the Spinning room;
Go wash your face and comb your hair,
Prepare to leave the room.

No more I'll oil my picker rods,
No more I'll brush my loom,
No more I'll scour my dirty floor
All in the Weaving room.

No more I'll draw these threads
All through the harness eye;
No more I'll say to my overseer,
Oh! dear me, I shall die.

No more I'll get my overseer
To come and fix my loom,
No more I'll say to my overseer
Can't I stay out 'till noon?

Then since they've cut my wages down
To nine shillings per week,
If I cannot better wages make,
Some other place I'll seek.

No more he'll find me reading,
No more he'll see me sew,
No more he'll come to me and say
"Such works I can't allow."

I do not like my overseer,
I do not mean to stay,
I mean to hire a Depot-boy
To carry me away.

The Dress-room girls, they needn't think
Because they higher go,
That they are better than the girls
That work in the rooms below.

The overseers they need not think,
Because they higher stand;
That they are better than the girls
That work at their command.

'Tis wonder how the men
Can such machinery make,
A thousand wheels together roll
Without the least mistake.

Now soon you'll see me married
To a handsome little man,
'Tis then I'll say to you factory girls,
Come and see me when you can.

—Broadside in Harris Collection, Brown University.

I have been unable to date this song precisely, but the aged condition of the broadside, together with such internal evidence as can be detected, place its composition around the 1830's. The "nine shilling" wage of which the singer complains coincides with the average weekly earnings of $2.25 paid to New England cotton-factory operatives in 1830. Furthermore, the freedom to return to the farm was not generally possible after 1840, when a mill-dependent permanent labor community had begun to attach itself to the factories. After the panic of 1837, which wiped out many of the small New England farmers, the refuge that the "Lowell factory girl" sings of had vanished.

"The Lowell Factory Girl," incidentally, is a folksong according to the narrowest definitions of that troublesome term. Its composer is unknown, it has undergone oral transmission, it has spread over a wide geographical area, and it has been sung by more than two generations. In his article "Some Types of American Folk Song" in the *Journal of American Folklore* (Vol. 28, 1915) John Lomax records a song containing several identifiable stanzas of "The Lowell Factory Girl," to which he appends this note:

I heard [this] sung by a wandering singer plying her minstrel trade by the roadside in Fort Worth, during an annual meeting of the Texas Cattle Raisers Association. It is the song of the girl factory worker, and the singer told me she picked it up in Florida.

Another version collected more recently in North Carolina is aptly titled "No More Shall I Work in the Factory."

NO MORE SHALL I WORK IN THE FACTORY

(Tune: "Ten Thousand Miles")

No more shall I work in the factory
To greasy up my clothes;
No more shall I work in the factory
With splinters in my toes.

REFRAIN: *It's pity me my darling,*
It's pity me I say
It's pity me my darling,
And carry me away.

No more shall I hear the bosses say,
"Boys, you'd better daulf."
No more shall I hear those bosses say,
"Spinners, you'd better clean off."

No more shall I hear the drummer wheels
A-rolling over my head,
When factories are hard at work,
I'll be in my bed.

No more shall I hear the whistle blow
To call me up so soon;
No more shall I hear the whistle blow
To call me from my home.

No more shall see the super come,
All dressed up so proud;
For I know I'll marry a country boy
Before the year is out.

No more shall I wear the old black dress,
Greasy all around;
No more shall I wear the old black bonnet
With holes all in the crown.

—People's Songs Library

The deprivation of the farm as a refuge for mill workers who were dissatisfied with conditions impressed upon them the identity of their cause with that of labor as a whole, and so unions of greater stability came into existence. Early in their history these organizations became articulate, and the owners, recognizing the danger of such articulateness, attempted to divert it into censored factory magazines. The most famous of these organs was the *Lowell Offering*, which received enthusiastic commendation as an expression of the nobility of the American laborer from persons who should have known better, among them Charles Dickens, who praised it in his *American Notes*. The diverted surge of operatives' protest built up behind this obstacle, and in the 1840's overflowed into its own channels—genuine mill workers' journals like *The Factory Girl*, the *Factory Girl's Album and Operative's Advocate*, and *The Voice of Industry*, in which most of the extant early protest songs are preserved.

The avidity of the mill owners thrived on the ignorance of the people from whom the textile labor force has traditionally been drawn. In modern times many textile mills moved to the rural South in order to benefit by cheap labor, a euphemism for ignorant labor.[2]

[2] Even this aspect of labor dissatisfaction has been reflected in song (tune: "London Bridge Is Falling Down"):

Greenberg Shop is moving South,
Moving South, moving South,
Greenberg Shop is moving South,
Swell Employers!

After we slaved to make them rich,
Make them rich, make them rich,
After we slaved to make them rich,
Lousy employers!

The mountain folk who constitute the American peasantry had little opportunity to recognize the squalor of their existence as long as they remained isolated in cultural pockets; but when the mill employment agents began enticing whole families from their leisured and idle poverty (which at least was ameliorated by the salubrious effects of rural life) to regimented and exploited poverty of urban areas where an entirely new plane of prosperity could be seen but not shared, conflict arose. The mill owners, as the stories of the Gastonia and Marion strikes show, desperately and ruthlessly tried to hamper this orientation by further restrictions. "Foreign" organizers, who provided in a moment social enlightenment that might not appear for years without outside stimulation, were in constant danger of being killed by men of whom Jay Gould was thinking when he said, "I can hire one half of the working class to kill the other half." The violent conflict resulting from these conditions inevitably produced songs of protest.

Drawing a labor force from the rural South assured the textile industry still another fundamental source of song. The cultural isolation of the mountain people and its attendant restriction of other sources of entertainment resulted in a strong tradition of singing which not only preserved a rich store of English and Scottish ballads and songs, but facilitated native song-making. Thus, while the northern urban worker is likely to express his dissatisfaction with labor conditions by beating his wife, the southern rural worker is apt to sublimate some of his protest at least in singing. In an area where four or five guitarists may be found in every group of twenty persons, and where song improvisation is an unremarkable talent, topical songs are common. If strikes or similar labor troubles arise, the topical songs become songs of protest.

There are other reasons for the abundance of protest songs among the textile workers, less fundamental perhaps, but still of contributory importance. The location of many textile mills in mining areas, where a separate body of protest song has already grown up, is one such reason. Another is the nature of the work in the textile industry. The textile worker is properly a machine tender whose duties are mechanical and monotonous; such work has already been conducive to singing simple, rhythmic, inconsequential songs.[3] Fitting union words to these songs is almost a subconscious process. As the worker sings or hums a well-integrated melody, the tune is acted upon by the force uppermost in his mind—in many cases the union, whose importance in the life of the textile worker is greatly underestimated by those whose lives are fuller. A young woman, possibly not far from childhood, singing the catchy children's song, "I Love Little Willie," may easily substitute "my union" for Willie:

> *I love my union, I do, Mama;*
> *I love my union, I do, ha ha;*
> *I love my union, and you can tell Pa,*
> *For he will like it you know.*
>
> *It fights for me, it does, Mama;*
> *It fights for me, it does, ha ha;*
> *It fights for me, and you can tell Pa,*
> *For he will like it you know.*

Another girl, while humming a tune before her machine, may be thinking of an inconsistent statement made earlier in the day by her boss; imperceptibly the thought affixes itself to the melody:

> *Semaria says he loves his girls*
> *Doo da, doo da;*
> *He wants to give them jewels and pearls*
> *All the doo da day.*
> *All the doo da day,*
> *All the doo da day,*
> *He wants to give them jewels and pearls*
> *Instead of union pay.*

A man (approximately half of textile workers are men) can quickly divest himself of an overpowering disgust for his job in a blues, when the materials for his song are all around him:

WEAVE ROOM BLUES

> *Working in a weave room, fighting for my life,*
> *Trying to make a living, for my kiddies and my wife,*
> *Some are needing clothing and some are needing shoes,*
> *But I'm getting nothing but these weave room blues.*

[3] The modern urban industrial worker has this singing done for him by recorded musical programs "piped" into the factory.

REFRAIN: *I've got the blues, I've got the blues,*
I've got them awful weave-room blues.
I've got the blues, the weave room blues.

When your loom's a slamming, shackles bouncing on the floor,
And when you flag a fixer you can see that he is sore.
I'm trying to make a living but I'm thinking I will lose,
For I'm going crazy with them weave room blues.

The harness eyes are breaking with the double coming through,
The Devil's in your alley and he's coming after you.
Our hearts are aching, let us take a little booze,
For we're going crazy with them weave room blues.

Slam, break out, makeouts by the score,
Cloth all rolled back and piled up on the floor.
The bats are running into strings, they are hanging to your shoes,
I'm simply dying with them weave room blues.

But the best songs, as always, are born of conflict. Strikes in the Deep South before the New Deal fostered the growth and consolidation of powerful labor unions were not merely good-natured gambits offered by the workers and accepted by the employers as preludes to peaceful arbitration; they were small-scale wars of attrition in which the employer tried to exterminate not merely the union, but the men behind it. Two such bloody conflicts were the Marion and Gastonia strikes of 1929.

THE MARION STRIKE

At the beginning of 1929 the Marion Manufacturing Company of Marion, North Carolina, had assets of $1,169,925 and was about to pay a dividend of $11.50 on each share of common stock. At the same time it was paying its seven hundred workers an average of $11 for a seventy-hour week, and some women were making less than $5.00 weekly.

In April three young workers, hearing of a textile strike in nearby Elizabethton, went to see Alfred Hoffman, southern organizer for the United Textile Workers' Union (AFL) in that city and inquired how they might get a union. He outlined plans for them, and after they had completed preliminary organization, took charge of the situation. On July 10 the new union presented a petition to R. W. Baldwin, the mill president, asking a reduction of the work shift to ten hours. He refused, and on July 11 the union struck.

In September the strike collapsed for a number of reasons—the hostile attitude of the conservative Marion citizenry, the inherent weakness of the union, the inexperience of its leaders, and the abandonment of the strike by the AFL policy commission. Before its collapse, however, the union obtained certain concessions agreed to by Baldwin after their recommendation by a mediation board led by the personal representative of North Carolina's Governor Gardner, himself the owner of a textile mill. The settlement agreement provided for a fifty-five-hour week with a corresponding decrease in pay, and permitted Baldwin to fire fourteen of the union leaders.

But after the strikers returned to their jobs Baldwin ignored even these empty concessions, and fired 102 union members. Unrest began again to spread through the Marion plant. Sensing impending trouble, Baldwin returned from his Baltimore home on October first and told Sheriff Oscar F. Adkins to assemble his deputies—a recently recruited band of notorious local toughs—and protect the plant. The deputies entered the mill the same day, and during a drinking spree that lasted from 8 P.M. until 1 A.M., goaded the workers, threatening to shoot them if they dared leave their jobs. At 1:30 a twenty-two-year-old worker, his patience strained to the breaking point, defied their threats, threw the main power switch, and ran through the plant, calling the workers out. The second strike was on.

Since the walk-out had been unplanned, many of the struck workers remained outside the mill gates to notify the day shift when it arrived. As the day workers appeared, the crowd grew and soon numbered 250. Meanwhile Adkins and his men, sobering, began to feel uneasy. At 7:30 Adkins panicked and fired a tear-gas charge into the crowd. A fifty-seven-year-old cripple, John Jonas, attacked the sheriff with his cane, and was promptly shot by one of the deputies. The crowd broke, trying to escape the tear-gas fumes, and the deputies fired at the unarmed, fleeing men, dropping more than a score. Six men died, all shot in the back.

Interviewed two days later, Baldwin told reporters:

I understand sixty or seventy-five shots were fired in Wednesday's fight. If this is true, there are thirty or thirty-five of the bullets accounted for. I think the officers are damned good marksmen. If I ever organize an army they can have jobs with me. I read that the death of each soldier in the World War consumed more than five tons of lead. Here we have less than five pounds and these casualties. A good average, I call it.[4]

On October fourth the people of Marion held a funeral for four of their dead. They brought flowers from the hills and decorated the caskets. A ribbon, their union colors, linked the coffins. No minister of the town of Marion or of the neighboring towns had come near the dead or their families. A stranger from another state had come to perform last rites. But during the services an old mountain preacher, Cicero Queens, who stood among the people, dropped to his knees before the coffins, and prayed:

O Lord Jesus Christ, here are men in their coffins, blood of my blood, bone of my bone. I trust, O God, that these friends will go to a better place than this mill village or any other place in Carolina. O God, we know we are not in high society, but we know Jesus Christ loves us. The poor people have their rights too. For the work we do in this world, is this what we get if we demand our rights? Jesus Christ, your son, O God, was a working man. If He were here to pass under these trees today, He would see these cold bodies lying here before us. O God, mend the broken hearts of these loved ones left behind. Dear God, do feed their children. Drive selfishness and cruelty out of your world. May these weeping wives and little children have a strong arm to lean on. Dear God, what would your Jesus do if He were to come to Carolina?

THE MARION MASSACRE

A story now I'll tell you
Of a fearful massacre,
Which happened down in Dixie
On the borders of the sea.

REFRAIN: *There'll be no sorrow there,*
There'll be no sorrow there,
In heaven above
Where all is love,
There'll be no sorrow there.

'Twas in Marion, North Carolina,
In a little mountain town;
Six workers of the textile
In cold blood were shot down.

[4] Asheville *Citizen*, October 4, 1929.

'Tis ever the same old story,
With the laborers of our land,
They're ruled by mighty powers,
And riches they command.

It started over money,
The world's most vain desire.
Yet we realize the laborer
Is worthy of his hire.

These men were only asking
Their rights and nothing more;
That their families would not suffer
With a wolf at every door.

Why is it over money,
These men from friends must part?
A-leaving home and loved ones,
With a bleeding, broken heart?

But some day they'll meet them
On that bright shore so fair,
And live in peace forever,
There'll be no sorrow there.

—People's Songs Library.

THE MARION STRIKE

This song is a remarkable example of economical, straightforward ballad making, free from conventional phraseology.

(Tune: "Wreck of the Altoona")

When they had that strike in North Carolina
Up there at the Marion mill,
Somebody called for the sheriff
To come down there on the hill.

The sheriff came down there to the factory,
And brought all of his men along,
And he says to the mill strikers,
"Now boys, you all know this is wrong."

"But sheriff, we just can't work for nothing,
For we've got a family to feed.
And they've got to pay us more money,
To buy food and clothes that we need.

"You've heard of the stretchout system,
A-going through this country today,
They put us on two men's jobs,
And just give us half enough pay.

"You know we helped give you your office,
And we helped to give you your pay;
And you want us to work for nothing,
That's why we are down here today."

So one word just brought on another,
And the bullets they started to flying.
And after the battle was over,
Six men lay on the ground a-dying.

Now, people, labor needs protection,
We need it badly today;
If we will just get together,
Then they can't do us that way.

Now, I hear the whistle blowing,
I guess I'd better run along.
I work in the factory,
That's why I wrote this little song.

—People's Songs Library.

THE GASTONIA STRIKE[5]

The 1929 strike at the Loray mills in Gastonia, North Carolina, began like hundreds of others in the southern textile industry, but ended as the South's greatest labor trial—a trial which but for the martyrdom of a union worker and the fact that a juror suddenly went insane, might have become another Sacco-Vanzetti travesty. The story of the strike itself is so usual that it does not need retelling: a mill community, exploited, oppressed, discouraged, and sullen in its discouragement, is aroused to action by Northern organizers—in this case, Communists.

The strike dragged on through the summer months, and the mill owners turned the strikers out of the company-owned houses. The evicted workers set up a tent colony on the edge of town. As the loss of the strike appeared imminent, the strikers formed a picket line in defiance of an unconstitutional local ordinance and prepared to march to the mill a mile away, where the night shift

[5] See also the story and songs of Ella May Wiggins, p. 244.

still carried on operations. They had gone only a short distance when a band of deputy sheriffs and police attacked them and drove them back to the tent town. Five policemen, two of whom were later indicted for drunkenness while on duty, followed them, threatening to "clean out the white trash." Without a warrant (which gave the strikers a legal right to resist them) the police entered the premises of the strikers' colony and blackjacked a union guard. One of the officers then fired at the strikers' headquarters, and answering shots killed O. F. Aderholt, Gastonia police chief.

Fifteen men and women were arrested and indicted for "conspiracy to commit murder," for no evidence existed to show that any of the fifteen was implicated in the actual shooting. The local union leader, Fred Beal, was not even present at the time of the disturbance; the evidence against him consisted of "inflammatory" excerpts from his speeches.

The venire faced by the indicted strikers was more prejudiced than the one which convicted Sacco and Vanzetti. The area, except for the mill workers (who were largely excluded from jury service because of a qualification which disqualified veniremen who were not property holders) consisted mostly of fundamentalist farmers and businessmen who lived in constant fear that their properties were threatened by the doctrines imported by the Northern organizers. Newspapers in Charlotte and Gastonia deliberately incited the solid citizens to perpetrate acts of violence against the strikers. Nearly the only concession to American ideals of justice made by these papers appeared in the Charlotte *News* just before the opening of the first trial:

> The leaders of the National Textile Workers' Union are communists, and are a menace to all that we hold most sacred. They believe in violence, arson, murder. They want to destroy our institutions. They are undermining all morality, all religion. But nevertheless they must be given a fair trial, although everyone knows that they deserve to be shot at sunrise.

A few papers, however, preserved some measure of sanity. The Charlotte *Daily News* observed on July 1,

> Gaston County is desperately near the mood to try a dozen or more malcontents for murder and condemn them by what they think about

God, marriage, and the nigger—and the history of the world has shown that on the first and last of these subjects the human race, when it has tried to think, has invariably gone insane.

A change in venue from inflamed Gastonia to Charlotte in neighboring Mecklenburg County made the outlook for the defendants somewhat more favorable, but when the first trial ended with the sudden insanity of one of the jurors, the reaction in the strike area approached anarchy. Mobs of hundreds prowled the countryside, beating and intimidating union members, under the goading of the Gastonia *Gazette*. Finally Ella May Wiggins was murdered, and a flood of nation-wide protest inundated the region.

By the time the second trial began, charges against eight of the accused strikers were dropped, and the charge against the others was reduced to second-degree murder, clearly demonstrating the weakness of the prosecution's case. But the inherent flimsiness of the accusation was compensated for by Solicitor John G. Carpenter's zeal. He endeavored, for example, to introduce before the jury a dummy of the dead police chief, dressed in his bloody uniform and loosely covered by a shroud; he rolled on the floor, knelt as in prayer, and castigated the defendants as "fiends incarnate . . . devils with hoofs and horns."

The intellectual level of the jury can easily be gauged by the fact that it returned convictions against the seven men. Significantly, the three Southerners received sentences of from five to fifteen years, while the Northern agitators, convicted on the same evidence, were given terms of from seventeen to twenty years.

The Gastonia strike has been especially rich in the production of song; at least eleven songs and ballads chronicling the mill troubles have found their way out of mountain-locked Gaston County.

UP IN OLD LORAY[6]

(Tune: "On Top of Old Smoky")

Up in old Loray,
Six stories high,
That's where they found us,
Ready to die.

[6] The Gastonia Textile Mills.

REFRAIN: *Go pull off your aprons,*
Come join our strike.
Say "Goodbye, old bosses,
We're going on strike."

The bosses will starve you,
They'll tell you more lies
Than there's crossties on the railroads.
Or stars in the skies.

The bosses will rob you,
They will take half you make,
And claim that you took it up
In coupon books.

Up in old Loray,
All covered with lint,
That's where our shoulders
Was crippled and bent.

Up in old Loray,
All covered with cotton,
It will carry you to your grave
And you soon will be rotten.

—From People's Songs Library.

THE SPEAKERS DIDN'T MIND

(Tune: "Wreck of the Old 97")

On a summer night as the speaking went on,
All the strikers were satisfied,
The thugs threw rotten eggs at the speakers on the stand,
It caused such a terrible fright.

The speakers didn't mind that and spoke right on,
As speakers want to do,
It wasn't long till the police came,
To shoot them through and through.

On that very same night the mob came down
To the union ground you know,
Searching high and low for the boys and men,
Saying "Damn you, come on, let's go."

"We'll take you to jail and lock you up,
If you're guilty or not we don't care;
Come git out of these tents, you low down dogs,
Or we'll kill you all right here."

They arrested the men, left the women alone,
To do the best they can;
They tore down their tents, run them out in the woods,
"If you starve we don't give a damn."

Our poor little children they had no homes,
They were left in the streets to roam;
But the W.I.R. put up more tents and said,
"Children, come on back home."

Some of our leaders are already free
Hoping all the rest will be soon,
And if they do we'll yell with glee,
For the South will be on a boom.

Fred Beal and Sophie and all the rest,
Are our best friends, we know;
For they come to the South to organize
When no one else would go.

They've been our friends and let's be theirs,
And help them organize,
We'll have more money and better homes,
And live much better lives.

—People's Songs Library. By Daisy MacDonald.

W. I. R.: Workers' International Relief; Beal: Fred Beal, Northern organizer and strike leader; Sophie: Sophie Melvin, a beautiful girl who was one of the original fifteen defendants.

Another ventriloquism song: The scabs who have been evicted by Manville Jenckes beg to be forgiven and taken back into the tent colony. The strikers admonish them for helping to wreck the union headquarters.

LET ME SLEEP IN YOUR TENT TONIGHT, BEAL

(Tune: "Let Me Sleep in Your Barn Tonight, Mister")

Let me sleep in your tent tonight, Beal,
For it's cold lying out on the ground,
And the cold wind is whistling around us,
And we have no place to lie down.

Manville Jenckes has done us dirty,
And has set us out on the ground,
We are sorry we did not join you,
When the rest walked out and joined.

Oh Beal please forgive us,
And take us into your tent;
We will always stick to the union,
And not scab on you no more.

You have tore up our hall and you wrecked it
And you've went and threw out our grub,
Only God in his heaven,
Knows what you scabs done to us.

—By Odel Corley (age 11).

COME ON YOU SCABS IF YOU WANT TO HEAR

(Tune: "Casey Jones")

Come on you scabs if you want to hear,
The story of a cruel millionaire.
Manville Jenckes was the millionaire's name,
He bought the law with his money and frame (frame-up)
But he can't buy the union with his money and frame.

Told Violet Jones if she'd go back to work
He'd buy her a new Ford and pay her well for her work;
They throwed rotten eggs at Vera and Beal on the stand
They caught the man with the pistol in his hand,
Trying to shoot Beal on the speaking stand.

ON A SUMMER EVE

(Tune: "Wreck of the Old 97")

On a summer eve as the sun was setting
And the wind blew soft and dry,
They locked up all our union leaders
While tears stood in our eyes.

Fred Beal's in jail with many others,
Facing the electric chair,
But we are working with the I.L.D.
To set our leaders clear.

Come on fellow workers and join the union,
Also the I.L.D.
Come help us fight this great battle
And set our leaders free.

Come listen fellow workers about poor Ella May;
She lost her life on the state highway.
She'd been to a meeting as you all can see,
Doing her bit to get our leaders free.

She left five children in this world to roam,
But the I.L.D. gave them a brand new home.
So workers come listen and you will see,
It pays all workers to join the I.L.D.

If we love our brothers as we all should do,
We'll join this union help fight it through.
We all know the boss don't care if we live or die,
He'd rather see us hang on the gallows high.

Our leaders in prison are our greatest friends.
But the I.L.D. will fight to the end.
Come on fellow workers, join the I.L.D.
And do your part to set our leaders free.

We need them back on the firing line,
To carry on the work that they left behind,
When they were put in the dirty cell,
In the Gastonia jail we all know well.

—By Daisy MacDonald. In Margaret Larkin
Collection, People's Songs Library.

MISCELLANEOUS TEXTILE SONGS

The mill owners discovered early the weapon later given the name "lockout" to combat indirectly the encroachment of the unions.

THE MILL HAS SHUT DOWN

"The mill has shut down! Good God, shut down!"
Like cry of flood or fire the cry
Runs swifter than lightning through the town.
"The mill has shut down! Good God, shut down!"
Men wring their hands and look at the sky;
Women fall fainting; like dead they lie.
At the very best they earned but bread,
With the mill shut down they'd better be dead.

Last year with patience a lessened wage
They helplessly took—better than none;
More children worked, at tenderer age—
Even their mite helped the lessened wage.
The babies were left at their home alone.
'Twas enough to break a heart of stone
To see how these people worked for bread!
With the mill shut down they'd better be dead!

"The mill has shut down! Good God, shut down!"
It has run at loss this many a day.
Far worse than flood or fire in the town
Will be famine, now the mill has shut down.
But to shut mills down is the only way,
When they run at a loss, the mill owners say.
God help the hands to whom it meant bread!
With the mill shut down they'd better be dead!

—Broadside in Harris Collection, Brown University.

LET THEM WEAR THEIR WATCHES FINE

This song was transcribed by Will Geer, the actor, from the singing of a woman in the mountains of West Virginia. She said she had made it up herself and put it to the tune of "Warren Harding's Widow."

I lived in a town away down south
By the name of Buffalo;
And worked in the mill with the rest of the trash
As we're often called, you know.

You factory folks who sing this rime,
Will surely understand
The reason why I love you so
Is I'm a factory hand.

While standing here between my looms
You know I lose no time
To keep my shuttles in a whiz
And write this little rime.

We rise up early in the morn
And work all day real hard;
To buy our little meat and bread
And sugar, tea, and lard.

We work from week end to week end
And never lose a day;
And when that awful payday comes
We draw our little pay.

We then go home on payday night
And sit down in a chair;
The merchant raps upon the door—
He's come to get his share.

When all our little debts are paid
And nothing left behind,
We turn our pockets wrong side out
But not a cent can we find.

We rise up early in the morn
And toil from soon to late;
We have no time to primp or fix
And dress right up to date.

Our children they grow up unlearned
No time to go to school;
Almost before they've learned to walk
They learn to spin or spool.

The boss man jerks them round and round
And whistles very keen;
I'll tell you what, the factory kids
Are really treated mean.

The folks in town who dress so fine
And spend their money free
Will hardly look at a factory hand
Who dresses like you and me.

As we go walking down the street
All wrapped in lint and strings,
They call us fools and factory trash
And other low-down things.

Well, let them wear their watches fine,
Their rings and pearly strings;
When the day of judgment comes
We'll make them shed their pretty things.

"Hard Times in Cryderville Jail" is one of the most popular tunes for protest song adaptations in the South. Every Southern industry has dozens of songs written to this tune.

HARD TIMES AT LITTLE NEW RIVER

Now New River Mills is between two hills,
It's hard times at the New River Mills.

REFRAIN: *Hard times on Little New River,*
Hard times, poor boy.

Little Jimmy Kelly, he thought he was mighty smart
He went down and brought him out a part.

—From Mrs. Coker, Townley, Alabama.
(For music, see "Hard Times in Colman's Mines," p. 262.)

HARD TIMES IN THE MILL

Every morning at half-past four
You hear the cook's hop on the floor.

REFRAIN: *It's hard times in the mill, my love,*
Hard times in the mill.

Every morning just at five,
You gotta get up dead or alive.

Every morning right at six,
Don't that old bell just make you sick?

The pulley got hot, the belt jumped off,
Knocked Mr. Guyon's derby off.

Old Pat Goble think's he's a hon
He puts me in mind of a doodle in the sun.

The section hand thinks he's a man,
And he ain't got sense to pay off his hands.

They steal his ring, they steal his knife,
They steal everything but his big fat wife.

My bobbin's all out, my ends all down
The doffer's in my alley and I can't get around.

The section hand's standing at the door
Ordering the sweepers to sweep up the floor.

Every night when I go home,
A piece of cornbread and an old jaw bone.

Ain't it enough to break your heart?
Hafta work all day and at night it's dark.

(For music, see "Hard Times in Colman's Mines," p. 262.)

Transcribed from the singing of Lessie Crocker, worker in the Columbia, South Carolina, knitting mills, and now a member of Local 252 of her union. Of the song she says, "This was composed by my mother and some of the old spoolers in the mill forty years ago."

The "Ballad of the Blue Bell Jail" was composed by Blanch Kinett, of Greensboro, North Carolina, on February 28, 1939. The "Blue Bell Jail" is the Blue Bell Garment Factory.

BALLAD OF THE BLUE BELL JAIL

(Tune: "Hand Me Down My Walking Cane")

Oh, come on union, go my bail,
Oh, come on union, go my bail,
Oh, come on union, go my bail,
Get me out of this Blue Bell jail,
For all my freedom's taken away, taken away.

If we had the sense of fools (3)
We wouldn't set here like a fool
All our freedom's taken away, taken away.

For we know that a mule will balk (3)
Let's get busy with this union talk
All our freedom's taken away, taken away.

We are worn and the place is tough (3)
Oh, my Lord, we've had enough,
All our freedom's taken away, taken away.

This union sure will do the trick (3)
It will make the bosses sick
All our freedom's taken away.

SHIRT FACTORY BLUES

(Tune: "Brown's Ferry Blues")

I wanna go home but there ain't no use,
The union gals won't turn me loose,

REFRAIN: *Lawd, lawd, got them shirt factory blues.*

Litoff wants to work but there ain't no use,
Flips his wings like an old gray goose.

They called a strike and we came out
He walked the streets and we kept them out.

We were down and just about out
When Charlie Handy helped us out.

Sherman knocked Chelo on the head,
Chelo thought that he was dead.

—By Cleda Helton and James Pyl,
LaFollette, Tennessee.

WINNSBORO COTTON MILL BLUES

Old man Sargent, sitting at the desk,
The damned old fool won't give us no rest.
He'd take the nickels off a dead man's eyes
To buy a Coca-Cola and an Eskimo Pie.

REFRAIN: I got the blues, I got the Winnsboro Cotton Mill Blues;
Lordy, Lordy, spoolin's hard;
You know and I know, I don't have to tell,
You work for Tom Watson, got to work like hell.
I got the blues, I got the Winnsboro Cotton Mill Blues.

When I die, don't bury me at all,
Just hang me up on the spool room wall;
Place a knotter in my hand,
So I can spool in the Promised Land.

When I die, don't bury me deep,
Bury me down on 600 street;
Place a bobbin in each hand
So I can daulf in the Promised Land.

—From People's Songs Library.

"Here We Rest" was recorded at the Merrimac Mill Village in Huntsville, Alabama, during the textile strike of 1934. Dean, the strike leader, was killed during an outbreak of violence.

HERE WE REST

(Tune: "Hallelujah, I'm a Bum")

We praise thee, O God,
For the strike of the South,
And we thank you, Mr. Dean
For calling us out.

REFRAIN: *Hallelujah, here we rest;*
Hallelujah, Mr. Dean;
Uncle Sammy, give us a handout
'Cause we're tired of these beans.

We are standing on guard
Both night and day,
We are doing our best
To keep scabs away.

We are 1200 strong
And the strike still is on,
And the scabs still are standing
But they won't scab for long.

Hallelujah, we are union,
Hallelujah, here we rest;
Mrs. Semour sends our checks out
We are standing the test.

The scabs are all sore
Cause we brought back Mr. Dean,
And they swore to heaven
They would get him again.

Hallelujah, we are union;
Hallelujah, here we rest;
Hallelujah, come and get him
We are armed for the test.

We thank you Mr. Dean,
Miss Berry and Miss Dowd,
For staying here with us,
Through this strike you've called out.

4. Songs of the miners

We have eyes to see like yours
Way down in the deep, deep mine;
But there's nothing to see but the dreadful dark
Where the sun can never shine
On the banks of the clammy coal.
Our lamps cast a flickering light
At the dreary bottom of the moist black hole
In the land of the noonday night.[1]

America's Hundred Years' War was fought in the coal fields. Since 1849, when an English Chartist named John Bates formed in Pennsylvania's Schuylkill County the first American miners' union, there have been hundreds of battles in this continuous struggle, and "battle" when used to describe the contention between the miners and operators is not a figure of speech. "There's blood on the coal and blood on the mines," one song says, "and blood on the mine owners' hands." The miners lost most of these

[1] From the *Amalgamated Journal,* December 25, 1902.
George Korson's research among the coal miners has been the only work of any thoroughness in the field of labor protest song. Since this chapter is to be read as a supplement to his studies *(Songs and Ballads of the Anthracite Miner,* New York, 1927; *Minstrels of the Mine Patch,* Philadelphia, 1938; *Coal Dust on the Fiddle,* Philadelphia, 1943; *Pennsylvania Songs and Legends,* Philadelphia, 1949) I have not included any of these songs except "Mother Jones" and "Miner's Life."
See also Aunt Molly Jackson's songs.

clashes, as defeat and victory are commonly defined, but every concession made by the operators—even if it were to spend three months breaking a strike instead of ten weeks—was a step forward toward complete unionization; and a lost strike always resulted in the next union being bigger and stronger. Many tangible victories were won: The miner no longer has to compete with convict labor, the heavily guarded mine patch and coal camp are gone, and the operators' feudal control over local and state government is being broken down. Most important, the miners have their union now, a powerful agency that has carried the war with the operators to the bloodless plane of diplomacy. "The boss won't listen when one guy squawks, but he's got to listen when the union talks." The operators listen now, and the miners have good pay and sufficient food. "Nobody starves to death in Kentucky now," says Aunt Molly Jackson. But it has not been long since people starved to death in Kentucky, and were shot to death in Kentucky, and were beaten, and blacklisted, and exiled in Kentucky, as in other coal states.

It is shameful to say that our folk music is immeasurably the richer for this terrible strife suffered by the miners, but this is a fact. The songs and ballads which follow represent scarcely one-tenth of the extant pieces proceeding from incidents of violence and bloodshed, and an incalculably small part of those that have vanished. Hundreds of strikes have marked the path of the union's march through the coal fields, and each of these conceivably produced from one to perhaps a dozen songs, depending on its length and bitterness. I have represented fully only two strikes in this study—the Davidson-Wilder and the Gastonia strikes—and I am far from confident that there were not other songs commemorating these great struggles.

Not only the long history of union activity in the mine country, but other factors account for the great body of protest song among the miners, which, incidentally, is the largest of any labor group. The same reason for the prolificacy of these songs among the textile workers obtains for the miners also: the rich tradition of folk singing in the Southern mountains, the long cultural isolation of the people, the uncompanionate nature of the work, and of course the bitter conflict with employers. In addition, the mine community, which until recently was a colony of shacks huddled around the breaker, with a company store and perhaps a ramshackle church the only public buildings, had no diversion for the miners—no theatres, no movies, no radio, no television, and often no liquor.

> It's a long way to Harlan,
> It's a long way to Hazard,
> Just to git a little booze,
> Just to git a little booze.

What entertainment they had they produced themselves; and singing is the first of the creative amusements. Subject matter is always drawn from that which is uppermost in the singer's mind, and since the miner's life revolved around the mine, his songs were of its relation to himself. Not always were his lyrics woeful, but labor strife is a category which takes an impressive place among his songs.

The loneliness of his work[2] had much to do with making the miner reflective, and therefore a questioner of his economic and social status. Loneliness and monotonous labor lead directly to singing as a diversion of encroaching thought, and these two forces —diversive singing and frustrated thinking—easily join to form a song of discontent. When all of these factors are considered, one may ask not why there are so many songs of strife among the miners, but why there are so few.

Many have been lost, unquestionably. To an even greater extent than those of other labor groups, the miners' songs of protest are transitory. Like the songs of discontented labor as a whole, they deal with specific incidents of interest only to the persons involved. If in the old days a miner in Bell County struck against his employer, it was of no great concern to a miner over in Breathitt who had his own troubles to think about, and make songs about. The element of time also exerted its influence on the life expectancy of the miners' protest songs. This year's strike was likely to be more widespread and more serious than that of two years ago, and so the song produced by the latter was easily displaced, especially if, as often happened, it was sung to the same tune. Poor communication was another factor peculiar to mine country. The location of coal villages did not follow natural lines of communi-

[2] The chief grievance of the Calumet strikers was the introduction of the one-man drill into the mines, an innovation that denied the workers any companionship underground.

cation, as the location of other industrial communities did, and consequently roads were bad. The poverty of the miners made automobiles hard to come by, and because of the poor roads, cars were a bad investment anyhow, even if $25 could somehow be accumulated. Nor was there any place near-by to go, except other mine villages, which differed only in name and arrangement of the shanties.

The *United Mine Workers Journal,* the great instrument of education and enlightenment among the miners, has disseminated many songs of a wider appeal, but usually the tune was not given, and unless the reader was energetic and interested enough to fit the words to compatible folk tunes, the song never got off the printed page. The *Journal* has preserved more miners' protest and strike songs than any other agency during its half-century of publication, but since it is often impossible to tell whether a printed stanza is a poem or a song—or, if it was a song, whether it was actually sung—the most valuable source of material remains the collectors who go into the coal fields and catch these songs as they pass by on their way to oblivion. Unfortunately collectors willing to share the hard life of the miners, even long enough to dig out a few nearly forgotten songs, have been all too rare.

THE LUDLOW MASSACRE

Woody Guthrie's ballad "The Ludlow Massacre"[3] recalls the most wanton atrocity in the history of American unionism, an incredible example of the ferocity with which predatory coal barons fought to maintain their feudal hold on the lands they mined. In 1913 the coal fields of southern Colorado were only nominally in the United States. In every practical sense they were autonomous states in which every function of government was controlled by the operators. Houses, stores, churches, streets, towns, land, were company-owned. Company guards policed the streets and enforced the law of the operators. Guards were stationed on the outskirts of some towns to investigate the credentials of strangers wishing to enter. Miners leased only the right of entry to their houses, so that the company could prohibit anyone it pleased from visiting the occupants. Miners were paid not in

[3] There have been other ballads made of the Ludlow massacre, but since they lack the distinction of Guthrie's version, I have not included them.

United States currency, but in company scrip, in defiance of the law.

The company controlled the life of the community not only through its domination of the economy, but also by its usurpation of the law. A federal grand jury, appointed to investigate the dispute between miners and operators, reported in December 1913 that the mine owners were in complete control of southern Colorado politics. Colorado congressman Keating, himself beyond the power of the operators, declared:

Industrial and political conditions in Las Animas and Huerfano counties have for many years been a menace and a disgrace to our state. For more than ten years the coal companies have owned every official in both counties. Last fall they lost the district judge and district attorney, but that has been their sole defeat. Business men who have dared to protest have been prosecuted and in many cases driven out. The administration of law has been a farce. As an example: Hundreds of men have been killed in the Southern Colorado coal mines during these ten years, yet no coroner's jury, except in one case, has returned a verdict holding the companies responsible, the blame being placed on the dead miner.[4]

It is no surprise in view of such conditions that when the miners struck on September 23, 1913, many of their demands had been guaranteed by law, among them the right to organize; an eight-hour day; their own checkweighmen; freedom to patronize any store, boarding house, or doctor of their own choosing; enforcement of Colorado laws. Their other demands were scarcely less reasonable. The real point of contention, as in the Calumet strike, was the union. On this question the owners were adamant.

The state governor, as Guthrie implies in this ballad, was a futile recourse, displaying in all his statements and actions relating to the strike a shameful timidity before the mine owners. For example, in the one conference in which they deigned to participate, the operators refused to admit to the meeting any union representatives. Governor Ammons, presiding, thus permitted them to flout his laws in his own presence.

The state militia acted similarly in disrespect of the law. After his illegal imprisonment of Mother Jones, a thousand women and children gathered in Trinidad to protest against Adjutant General

[4] Quoted in *Survey,* December 30, 1913, Vol. 31, p. 321.

Chase's conduct. General Chase assembled a company of soldiers and rode out to meet the women. As he approached, he fell off his horse. Angered by the women's laughs and jeers, he ordered the mounted troops to charge; and they did so, inflicting sabre wounds on four women and a ten-year-old boy.

But Chase's greatest crime was one committed after he and his militia retired from the coal fields in April 1914, when the strike was in its eighth month. There had been many acts of violence committed on both sides—by the Baldwin-Felts imported thugs who toured the strike area in armored cars mounting machine guns, and by the hard-bitten miners who retaliated viciously after each depredation committed against them. The operators had turned the miners out of the company-owned houses, and the dispossessed workers were living in tent colonies in Walsenburg, Trinidad, and Ludlow. Chase organized two companies of the National Guard out of the basest elements in southern Colorado, and then left the area at the mercy of these irresponsible gunmen.

April 20 was Ludlow's day of horror. Early in the morning the "Guardsmen" began riddling the tents with fire from a ring of machine guns which they had set up around the colony. The fact that such an attack had been anticipated saved the lives of many of the miners and their families, for they huddled in the trenches which had been dug under the tents. All that day the gunmen fired into the tents, and when night fell and the occupants tried to escape in the darkness, the soldiers set fire to the tents. In the morning the Ludlow miners counted twenty-four of their people dead.

LUDLOW MASSACRE

It was early springtime when the strike was on,
They drove us miners out of doors,
Out from the houses that the company owned;
We moved into tents up at old Ludlow.

I was worried bad about my children,
Soldiers guarding the railroad bridge;
Every once in a while the bullets would fly,
Kick up gravel under my feet.

We were so afraid you would kill our children,
We dug us a cave that was seven foot deep,
Carried our young ones and a pregnant woman
Down inside the cave to sleep.

That very night you soldiers waited,
Until us miners was asleep;
You snuck around our little tent town,
Soaked our tents with your kerosene.

You struck a match and the blaze it started;
You pulled the triggers of your gatling guns;
I made a run for the children but the fire wall stopped me,
13 children died from your guns.

I carried my blanket to a wire fence corner,
Watched the fire till the blaze died down;
I helped some people grab their belongings,
While your bullets killed us all around.

I never will forget the look on the faces
Of the men and women that awful day,
When we stood around to preach their funerals
And lay the corpses of the dead away.

We told the Colorado governor to phone the President,
Tell him to call off his National Guard;
But the National Guard belonged to the governer,
So he didn't try so very hard.

Our women from Trinidad they hauled some potatoes
Up to Walsenburg in a little cart;
They sold their potatoes and brought some guns back
And they put a gun in every hand.

The state soldiers jumped us in the wire fence corner;
They did not know that we had these guns.
And the red-neck miners mowed down these troopers,
You should have seen those poor boys run.

We took some cement and walled the cave up,
Where you killed these 13 children inside;
I said "God bless the mine workers' union,"
And then I hung my head and cried.

Mother Jones was the greatest of the great women among the early mine union organizers; Aunt Molly Jackson, Fannie Sellins, and Sarah Ogan were as strong and as fearless as she, but they lacked the education that enabled Mother Jones to make her name famous as a champion of the miners. She lived for a hundred years, and was an active organizer for fifty of them, participating in her last strike in her eighty-ninth year.

Always at the front in the most serious troubles faced by her "children," as she called them, Mother Jones moved into Trinidad on January 5, 1913. She was seized immediately and was put aboard an outgoing train. General Chase characteristically explained his action in the following statement:

Mother Jones was met at the train this morning by a military escort acting under instructions not to permit her to remain in this district. The detail took charge of Mrs. Jones and her baggage, and she was accompanied out of the district under guard after she had been given breakfast. The step was taken in accordance with my instructions to preserve peace in the district. The presence of Mother Jones here at this time cannot be tolerated. She had planned to go to the Ludlow tent colony of strikers to stop the desertion of union members. If she returns she will be placed in jail and held incommunicado.[5]

She returned.

MOTHER JONES

The world today is mourning
The death of Mother Jones;
Grief and sorrow hover
Over the miners' homes;
This grand old champion of labor
Has gone to a better land,
But the hard-working miners,
They miss her guiding hand.

[5] Quoted in *Survey,* Vol. 31 (February 14, 1913), p. 614.

Through the hills and over the valleys,
In every mining town,
Mother Jones was ready to help them—
She never turned them down.
In front with the striking miners
She always could be found,
She fought for right and justice,
She took a noble stand.

With a spirit strong and fearless
She hated that which was wrong;
She never gave up fighting
Until her breath was gone.
May the workers all get together
To carry out her plan,
And bring back better conditions
To every laboring man.[6]

THE 1913 MASSACRE

Violence in the mines is not limited to the coal fields. The men who worked the Western metal mines were drawn from the same national stocks as the Eastern coal miners—Cornishmen, Englishmen, and Slavs—and worked under conditions almost identical with those of their Eastern brothers.

The bitterest strike in the upper Michigan copper country came in 1913, when the Western Federation of Miners endeavored to unionize the industry. There had been considerable discontent among the miners during the fifty-year history of the Michigan mines, but the thirty-eight nationalities represented among the miners were divided by the usual frictions developed by national heterogeneity and provided no basis for organization. Only the Finns, many of whom were Socialists, were articulate, but their influence was not great enough to unite the miners.

The Western Federation of Miners had a bad reputation among operators, and the invasion of the copper country by its organizers was fiercely resisted. When, early in 1913, the Federation became the bargaining agency for the miners, the operators refused to recognize it; official letters were returned unopened, and its threats to pull the miners out were ignored. Within a week after

[6] I have included "Mother Jones" here, though it is in Korson's collection, because this is a version different enough to prove folk transmission, and because this corrects the incoherent third line in Korson's version (*Coal Dust on the Fiddle,* p. 348) "When mankind has hovered."

the sixteen thousand miners struck on July 23, 1913, the owners called in the state militia force of 2,700 soldiers to guard strike-breakers, and soon afterward began to import labor detectives and professional gunmen from the East. Undoubtedly much of the violence that ensued was caused by these mercenaries, whose jobs depended on their ability to preserve disorder. The W.F.A., despite its reputation as a dangerous organization which could give as much trouble as it took, made a diligent effort to keep the strike peaceful. Members were cautioned not to drink, carrying of firearms was prohibited on penalty of expulsion from the union, and the union complied with discriminatory injunctions which denied the miners their constitutional rights. But when the W.F.A. petition for an injunction against the companies' importation of Waddell-Mahon gunmen was denied, and after two miners were killed and three wounded in an unprovoked attack by Waddell-Mahon detectives on a miner's home, the union struck back, and each murder or lesser act of violence on the part of the company police was answered with similar reprisals on a tooth-for-a-tooth basis.

Most of the demands fought for by the miners were either palpably reasonable or required by law, as some of the managers freely admitted, and the operators were secretly willing to grant them. But the owners would consider no arguments for the establishment of the union.

At Christmas, 1913, the strike was in its sixth bitter month, and feeling was tense. The Calumet business men had formed a Citizens' Alliance, whose avowed purpose was to drive the W.F.A. out of the copper country. Woody Guthrie tells the story of the Christmas tragedy which ensued when a man wearing a Citizens' Alliance button opened the door leading to the second floor auditorium where the miners were holding their Christmas party. There are some slight inaccuracies resulting from Guthrie's exercise of poetic license: the average daily wage for a 10½ hour shift was $3.48, though some teen-age workers made as little as $1.25 daily; seventy-two persons died, not seventy-three, and some of these were adults. "The 1913 Massacre" illustrates another aspect of Woody Guthrie's genius as a folk-ballad maker, another reason for his ranking with the nameless composers of "Chevy Chase" and "Lord Randal." Like his other ballads, this is clear, direct, and economical in the classic tradition, but its best feature is in the approach. By making the listener a participant in the tragedy he achieves great dramatic effect, and makes its poignancy a very real thing. "I will take you in a door and up a high stairs" gives in one line a good picture of the place in which the tragedy occurred.

1913 MASSACRE

Take a trip with me in 1913,
To Calumet, Michigan, in the copper country.
I will take you to a place called Italian Hall,
Where the miners are having their big Christmas ball.

I will take you in a door and up a high stairs;
Singing and dancing is heard everywhere.
I will let you shake hands with the people you see,
And watch the kids dance round the big Christmas tree.

You ask about work and you ask about pay;
They tell you they make less than a dollar a day
Working the copper claims, risking their lives,
So it's fun to spend Christmas with children and wives.

There's talking and laughing and songs in the air,
And the spirit of Christmas is there everywhere.
Before you know it you're friends with us all,
And you're dancing around and around in the hall.

Well, a little girl sits down by the Christmas tree lights
To play the piano, so you gotta keep quiet.
To hear all this fun you would not realize
That the copper boss thugmen are milling outside.

The copper boss thugs stuck their heads in the door;
One of them yelled and he screamed, "There's a fire!"
A lady she hollered, "There's no such a thing,
Keep on with your party, there's no such a thing."

A few people rushed and it was only a few,
"It's just the thugs and the scabs fooling you."
A man grabbed his daughter and carried her down,
But the thugs held the door and they could not get out.

And then others followed, a hundred or more,
But most everybody remained on the floor.
The gun thugs they laughed at their murderous joke,
While the children were smothered on the stairs by the door.

Such a terrible sight I never did see;
We carried our children back up to their tree.
The scabs outside still laughed at their spree,
And the children that died there were 73.

The piano played a slow funeral tune;
And the town was lit up by a cold Christmas moon.
The parents they cried and the miners they moaned,
"See what your greed for money has done."

THE DAVIDSON-WILDER STRIKE

Dr. J. B. Thompson tells how he recorded the text of the "Wilder Blues":

In January or February of 1933 I went down to the Highlander Folk School to help Myles Horton get his school started. The whole school had a budget of $1400 for the first year; we nearly starved, literally. But that's another story.

One of the first services we performed was at the lock-out of the miners in a little valley town, Wilder, Tennessee. There was nothing in Wilder but the coal mines, the miserable little shacks the company rented to the miners, the company store, and one or two sad, unpainted churches. The company paid the miners in scrip instead of money, so they had to buy their food and other necessities in the company store where the prices were much higher than at independent stores. The company made deductions for a bath house which did not exist, for doctor's services which seldom were available, for house rent, etc., etc. The miners worked hard and dangerously, but sank deeper and deeper into debt. They didn't have enough to keep their children alive, so finally they went out on strike. They were affiliated with no outside organization; they just had a little union of their own.

When they struck, the company turned off the electricity and took the doors off the houses. It was mid-winter and terribly cold. But still the company could not break the morale of the union, which was led by a mountaineer named Barney Graham. In desperation the company dynamited an old decayed trestle and said the miners were committing acts of violence, but anyone knew if the miners wanted to destroy company property they would have blown up a good bridge. But to "protect property" the governor sent in the National Guard, and in three months spent more to guard the mines than the company had paid to the state in taxes for 20 years. These young soldiers were fresh and cocky; they had never had authority before; they got drunk, they swaggered, they incited the strikers. Then the company brought in strikebreakers—scabs. We saw the advertisements the company ran in mountain newspapers and circulated in handbills. They offered the scabs much better wages than they had paid the strikers, board and room, guard, and "a woman at night." So they got plenty of scabs. The Red Cross gave out relief flour and food to the scabs but not to the starving strikers, for the county chairman of the Red Cross was the wife of the operator.

Myles discovered this situation and wrote letters which were published in the state's leading newspapers calling attention to the plight of the strikers. A little group of Socialists in Nashville gathered food and clothing and a little money, which Myles and I hauled over the mountain roads into Wilder every Saturday. I will never forget the long line of gaunt, haggard, brave people who lined up to receive the scant rations we handed out to last them a week. Each family got a pound of dried beans, a half-pound of coffee, two tins of canned milk (if they had a baby), half a pound of sugar. These rations saved many lives, but meanwhile many babies had died of starvation.

The company had let it be known that if Myles ever came back he would not get out alive. But the next Saturday I drove him back into town and we distributed the stuff again. We were unarmed. When we went into the company store about a dozen scabs put their hands on their guns, but the strikers followed us around and about two dozen of them fingered their pistols. So we walked around innocently and safely, like Ferdinand.

One very cold Saturday, after giving out all our groceries, we went into a stuffy, dirty little frame hotel where a poor meal was put on a long table, and for fifty cents you could sit down at the greasy table and help yourself along with anyone else who had fifty cents. While I ate I heard music and commotion in a front room, a bed room. I edged my way in. A man, about 50 or 60 years old, wearing an old black hat, and with a two-weeks beard, sat on the bed strumming his

guitar. As he played he sang stanza after stanza of a song he had composed about the Wilder strike. (The mines were at Davidson and
Wilder.) Whenever he ended a particularly good stanza, the men—20
or more—would cheer and say, "Uh-huh!" or "Amen!" He made some
new stanzas in my presence, but when he saw me and my city clothes,
he stopped. I told a union official I would very much like to write
the song down. They asked the bard, Ed Davis, but he was timid and
refused. I begged a bit, but it did no good. So I went outside and
got a couple of dirty little kids who were running around the house,
and told them to go in and ask Uncle Ed to sing it again. Ten minutes
or so later they did, and it worked. I sat outside the door, most of
the men realizing what was happening. The kids begged him; he sang
it again and I got the chorus and some of the stanzas. Then I had
them go in and ask him again, and that's the way we worked it; he
just kept singing it for those kids and the fellow strikers who sat
around cheering him and joining in the chorus. Finally, I got it all
down and had the tune well enough in mind to go back to the dining
table and write it down. Then the men told him I had written it down,
and to my surprise, he was very much pleased. He had just been too
self-conscious to sing it for me. Two weeks later we had Norman
Thomas come down to speak at a mass meeting. We had Ed sing the
song again and the audience cheered and ate it up. It was their song;
it was their life.

Ed Davis, who wrote this song, could neither read nor write, but
he sure could play that guitar.

THE WILDER BLUES

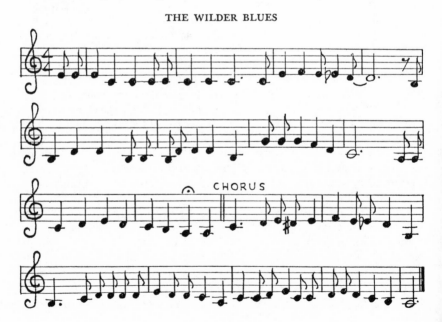

Mr. Shivers said if we'd block our coal
He'd run four days a week.
And there's no reason we shouldn't run six,
We're loadin' it so darn cheap.
It's the worst old blues I ever had.[7]

CHORUS: *I've got the blues,*
        I've shore-God got 'em bad.
        I've got the blues,
        The worst I've ever had!
        It must be the blues
        Of the Davidson-Wilder scabs.

He discharged Horace Hood
And told him he had no job;
Then he wouldn't let Thomas Shepherd couple
Because he wouldn't take the other fellow's job.

Mr. Shivers he's an Alabama man,
He came to Tennessee;
He put on two of his yeller-dog cuts,
But he failed to put on three.

Mr. Shivers, he goes to Davidson,
From Davidson on to Twin;
And then goes back to Wilder
And then he'd cut again.

Mr. Shivers told Mr. Boyer,
He said, "I know just what we'll do;
We'll get the names of the union men
And fire the whole durn crew."

We paid no attention to his firing,
And went on just the same;
And organized the holler
In L. L. Shivers' name.

Mr. Shivers, he told the committeemen,
He said, "Boys, I'll treat you right;"
He said, "I know you're good union men,
And first class Camelites."[8]

[7] Every stanza ends with this refrain line.
[8] Camelite: Campbellite—a member of a religious sect.

I felt just like a cross-breed
Between the devil and a hog;
And that's about all I could call myself
If I sign that yeller-dog.

There's a few things right here in town
I never did think was right;
For a man to be a yeller-dog scab
And a first-class Camelite.

There's a few officers here in town
And never let a lawbreaker slip;
They carried their guns when scabbing begun
Till the hide come off their hips.

Phlem Bolls organized the holler
About a hundred strong;
And stopped L. L. Shivers
From putting the third cut on.

They wanted to cut our doctor
Because the salary was too high;
And Shivers said, "You can't do that,
And there's no use to try."

They met again to hold it off
And they voted it with ease;
They added on fifty cents a month
And called it hospital fees.

Dr. Collins grinned all over his face;
He said, "I know just what I'll do;
Get a dollar and a half off the Wilder scabs
And all of Davidson too."

Mr. Shivers got rid of his nigger,
And a white man took his place;
And if you want me to tell you what I think of that,
It's a shame and a damned disgrace.

Dick Stultz is for the union men,
And Bully Garret against us all;
Dick kicked Bully in the stomach,
And you'd oughta heered Bully squall.

Bully Garret got excited,
And run into Bill Mack's store;
And that's just half of what he done,
And backed to Baltimore.

Paw Evans has got a 'tater patch,
Away out on the farm;
Alek Sells guards that 'tater patch
With a gun as long as your arm.

I'd rather be a yeller-dog scab
In a union man's back yard,
Than to tote a gun for L. L. Shivers,
And to be a National Guard.

Ed Davis was not the only Davidson-Wilder bard. Over in the twin city of Davidson, miner Tom Lowery was composing his blues:

LITTLE DAVID BLUES

Little Cowell worked for John Parish
For 35 cents a day;
He ate so many cheese and crackers
He fell off a pound every day.

REFRAIN: *It's all night long,*
From the midnight on.

Then he came to Davidson a-working
For Mr. Hubert and E. W. too,
And Cowell knows just exactly, boy,
How to deny you.

You go in the mines and find water
It's right up to your knees;
You surely don't like to work in it,
But you don't do as you please.

They'll take you by the collar
They'll mall you in the face;
They'll put you in the water hole
It's right up to your waist.

You come out of the office
After working hard all day;
Your sheriff dues and your doctor bill
You surely got to pay.

Men go through the office
They go through one by one;
They'll ask you for two dollars in scrip,
And Oh, gee! Make it one.

You get your handful of scrip,
And you go right in the store,
You find a fellow with a black mustache,
Writing it down on the floor.

You ask for a bucket of lard
And "What's meat worth a pound?"
"We sell it to you at any price,
'Cause we're spizwinkin'⁹ now."

You ask for a sack of flour,
And then you'll ask the cost.
It's a dollar and a quarter a sack
And fifty cents a yard for cloth.

I went into the store one day,
Mr. Cowell was frying some steak;
I warned it would give him
Scab colic and the bellyache.

The strike dragged on through the spring; at the end of April a Chicago thug brought in by the company shot Barney Graham, the union leader, in the back. The poignant "Ballad of Barney Graham" was composed by Graham's daughter, Della Mae.

⁹ "spizwinker": scab. Little Cowell was a spizwinker.

THE BALLAD OF BARNEY GRAHAM

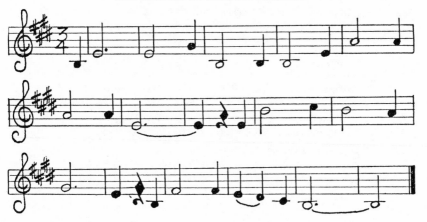

On April the thirtieth,
In 1933,
Upon the streets of Wilder
They shot him, brave and free.

They shot my darling father,
He fell upon the ground;
'Twas in the back they shot him;
The blood came streaming down.

They took the pistol handles
And beat him on the head;
The hired gunmen beat him
Till he was cold and dead.

When he left home that morning,
I thought he'd soon return;
But for my darling father
My heart shall ever yearn.

We carried him to the graveyard
And there we lay him down;
To sleep in death for many a year
In the cold and sodden ground.

Although he left the union
He tried so hard to build,
His blood was spilled for justice
And justice guides us still.

And still another folk composer appears in this little strike in two little towns, a woman named Eleanor Kellogg.

MY CHILDREN ARE SEVEN IN NUMBER

(Tune: "My Bonnie Lies Over the Ocean")

My children are seven in number,
We have to sleep four in a bed;
I'm striking with my fellow workers,
To get them more clothes and more bread.

REFRAIN PATTERN:

Shoes, shoes, we're striking for pairs of shoes,
Shoes, shoes, we're striking for pairs of shoes.

Pellagra is cramping my stomach,
My wife is sick with T.B.;
My babies are starving for sweet milk,
Oh, there's so much sickness for me.
Milk, milk, we're striking for gallons of milk. . . .

I'm needing a shave and a haircut,
The barbers I cannot afford;
My wife cannot wash without soapsuds,
And she had to borrow a board.
Soap, soap, we're striking for bars of soap. . . .

My house is a shack on the hillside,
Its floors are unpainted and bare;
I haven't a screen to my windows,
And carbide cans do for a chair.
Homes, homes, we're striking for better homes. . . .

Oh, Aid Truck go over the mountain,
Oh, Aid Truck come back with a load;
For we are just getting a dollar
A few days a month on the road.
Gas, gas, we're bumming a gallon of gas. . . .

They shot Barney Graham our leader,
His spirit abides with us still;
The spirit of strength for justice,
No bullets have the power to kill.
Barney, Barney, we're thinking of you today. . . .

Oh, miners, go on with the union,
Oh, miners, go on with the fight;
For we're in the struggle for justice
And we're in the struggle for right.
Justice, justice, we're striking for justice for all. . . .

MISCELLANEOUS SONGS FROM THE COAL FIELDS

MINER'S FLUX

They are shooting starving miners here,
And framing men to jail.
They cheat us in the company store,
And cheat us at the scale!
And the bosses spend a million bucks,
On jewels and on silk
While our children die of bloody flux
Because they have no milk.
They are clubbing men and women here,
Because they ask "more bread."
The bosses' justice orders cops
And thugs to give them lead.

COME ALL YOU HARDY MINERS

Come all you hardy miners and help us sing this song,
Sung by some union men, four hundred thousand strong.
With John White, our general, we'll fight without a gun,
He'll lead us on to victory and 60 cents a ton.

Come all you hardy miners and help us sing this song;
On the 21st day of April we struck for 60 cents a ton;
The operators laughed at us and said we'd never come
Out in one body and demand that 60 cents a ton.

Come out, you scabs and blacklegs and join the men like one;
Tell them that you're in the fight for 60 cents a ton;
There now in old Virginny they're scrambling right along,
But when we win they're sure to try for 60 cents a ton.

Come all you hardy miners, let's try to do our best,
We'll first get old Virginny, Kentucky, and then we'll get the rest;
There's going to be a meeting, right here in this land;
When we reach across the river and take them by the hand.

—By Finlay "Red Ore" Donaldson.

OUR CHILDREN THEY WERE SICKLY

You didn't do no wrong,
You didn't do no crime;
You gave away your young years
To slavery in the mines,
To slavery in the mines.

Our children they were sickly,
They had no clothes to wear;
Our little ones were sickly,
And no one seemed to care,
And no one seemed to care.

"I'll go join the union, then,"
These were the words you said,
And I knew they'd bring you to me
A-lying cold and dead,
A-lying cold and dead.

Go tell that sheriff
And his gunmen too,
That the reason my life is broken,
Is because they murdered you,
Is because they murdered you.

Sarah Ogan, like her fiery sister, Aunt Molly Jackson, was a union organizer and composer of militant miners' songs.

I AM A GIRL OF CONSTANT SORROW

I am a girl of constant sorrow,
I've seen trouble all my days.
I bid farewell to old Kentucky,
The place where I was born and raised.

My mother, how I hated to leave her,
Mother dear, she now is dead;
But I had to go and leave her,
So my children could have bread.

Perhaps, dear friends, you are a-wondering
What the miners eat and wear;
This question I will try to answer
For I am sure that it is fair.

For breakfast we had bulldog gravy,
For supper we had beans and bread.
The miners don't have any dinner,
And a tick of straw they call a bed.

Well, our clothes are always ragged,
And our feet are always bare;
And I know that if there's a heaven
That we all are going there.

Well, we call this Hell on earth, friends,
I must tell you all good-bye.
Oh, I know you all are hungry,
Oh, my darling friends, don't cry.

Harvey Matt, formerly head of the People's Songs Music Center, recalls an incident that occurred on the troopship which was returning him and other soldiers from Germany in 1946. While he was singing folk songs with a group of other GI's in their bunks, a chaplain approached and told the group that he was very much opposed to folk music because he was from Harlan County, Kentucky, explaining that every time a picket line would form "Somebody would start singing, and by God, we'd have a riot."

Had the chaplain claimed any other county in the United States as his home, this anecdote would be discarded as apocryphal, for clergymen ordinarily do not use oaths in secular contexts, but since he was from Harlan, the only questionable part of the story is the mildness of his language. Undoubtedly the last frontier is Bloody Harlan; next to the dependability of death and taxes, nothing is more certain than murder in Harlan on election day.

The most famous song to come out of the coal fields was written by Mrs. Sam Reece, the wife of a Harlan organizer. During the height of the strike violence in that county in 1931, a band of deputies under High Sheriff J. H. Blair broke into her home, looking for Sam. After vainly ransacking the cabin, the deputies left, and Mrs. Reece was able to get warning to her husband.

Several days later Mrs. Reece tore off a sheet from the wall calendar and wrote "Which Side Are You on?" to the tune of an old Baptist hymn, "Lay the Lily Low." Since then the song has spread throughout the United States, and has undergone many changes. As a coal-mine song, the version most common today retains only the first, fifth, and sixth stanzas, substituting for the others stanzas like

> *Don't scab for the bosses,*
> *Don't listen to their lies;*
> *Us poor folks just ain't got a chance*
> *Unless we organize.*

"Which Side Are You on?" has been taken over by numerous other groups who find the simple stanzas easily adaptable to all situations. Perhaps the most compatible is this stanza, sung in the motion picture strike of 1946. Compare this with the fifth stanza of the original.

> *They say in Culver City*
> *There are no neutrals there;*
> *You either are a union man*
> *Or a scab for Louis B. Mayer.*

Even the stanzas substituted for the originals during the song's first period of transmission have also gone through the folk process:

> *Don't let Jack Tenny fool you,*
> *Don't listen to his lies;*
> *We'll never get a decent home*
> *Unless we organize.*[10]

WHICH SIDE ARE YOU ON?

[10] From a Sacramento, California, housing protest meeting.

Come all of you good workers,
Good news to you I'll tell,
Of how the good old union
Has come in here to dwell.

REFRAIN: *Which side are you on?*
     Which side are you on?

We've started our good battle,
We know we're sure to win,
Because we've got the gun thugs
A-lookin' very thin.

They say they have to guard us
To educate their child;
Their children live in luxury
Our children's almost wild.

With pistols and with rifles
They take away our bread,
And if you miners hinted it
They'd sock you on the head.

They say in Harlan County
There are no neutrals there;
You either are a union man
Or a thug for J. H. Blair.

Oh workers, can you stand it?
Oh tell me how you can.
Will you be a lousy scab
Or will you be a man?

My daddy was a miner,
He is now in the air and sun[11]
He'll be with you fellow workers
Until the battle's won.

Merle Travis, one of the better hillbilly singers, prefaces his record of his fine composition "Dark as a Dungeon" with this note:

I never will forget one time when I was on a little visit down home in Ebenezer, Kentucky, I was talking to an old man that had knowed me ever since the day I was born and a friend of the family. He says, "Son, you don't know how lucky you are to have a nice job like you got and don't have to dig out a living from under these old hills and hollers like me and your pappy used to." When I asked him

---

[11] Blacklisted and without a job.

why he never had left and tried some other kind of work he said, "Nossir, you just won't do that. If you ever get this old coal dust in your blood, you're just going to be a plain old coal miner the rest of your days." He went on to say, "It's a habit—sorta like chewin' tobacco."[12]

DARK AS A DUNGEON

Come and listen, you fellers so young and so fine
And seek not your fortune in the dark dreary mine;
It'll form like a habit and seep in your soul
Till the stream of your blood is as black as the coal.

REFRAIN: *It's dark as a dungeon, and damp as the dew,*
Where the dangers are doubled, and the pleasures are few;
Where the rain never falls and the sun never shines,
It's dark as a dungeon, way down in the mines.

There's many a man that I've known in my day
Who lived but to labor his whole life away;
Like a fiend with his dope and a drunkard his wine
A man will have lust for the lure of the mine.

I hope when I die and the ages will roll
My body will blacken and turn into coal;
Then I'll gaze from the door of my heavenly home
And pity the miners, a-diggin' my bones.

[12] From "Folk Songs from the Hills," Capitol Records album AD 50. Copyright 1947 American Music Co. Used by permission.

5. The migratory workers

The Wobblies, Hoboes, and Migrants

> *He built the road,*
> *With others of his class he built the road.*
> *Now o'er it, many a weary mile, he packs his load,*
> *Chasing a job, spurred on by hunger's goad.*
> *He walks and walks and walks and walks*
> *And wonders why in Hell he built the road.*

THE MAKING OF A MOVEMENT: THE WOBBLIES

The Industrial Workers of the World, the revolutionary organization founded to destroy the forces of avarice, and the "one big union" which first made songs of militant action out of songs of discontent, ironically enough became a singing movement through the mercenary scheme of a professional spellbinder.

In the fall of 1906, a year after its inception as a combination of such radical groups as the Socialist Labor Party, the Western Federation of Miners, and the American Labor Union, the IWW went through its first great crisis. A disagreement in philosophy between the syndicalistic ("red") and the socialistic ("yellow") factions split the union in two. The red faction, comprised of the few most capable leaders, settled in Chicago, "fired" the elected officers, rewrote the constitution, and, in a word, took the organization away from the more numerous but less talented Detroit group, who later became known as the Workers International Industrial Union. The change in official policy alienated the Western Federation of Miners, the largest and most influential of the affiliated member organizations, and it withdrew, taking the exchequer. Cut off at the pockets, the nuclear IWW began to die, local by local.

Among the locals which still retained sufficient funds to keep afloat was the Spokane branch, prosperously situated on the crossroads of the Northwest; but it too felt the pinch of hard times. Like the other IWW locals it did not have enough money to continue the salaries of experienced missionaries, and organization came to a standstill. At this crucial juncture, a professional orator for the Socialist Party, one Jack Walsh, approached the Spokane officials and submitted a plan which he guaranteed would bring in many new members at no cost to the union. His idea was to introduce the methods of politics to unionism, to preach industrial revolution from the soapbox, and to recruit new members for $2.00 a head—which, he adroitly demonstrated, would cost the IWW nothing, since his commission would come out of the initiation fee of $2.50. Reluctantly, but with little choice in the matter, the Spokane local consented, and Walsh set up his "pitch" in Spokane's tenderloin district, where the hoboes, tramps, and other ambulant unemployed congregated.

His idea was successful; large crowds gathered to watch this unique labor organizational approach, and many somehow dug up the $2.50 initiation fee despite the depression which at that time was paralyzing American industry. But the revolutionary philosophy that Walsh was peddling conflicted with the principles of religious complacency being preached simultaneously up the street by the Salvation Army and the Volunteers of America, and these two bands marched down, surrounded Walsh, and proceeded to drown him in a cacophony of cornets and tambourines. Walsh, however, was equal to the crisis, and retired only long enough to organize a brass band of his own, in which Mac McClintock played an E-flat baritone horn and a giant lumberjack beat, as

McClintock recalls, the "b'jeezuz" out of a bass drum. Walsh's band learned four tunes and hammered away at these over and over until the evangelists capitulated.

Instead of abandoning his noise-making aggregation with the achievement of his purpose, as a less alert man might have done, Walsh saw in it possibilities of its development into another money-making machine. At that time a popular feature of burlesque shows was a take-off on the Salvation Army, whose recently intro-duced street-corner evangelism was in a precarious stage of its career. Not yet accepted by the unfortunates whom the Salvation Army tried to salvage, and vigorously denounced by more stable and dignified religious purveyors, it was a large and immobile target for ridicule. A troupe of burlesque comedians, dressed in garish uniforms caricaturing the evangelical military and carry-ing the popular Salvation Army musical instruments, would march on the stage to the booming of a bass drum and the rattle of tambourines, and line up before the audience. In turn each in-strumentalist would "testify" with a quatrain of risqué doggerel such as

> *Oh I courted a gal with a wooden leg;*
> *With her I used to linger.*
> *The way I knew she had a wooden leg,*
> *I ran a splinter in my finger.*

"Then," Mac McClintock remembers, "they did a walk-around while one performer brayed the tune on a cornet or trombone, another banged the bass drum, and the rest swatted and jangled their tambos until they were in position for the next solo verse."

It occurred to Walsh that this satirical mimicry of the singing evangelists might be extended to further IWW doctrines, and incidentally stimulate the flow of the $2.00 initiation fees. Luckily for his idea, his group included McClintock, already known in hobo circles as the composer of "Hallelujah, I'm a Bum," "The Big Rock Candy Mountain," and the "Bum Song," and Richard Brazier, a gifted parodist who was to become one of the IWW's most prolific composers. To McClintock's "Hallelujah, I'm a Bum," the band added a parody of another gospel hymn, "When the Roll is Called up Yonder," and parodies of the popular Salvation Army secular nickel-getters, "Where the Silvery Colorado Wends Its Way" and "Where is My Wandering Boy Tonight?":

> *Where is my wandering boy tonight,*
> *The boy of his mother's pride?*
> *He's counting the ties with his bed on his back*
> *Or else he is bumming a ride.*
>
> *Oh, where is my wandering boy tonight?*
> *Oh, where is my wandering boy tonight?*
> *He's at the head of an overland train—*
> *That's where your boy is tonight.*

The four songs were printed in a 10c leaflet which grew into the famous *Little Red Song Book,* the Wobblies' Bible, which is now in its twenty-eighth edition.

When the point of diminishing returns was reached in Spokane, Walsh led his band through the Northwest coastal towns on an exceptionally remunerative tour. But "fattening hogs ain't in luck," as Walsh was soon to discover. The Seattle local, one of the most influential western branches of the IWW, had never approved Walsh's street-corner organizing because such methods were to be identified with the tactics of political action, which the IWW policy makers had condemned as a perpetuation of the capitalistic system. Furthermore, the IWW locals realized that they had been taken by the shrewd Walsh, and complained that few of his recruits had ever paid more than the first month's dues. Walsh replied that he had contracted only to bring the members in, not to keep them.[1] His contention was ignored, the IWW took back its instruments and uniforms, and Walsh was fired.

But his idea had taken root, and before long street singing and organization became the principal activity of the struggling Pacific locals. The national policy board bestowed its benediction on topical singing as a weapon of revolt, and Walsh's four-page leaflet grew larger year by year.

Perhaps the greatest importance of the "little red song book"[2]

---

[1] The principal reason for the supplanting of the IWW by other industrial unions was this inability to hold its members. Its organizers succeeded easily enough in convincing migrant workers that the capitalistic system was an evil excrescence of greed, but they offered no constructive plan for the future other than abstract and bombastic exhortations for the workers to "cast off [their] chains."

[2] Its title through the years has been *IWW Songs: To Fan the Flames of Discontent.*

was its function as a vehicle for the IWW *Preamble*. "He who travels lightest, travels fastest," the Wobblies believed, so their movement, great as were its conceptions of a new world order, was founded on no elaborate constitution, no pretentious, orotund manifesto, no *Das Kapital,* but on a simple one-page statement:

THE PREAMBLE
Of the Industrial Workers of the World

The working class and the employing class have nothing in common. There can be no peace so long as hunger and want are found among millions of working people and the few, who make up the employing class, have all the good things of life.

Between these two classes a struggle must go on until the workers of the world organize as a class, take possession of the earth and the machinery of production, and abolish the wage system.

We find that the centering of management of the industries into fewer and fewer hands makes the trade unions unable to cope with the ever-growing power of the employing class. The trade unions foster a state of affairs which allows one set of workers to be pitted against another set of workers in the same industry, thereby helping defeat one another in wage wars. Moreover, the trade unions aid the employing class to mislead the workers into the belief that the working class have interests in common with their employers.

These conditions can be changed and the interest of the working class upheld only by an organization formed in such a way that all its members in any one industry, or in all industries if necessary, cease work whenever a strike or lockout is in any department thereof, thus making an injury to one an injury to all.

Instead of the conservative motto, "A fair day's wage for a fair day's work," we must inscribe on our banner the revolutionary watchword, "Abolition of the wage system."

It is the historic mission of the working class to do away with capitalism. The army of production must be organized, not only for the every-day struggle with capitalists, but also to carry on production when capitalism shall have been overthrown. By organizing industrially we are forming the structure of the new society within the shell of the old.

These were catastrophic ideas, and upon them was founded not only their philosophy, but their songs also, each of which was designed to illustrate and dramatize some phase of the struggle. Ideas this big, however, are apt to lead literary versifica-

tion into bombast and heavy rhetoric—precisely what happened
to the IWW songs which attempted to versify the *Preamble:*

> *The workers of the world are now awaking;*
> *The earth is shaking with their mighty tread.*
> *The master class in fear now is quaking,*
> *The sword of Damocles hangs o'er their head.*
> *The toilers in one union are uniting,*
> *To overthrow their cruel master's reign.*
> *In One Big Union now they all are fighting,*
> *The product of their labor to retain.*

To the "blanket stiffs" and "jockers" who comprised the membership of the early IWW, words like these were impressive, but
no more within their comprehension than the Salute to the Flag
is to the first-grade pupil who recites it after his teacher. And
when members of this social stratum attempt to imitate these
high-sounding phrases, the result is likely to be absurd. There is
something ridiculous, for example, in attempting to fit to the
tune of "Wabash Cannonball" stanzas like this:

> *Hail! ye brave Industrial Workers,*
> *Vanguard of the coming day,*
> *When labor's hosts shall cease to oblige*
> *And shall dash their chains away.*
> *How the masters dread you, hate you,*
> *Their uncompromising foe;*
> *For they see in you a menace,*
> *Threatening soon their overthrow.*

The only excuse that can be offered for such an unnatural
misalliance is that it was made deliberately, in accordance with
the formula that guided all the IWW song making: Take a tune
known intimately by the most unmusical of the migrants, and
fit to it revolutionary words—and the more bloodthirsty the words,
the better.

The Wobbly composers sinned in the other extreme also; some
of their songs are the worst doggerel that has ever got into print:

> *In the prison cell we sit*
> *Are we broken-hearted—nit—*
> *We're as happy and as cheerful as can be;*
> *For we know that every Wob*
> *Will be busy on the job,*
> *Till they swing the prison doors and set us free.*

But what is left of the IWW songbook after these defects are considered makes it the first great collection of labor songs ever assembled for utilitarian purposes—indeed, few collections since the publication of the first "little red songbook" equal it. In it first appeared the greatest American labor song, "Solidarity Forever," and such worthy songs of lesser stature as "The Workers' Funeral Hymn" and "The Red Flag." Historically, it is of first importance as a record of a conscious effort to carry economic and social discontent to the singing stage, which some writers believe is a necessary precedent to action. In the field of folksong scholarship, the IWW songbook is significant for its preservation of original compositions which potentially are folk material. Some observers might page through the Wobbly book and condemn the entire collection as either bombast or doggerel, neither of which can conceivably get into the stream of folklore, but such arbitrary judgments are always rash. The Wobblies' "Where the Fraser River Flows" has little to recommend it, for example. It is not the worst of the IWW parodies, certainly, but neither does it have any of those qualifications that seem to be prerequisites for admission to the highly selective folk tradition:

> *Fellow workers pay attention to what I'm going to mention,*
> *For it is the clear contention of the workers of the world;*
> *That we should all be ready, true-hearted, brave and steady,*
> *To rally round the standard when the Red Flag is unfurled.*
>
> REFRAIN: *Where the Fraser river flows, each fellow worker knows,*
> *They have bullied and oppressed us, but still our Union grows.*
> *And we're going to find a way, boys, for shorter hours and better pay, boys,*
> *And we're going to win the day, boys, where the river Fraser flows.*

But then Aunt Molly Jackson submits as her own composition a song containing these stanzas:

> *Fellow workers, pay attention*
> *To what I'm going to mention;*
> *Now this is the intention*
> *Of the workers of the world.*

> *To march in under our union banner,*
> *To sing and shout our slogan,*
> *And build one powerful union*
> *For the workers of the world.*
>
> *We are going to find a way, boys,*
> *To shorter hours and better pay, boys,*
> *Yes, we are learning the way, boys,*
> *As lots of bosses know.*[3]

The bulk of the songs contained in the IWW songbook are parodies of gospel hymns and sentimental songs which have firmly established themselves in American esteem, such as "Just Before the Battle, Mother," "Love Me and the World Is Mine," and "That Tumble Down Shack in Athlone." But no recognized composition, whatever its original nature, was safe from parody when the Wobbly song maker was hunting for a tune to fit a set of lyrics. Thus "Onward Christian Soldiers" becomes "Onward, One Big Union"; "Marching Through Georgia" becomes "Paint 'er Red";[4] "Barcarolle" becomes "Farewell Frank"; "The Toreador Song" becomes "We Come"; and even "Lillibullero," the seventeenth-century incendiary song that was said to have caused the loss of three kingdoms, turns up as "Workers of the World."

From a literary aspect, the most consistently good songs emanating from the Wobbly composers are the elegies written for their fallen comrades. The pretentiousness which results in bombast, the iconoclasm which results in compositions of poor taste, and the hack work which results in doggerel are rarely found in the elegies. The imminence of violent death which hung over all the Wobblies when most of these songs were written was brought close to them when they commemorated the victim of a lynching mob or vengeful justice, and consequently purged their songs of insincerity and questionable humor.

In spite of its defects, which are many, the many fine features of the "little red songbook" firmly establish it as a landmark in the history of singing labor.

---

[3] The direction of borrowing in this transmission is clearly determined in other stanzas of Aunt Molly's song by her use of certain words, not usually in her vocabulary, present in the Wobbly song.

[4] Attributed to Ralph Chaplin in the IWW songbooks, but Chaplin in his autobiography, *Wobbly*, shifts the responsibility for this embarrassing composition to an obscure song writer. "Paint 'er Red" was one of the Wobblies' great songs.

Unquestionably the greatest song yet produced by American labor is "Solidarity Forever," written to the tune of "John Brown's Body" by Ralph Chaplin. Chaplin was one of the leaders of the early Chicago faction of the IWW and right-hand man to Big Bill Haywood, but soon after his release from prison in 1923 he underwent that change of heart experienced by so many youthful radicals. He has lived to hear "Solidarity Forever" used against him.

SOLIDARITY FOREVER

When the union's inspiration through the workers' blood shall run,
There can be no power greater anywhere beneath the sun.
Yet what force on earth is weaker than the feeble strength of one?
But the union makes us strong.

> *Solidarity forever!*
> *Solidarity forever!*
> *Solidarity forever!*
> *For the union makes us strong.*

Is there aught we hold in common with the greedy parasite
Who would lash us into serfdom and would crush us with his might?
Is there anything left for us but to organize and fight?
For the union makes us strong.

It is we who plowed the prairies; built the cities where they trade;
Dug the mines and built the workshops; endless miles of railroad laid.
Now we stand, outcast and starving, 'mid the wonders we have made;
But the union makes us strong.

All the world that's owned by idle drones, is ours and ours alone.
We have laid the wide foundations; built it skyward stone by stone.
It is ours, not to slave in, but to master and to own,
While the union makes us strong.

They have taken untold millions that they never toiled to earn.
But without our brain and muscle not a single wheel can turn.
We can break their haughty power; gain our freedom while we learn
That the union makes us strong.

In our hands is placed a power greater than their hoarded gold;
Greater than the might of armies, magnified a thousand-fold.
We can bring to birth the new world from the ashes of the old,
For the union makes us strong.

Some of the turgid rhetoric of the latter stanzas of "Solidarity Forever" has been burned out in the alembic of folk transmission.

The pattern of the usual adaptation is a retention of the first stanza and chorus, intact, and a complete discarding of the subsequent stanzas for improvised stanzas less pretentious and more relevant to the situation at hand:

The men all stick together and the boys are fighting fine;
The women and the girls are all right on the picket line.
No scabs, no threats can stop us as we all march out on time,
For the union makes us strong.

From a strike at the Safeway Stores in West Oakland, California, to force the management to hire Negro clerks, comes this variant:

Safeway thinks America is only for one race;
To earn a living, white must be the color of your face.
But we believe in democracy for everyone
So we'll picket till our job is done.

Surprisingly enough, there were lady Wobs among the members of this toughest of all unions, and some of them, like Katie Phar and Elizabeth Gurley Flynn, attained prominence in the leadership. This song was composed in prison by Vera Moller, another member of this Amazonian band.

WE MADE GOOD WOBS OUT THERE

(Tune: "Auld Lang Syne")

Though we be shut out from the world
Here worn and battle-scarred,
Our names shall live where men walk free
On many a small red card.

So let us take fresh hope, my friend,
We cannot feel despair.
Whate'er may be our lot in here,
We made good Wobs out there.

When we were out we did our bit
To hasten Freedom's dawn.
They can't take back the seeds we spread,
The truths we passed along.

'Tis joy to know we struck a blow
To break the master's sway,
And those we lined up take the work
And carry on today.

Though we be shut out from the world,
And days are long and hard,
They can't erase the names we wrote
On many a small red card.

So let us take fresh hope, my friend,
Above our prison fare,
Whate'er may be our lot in here,
We made good Wobs out there.

"Dump the Bosses off Your Back" is a selection, taken at random, from the many gospel hymn parodies in the *Little Red Song Book.*

DUMP THE BOSSES OFF YOUR BACK
(Tune: "Take It to the Lord in Prayer")

Are you poor, forlorn, and hungry,
Are there lots of things you lack?
Is your life made up of misery?
Then dump the bosses off your back.

Are your clothes all patched and tattered,
Are you living in a shack?
Would you have your troubles scattered?
Then dump the bosses off your back.

Are you almost split asunder?
Loaded like a long-eared jack?
Boob—why don't you buck like thunder
And dump the bosses off your back?

All the agonies you suffer
You can end with one good whack.
Stiffen up, you orn'ry duffer,
And dump the bosses off your back.

One of the most successful organizing drives of the IWW was among the lumber and sawmill workers of the Northwest. After the AFL twice failed in attempting to establish a union, the Wobblies succeeded, but at the cost of the usual number of their shock troops. The most violent struggle took place at Everett, Washington, in the summer of 1916, after a long strike was about to collapse because of repeated beatings of strikers by police. August 19 saw the police begin an offensive designed to clear out the remaining pickets, but when the story of the beatings got abroad more Wobbly expendables moved into Everett. A strong force of police overwhelmed them also. Faithful to the principle of "one big union," the IWW gathered a force large enough to contend with the police, loaded two steamers full of men, and sailed from Seattle to Everett. But the police had been warned of the attempted invasion, and before the ships could dock they swept the decks with gunfire. Five Wobblies were killed and thirty-one were wounded, but they fought back, and when the battle ended, there were two dead and fourteen wounded among the deputies.

EVERETT, NOVEMBER FIFTH

". . . and then the fellow worker died, singing 'Hold the Fort' . . ."

Out of the dark they came; out of the night
Of poverty and injury and woe—
With flaming hope, their vision thrilled to light—
Song on their lips, and every heart aglow;

They came, that none should trample labor's right
To speak, and voice her centuries of pain.
Bare hands against the masters' armed might!
A dream to match the tolls of sordid gain!

REFRAIN: *Song on his lips, he came;*
Song on his lips, he went;
This be the token we bear of him—
Soldier of Discontent.

And then the decks went red; and the grey sea
Was written crimsonly with ebbing life.
The barricade spewed shots and mockery
And curses, and the drunken lust of strife.

Yet, the mad chorus from that devil's host,
Yea, all the tumult of that butcher throng,
Compound of bullets, booze, and coward boast,
Could not outshriek one dying worker's song!

At the height of the recent Flying Saucer furor, a letter to the editor of a Philadelphia newspaper ventured the explanation, "They're pieplates—left over from the pie in the sky we were promised years ago." Possibly many of the younger generation missed the implication, but the older readers recalled Joe Hill's most famous song.

One evening late in 1910 Joe Hill walked into the Portland, Oregon, IWW hall with a song he had written to the tune of the popular Salvation Army gospel hymn, "In the Sweet Bye and Bye." He gave it to the secretary of the local, George Reese, who handed it to Mac McClintock, the local's "busker," or tramp entertainer. Mac sang it to the men idling in the hall, and the tremendous applause that greeted its rendition convinced Reese that they had something. He and McClintock revised the song, and printed it in their little song leaflet which two years later was adopted by the IWW as the official songbook of the union. Hill was invited to join the Wobblies, and so began his fabulous career.

THE PREACHER AND THE SLAVE

Long-haired preachers come out every night
Try to tell you what's wrong and what's right;
But when asked about something to eat,
They will answer with voices so sweet:

REFRAIN: *You will eat, bye and bye*
In that glorious land above the sky (way up high)
Work and pray, live on hay,
You'll get pie in the sky when you die (that's no lie).

And the starvation army they play,
And they sing and they clap and they pray,
Till they get all your coin on the drum,
Then they tell you when you're on the bum:

If you fight hard for children and wife—
Try to get something good in this life—
You're a sinner and bad man, they tell,
When you die you will sure go to hell.

Workingmen of all countries, unite,
Side by side for freedom we'll fight;
When the world and its wealth we have gained
To the grafters we'll sing this refrain:

You will eat, bye and bye,
When you've learned how to cook and to fry;
Chop some wood, 'twill do you good,
And you'll eat in the sweet bye and bye.

Among labor unions Hill's version of "Casey Jones" has become more popular than the original railroad ballad. It is one of the few songs that no labor song anthologist would dare leave out. According to popular history, it was composed for a Southern Pacific strike in 1910, but company records and newspapers show no evidence of a strike of the magnitude described in Hill's story of the song's composition having taken place in that year. Harry McClintock says it was written for the "Harriman strike of 1911."

CASEY JONES, THE UNION SCAB

The workers on the S.P. line to strike sent out a call;
But Casey Jones, the engineer, he wouldn't strike at all.
His boiler it was leaking, and its drivers on the bum,
And his engine and its bearings, they were all out of plumb.

REFRAIN: *Casey Jones kept his junk pile running;*
Casey Jones was working double time;
Casey Jones got a wooden medal
For being good and faithful on the S.P. line.

The workers said to Casey, "Won't you help us win this strike?"
But Casey said, "Let me alone, you'd better take a hike."
Then Casey's wheezy engine ran right off the worn-out track,
And Casey hit the river with an awful crack.

Casey Jones hit the river bottom;
Casey Jones broke his bloomin' spine;
Casey Jones was an Angelino
He took a trip to heaven on the S.P. line.

When Casey Jones got up to heaven to the Pearly Gate,
He said, "I'm Casey Jones, the guy that pulled the S.P. freight."
"You're just the man," said Peter, "Our musicians went on strike;
You can get a job a-scabbing any time you like."

Casey Jones got a job in heaven;
Casey Jones was doing mighty fine;
Casey Jones went scabbing on the angels
Just like he did to workers on the S.P. line.

The angels got together, and they said it wasn't fair,
For Casey Jones to go around a-scabbing everywhere.
The Angels' Union Number 23, they sure was there,
And they promptly fired Casey down the Golden Stair.

Casey Jones went to Hell a-flying.
"Casey Jones," the Devil said, "Oh fine!
Casey Jones, get busy shoveling sulphur—
That's what you get for scabbing on the S.P. line."

A version of Joe Hill's "Casey Jones," collected by Duncan Emrich among the western miners, records an exercise of one of the Wobblies' chief weapons, sabotage:

The workers got together, they said it wasn't fair
For Casey to go around in his cabin everywhere.
Someone put a bunch of railroad ties across the track,
And Casey hit the river with an awful crack.[5]

After hearing a similar stanza sung by a group of Wobblies in 1913, Harry F. Ward was impressed by the vociferous applause that greeted the lines telling of the workers' revenge. He continues,

Still another ballad tells gleefully how the cheated laborer buys a piece of gaspipe to lie in wait for the employment shark who has robbed him. This is partly the naïve revelation by simple folk of that terrible disregard for human life which is one of the outstanding facts of our industrial process. More than that, we have here the voice of men with whom life is rarely safe . . . men for whose lives society has scant respect may be expected to reciprocate the feeling and make it concrete. "We care no more for your food supply in time of strike than you cared for ours in ordinary times," was what the English strikers told remonstrant England after they had tied up transportation. These men whom the I.W.W. is organizing have less restraint.[6]

"Workers of the World, Awaken!" is probably Joe Hill's best serious song. It is one of the long tradition of compositions written in jail.

WORKERS OF THE WORLD, AWAKEN!

Workers of the world, awaken!
Break your chains, demand your rights.
All the wealth you make is taken
By exploiting parasites.
Shall you kneel in deep submission
From your cradles to your graves?
Is the height of your ambition
To be good and willing slaves?

[5] "Songs of the Western Miners," *California Folklore Quarterly*, Vol. 1 (1942), p. 216.
[6] "Songs of Discontent," *Methodist Review*, September, 1913, p. 728.

REFRAIN: *Arise, ye prisoners of starvation!*
Fight for your emancipation;
Arise, ye slaves of every nation
In one union grand.
Our little ones for bread are crying,
And millions are from hunger dying;
The end the means is justifying,
'Tis the final stand.

If the workers take a notion,
They can stop all speeding trains;
Every ship upon the ocean
They can tie with mighty chains;
Every wheel in the creation,
Every mine and every mill,
Fleets and armies of the nation
Will at their command stand still.

Join the union, fellow workers,
Men and women, side by side;
We will crush the greedy shirkers
Like a sweeping, surging tide.
For united we are standing,
But divided we will fall;
Let this be our understanding—
"All for one and one for all."

Workers of the world, awaken!
Rise in all your splendid might;
Take the wealth that you are making,
It belongs to you by right.
No one will for bread be crying,
We'll have freedom, love, and health
When the grand red flag is flying
In the Workers' Commonwealth.

THE MAKING OF A LEGEND: JOE HILL

The first saint in the martyrology of labor is Joe Hill. Of the scores of men who have willingly given their lives to advance the cause of American labor, none remotely approaches Joe Hill's position in popular estimation. He has become not only the idol of a moribund union, but the apotheosis of militant labor, a modern Wat Tyler—but of the little that is known of him, nothing is more certain than his unworthiness of the honor lavished upon his memory.

Joe Hillstrom was responsible for his own beatification. The entire legend that has grown up around him derives from his conduct after his arrest for the murder of a Salt Lake City grocer—an astounding display of incredible self-detachment, apparent eagerness to die a martyr's death, and an almost unparalleled flair for self-dramatization. Taciturn, eremitic, and mysterious in his movements before his arrest, Hillstrom suddenly began to act as if he were playing the part of the quixotic hero of a fantastic melodrama—he refused to divulge, on the grounds of chivalry, the name of a woman allegedly implicated in his shooting; he refused to testify in his own defense; he refused to permit the IWW to hire lawyers to defend him; he fired his two defense attorneys in a sensational courtroom outburst; he rejected an unofficial offer of clemency; he wrote in his death cell poignant letters, poems, and songs full of the phrases that in such circumstances easily lend themselves to immortality; and he climaxed this unbelievable show of bravado by shouting to the firing squad the orders which executed him.

Before his indictment in Salt Lake City in 1914 virtually nothing was known of Joe Hillstrom; much of what has been learned since his execution has been based on hearsay, and extremely questionable hearsay at that. The popular biographical sketch of Hill which prefaces the various literary memorials dedicated to him—records, magazines, songs—varies only in the arrangement of words, and is always a paraphrase of idealized hearsay. A typical example is the preface to a recent recording of Alfred Hayes' and Earl Robinson's great ballad, "Joe Hill":

> Joe Hill was a migratory worker and labor organizer who composed songs which captured the stirring militant spirit of men on the picket line. Like many of his fellow organizers, Hill was convicted of murder on trumped-up charges. He was shot on November nineteenth, 1915. His last words were, "Don't mourn for me; organize."
>
> —Michael Loring, Theme Record T-100.

Even Ralph Chaplin, the number two man in the IWW during its period of greatest activity, confessed, "I never set eyes on Joe Hill alive. . . . All I know was that his full name was Joseph Hillstrom, that he lived in California, worked on odd jobs, and wrote poems or drew pictures in his spare time."[7] Chaplin assembled the only biographical information about Hillstrom collected before his execution, a few notes on which everything written on Hillstrom since then, with the exception of Wallace Stegner's recent investigations, has been based. Yet Chaplin's source was a drunken sailor whom he met in a Cleveland saloon. In his autobiography Chaplin tells the story of this encounter.

It was at Cleveland in the little saloon where we used to stop for beer and sandwiches after taking *Solidarity* over to the post office. It was close to midnight. We had loaded the heavy bags on our backs to beat the deadline. An I.W.W. lake seaman tapped me on the shoulder as I was leaving and asked me if I wanted to get the full story of Joe Hill's life. "Joe's cousin is here," he said. "His name is John Holland. Buy him a drink, and he'll tell all." I was at once skeptical and delighted—scarcely willing to believe that such good luck could be possible.

John Holland turned out to be a deeply-bronzed and somewhat inebriated deep-sea sailor whose blue eyes and blond air contrasted strikingly with his complexion. He had a true mariner's taciturnity, plus a classic Swedish accent. Word by word and drink by drink, I got the story out of him and wrote it down in my notebook. Incomplete as they are, these notes have served as the basis for every article ever published about Joe Hill. In fact, I believe they represent all that is known about his background.

Joe Hill was twenty years old in 1902 when he arrived in this country. He had a common school education and a fair knowledge of English which he had picked up at the Y.M.C.A. in his home town, Jevla, Westerjutland. Joe continued his education by reading while working as a seaman on freighters plying between Gothenburg and England. He left Sweden when his mother died

In New York City, Joe Hill worked for a couple of weeks as a porter in a Bowery saloon, then at any kind of odd job he could find. At the end of a year he and his cousin shoved off for Chicago via the boxcar route. They wanted to go to the West Coast. Joe Hill remained in Chicago two months and managed to save up twenty dollars for a road stake. His cousin had gone on to California. The boys met at San Pedro, where they lived for three years, alternating their time between longshoring and working freight steamers on the Honolulu run. Association with migratory workers at sea and ashore attracted Joe Hill to the I.W.W. He joined the organization in San Pedro and never transferred.

[7] Ralph Chaplin, *Wobbly*, University of Chicago Press, 1938, p. 184.

He could play almost any kind of musical instrument and delighted in improvising satirical parodies of well-known songs. At the Mission Church, 331 Beacon Street, San Pedro, he struck up a friendship with Mr. Macon, the director. There was a piano in the mission, where Joe Hill, between jobs, would sit by the hour picking out the words for his parodies line by line, to the amusement of his fellow maritime workers. He would polish up the verses at night and eventually assemble them into songs.

Everybody around the mission marveled at Joe Hill's untiring industry. He had the reputation of being a "harmless man" as well as notably unselfish. Frequently he would give away "his last rice." He never had a steady girl, always protesting that he was "too busy." His cousin, more typical of the maritime trade, urged him repeatedly, "Come on Joe, and have a good time." Joe never went. John Holland would find him late at night scribbling verse, "twisting the hair on his forehead with his finger as he figured out the rhymes." Joe Hill never smoked or drank. He was fond of Chinese dishes, which he prepared with great skill. It was said of him that he could "eat with chopsticks like a native."

It was during the great strike on the Southern Pacific Railroad in 1910 that Joe Hill first gained fame as a rebel songwriter. "Casey Jones, the Union Scab" was printed on cards and sold for strike relief in every West Coast city. Joe Hill could never understand why his parodies became so popular. He was greatly surprised to find himself in the limelight and his roughneck songs famous through the world. It was Joe Hill, more than any other songwriter, who made the I.W.W. a singing organization.

That this fragmentary biography, based on the testimony of an unreliable informant whose alleged relationship with Hill was unsubstantiated and who if he were indeed Hill's cousin would have been biased in his favor, should have been accepted as not only the truth but the whole truth is incredible. Yet not until Wallace Stegner began his research on the Hill legend was there any serious effort made to find out more about this mysterious champion of labor. Stegner reëxamined the court records and other documents pertaining to Hill's trial, searched through contemporary newspapers, and interviewed old Wobblies who remembered Hill. His conclusions, briefly, are that Hill's activities during his four years as a Wobbly are vague; that he was not a misogynist as Holland maintained, but on the contrary was continually in trouble because of women; that, far from being an expert instrumentalist, he could not learn to play the guitar; that the record of Hill's strike activities is questionable if not erroneous; that although Hill was always well dressed, he had no visible means of support; that it was the general impression among old time Wobblies that Hill was a crook; that Hill was probably guilty of the murder for which he was convicted.

Probably no Wobbly knew Joe Hill better than Harry McClintock. McClintock was present when Joe Hill brought his first composition, the now-famous "Preacher and the Slave," into the IWW hall at Portland, and later, as a resident of Hill's home port and as a leader in the early Wobbly singing movement, cultivated as close an acquaintance with him as anyone who has so far been found by researchers. McClintock told me that Stegner's biographical novel, *The Preacher and the Slave,* is the most accurate work, with certain qualifications, yet done on the Hill legend. He remembers Hill as a quiet man with a deadly equanimity that frightened even the hardened Wobblies. He was thought to be a robber, but looked more like a gambler in his conservative navy blue suit and black tie—"a real-life Raffles," Mac calls him—and if he were a criminal, Mac continues, "he robbed from the robbers." He had the reputation of being a dangerous character, yet to McClintock's knowledge, no one ever saw him get into a fight. He was known to the police before he joined the IWW, and though his only jail sentence came as a result of his organizational activities, he was picked up in 1910 in connection with a streetcar holdup. He proved, however, that he had been in Hilo while the robbery was being committed.

His intimate acquaintances, if he had any, were apparently drawn from outside the IWW, and his movements were frequently not known to the union leaders. In 1911 he apparently was in Mexico serving with the "International Brigade," and possibly was shot in the leg at the abortive action at Tijuana. Though he had no visible income sufficient to account for his impeccable dress, Hill was not entirely without visible means of support, for, according to McClintock, he was at least nominally employed as a seaman, and shipped out of San Pedro on offshore vessels, usually to Hawaii. Since he traveled under an alias and with false Norwegian seaman's papers, it is probable that many of his mysterious disappearances could be accounted for legitimately. McClintock confirms Stegner's refutation of Holland's claim that Hill was an expert instrumentalist, for he tried several times to teach Hill the guitar, but with no success. Hill could, however, pick tunes out on the piano.

Hill's real connection with the IWW remains in mystery. As Stegner's investigations show, most of the strikes in which Hill was allegedly an organizer either did not exist, or Hill's presence at them was not proved. The IWW did not send him to Utah as an organizer, and though his presence in that State was supposedly accounted for by his efforts to promote a strike in Bingham Canyon, there is no evidence extant to show that he was connected with any agitation there, and the strike itself never materialized. In an open letter maintaining his innocence written after his conviction, Hill claimed to have been working in the near-by Park City mines, but he was unemployed at the time of his arrest. It is probable, though, in view of the intense IWW activity in the Utah copper mines in 1913, that Hill had some connection with the movement there.

Since Hill's conviction is the most important single fact relating to his life, a summary of the evidence on which it was based may be worth inclusion here.

At approximately 10:30 P.M. on January 10, 1914, two armed men, masked in bandannas, walked into the store of J. G. Morrison, a prominent Salt Lake City grocer, and confronted him and his two sons. One of the men shouted, "We've got you now," and opened fire. Morrison fell, the youngest son, Merlin, fled into a rear room, and the other son, Irving, took his father's pistol and fired once before being shot down by the men. Neighbors who saw the men run from the store said that one of them clutched his chest and exclaimed, "Oh God, I'm shot." About two hours later Joe Hill walked into the office of a doctor two and a half miles away from Morrison's store bleeding profusely from a bullet wound in his left lung. As the doctor took off Hill's coat, a shoulder holster fell from Hill's clothes; the doctor saw it contained a pistol. Hill said that he had been shot in a fight over a woman, admitted partial responsibility for the fray, and asked the doctor to keep the affair quiet so that the woman's reputation would not be jeopardized.

That is the extent of the evidence on which Hill was convicted.

It is extremely damaging circumstantial evidence, undeniably; but all the other details appertaining to the shooting of Morrison seem to indicate that Hill was innocent. Witnesses described Morrison's assailants as being several inches shorter than Hill's six feet; Merlin Morrison refused to identify Hill as his father's slayer; no blood other than the dead men's was found in the store (though the police maintained that they discovered expectorated blood in the alley); though the bullet which wounded Hill passed completely through his body, no bullet was found in the store, and furthermore, the prosecution never established that Morrison's pistol had been fired; Morrison was shot with a .38 caliber pistol, and according to Hill, his own pistol, which he threw away after leaving the doctor, was a .30 caliber Luger. The doctor saw only the handle of Hill's pistol and could not describe either its caliber or appearance. The evidence that was not introduced at the trial also tended to exonerate Hill. The clerk from whom he said he purchased his Luger sent a telegram to Salt Lake City confirming that someone bought a Luger from him at the time Hill said he bought the pistol. Morrison had several enemies of whom he was mortally afraid; these men, he had told a reporter before he was shot, had attempted to kill him in September 1913. The reporter was not allowed to submit this evidence. A Wobbly named William Busby made a statement to the Seattle police that he had been with Hill the night Morrison was shot, and had while in Salt Lake City before Hill's trial inadvertently mentioned that he could prove Hill's innocence in the presence of a detective. He was arrested and imprisoned until the end of Hill's trial, when he was told to get out of the state. The police chief wired this information to Utah's Governor Spry, but Spry not only ignored the implication that Hill had been framed, but threatened to prosecute Busby. It is significant that this threat was not carried out, nor was any effort made by the Utah authorities to disprove Busby's charge.

The attitude of the court during Hill's trial was extremely hostile, and this hostility extended to Hill's own attorneys whom he discharged after shouting out in the courtroom, "I have three prosecutors here, and I intend to get rid of two of them." No motive for the murder was shown. No cognizance was taken of the fact that a man with Hill's serious chest wound could not have managed to stay on his feet for two hours and to have made his way two and a half miles to the doctor's office. After Hill's conviction a worldwide flood of protest poured into Utah. Prominent persons, among them the Swedish consul and President Wilson (who sent two telegrams to Governor Spry), interceded for Hill, but in spite of these appeals and the inherent flimsiness of the evidence on which Hill had been convicted, he was executed by a firing squad on November 15, 1919. His last words were not "Don't mourn for me; organize!" but "Yes, aim! Let her go! Fire!"

The more dramatic quotation appeared in a letter which Hill sent from his death cell to Big Bill Haywood:

Goodbye, Bill: I die like a true rebel. Don't waste any time mourning—organize! It is a hundred miles from here to Wyoming. Could you arrange to have my body hauled to the state line to be buried? I don't want to be found dead in Utah. Joe Hill.

This was not the only dramatic statement to come from Hill's death cell. He composed songs and poems which were later printed in the IWW songbook. One of these is his famous "Last Will" which he printed in a steady hand on the night before his death:[8]

> *My will is easy to decide,*
> *For there is nothing to divide.*
> *My kin don't need to fuss and moan,—*
> *"Moss does not cling to a rolling stone."*
> *My body? Ah, if I could choose,*
> *I would to ashes it reduce,*
> *And let the merry breezes blow*
> *My dust to where some flowers grow.*
> *Perhaps some fading flower then*
> *Would come to life and bloom again.*
> *This is my last and final will,*
> *Good luck to all of you,*
> > *Joe Hill.*

Joe Hill's body was brought to Chicago, where an enormous crowd waited to pay its homage. The auditorium where the funeral services were held was jammed with a throng which overflowed into the streets, until an estimated thirty thousand people were

[8] Unlike the many "written on the eve of his execution" poems actually composed several days later by a poor poet trying to make an honest penny, this death-watch poem is genuine.

there. After the ceremonies in the auditorium, the funeral procession marched a mile, through streets crowded with mourners, to the train which carried his body to the cemetery. There, in accordance with his "Last Will," Joe Hill was cremated and his ashes put into thirty envelopes, which were then sent to all parts of the world. One envelope was retained by the IWW in Chicago and was seized by the Department of Justice in 1918 during its raids for evidence preceding the trials which broke the back of the Wobbly movement. Thus, as Wallace Stegner puts it, "Although 97 percent of Joe Hill's mortal remains are somewhere free and fecund in the earth, three percent are still in the hands of the cops."

Whether or not Hill was actually guilty of the murder of Morrison, there can be no question that his conviction came as a result of his connection with the IWW. Probably no organization in America was so feared and hated as the IWW before and during the First World War, and the degree of fear and hatred which it enkindled in the copper-mine operators amounted almost to insanity. Nearly every labor dispute in which it engaged ended in bloody violence, and always most of the blood was lost by the Wobblies. When a migrant signed his little red membership card, he simultaneously signed a death warrant that might be picked up at any time; and this fact, curiously enough, was recognized by the Wobblies themselves, who seemed to be imbued with the spirit of martyrdom that Joe Hill exemplified during and after his trial. After the shameful trials conducted by the Department of Justice against the Wobbly leaders during the First World War, several of the top men in the organization jumped bail and fled to Russia. Of those who remained to serve their sentences, many refused to ally themselves with communism because they felt that the communists too were a "bunch of politicians." The whole movement, in fact, could be summed up as a screaming banzai charge at capitalism.

As Joe Hill's reputation as a labor hero appears somewhat tarnished under scrutiny, so does his reputation as a composer of "songs which captured the militant spirit of men on the picket line" appear less refulgent in the light of critical examination. It is unfortunate that his position at the top of the IWW martyrs (of whom there were many more genuine than he) has required the editors of the "little red song book" to include so many of his songs, for on the whole their quality detracts from the worth of a book which occupies a position of honor among collections of songs of protest. Only two of the score of songs attributed to him, "The Preacher and the Slave," and "Casey Jones, the Union Scab," have any permanent value. Both of these have attained the status of genuine folksong, the latter, for example, having been collected by folklorist Duncan Emrich in the Virginia City, Nevada, mines in a version somewhat different from that composed by Hill. Two or three, like "The Rebel Girl" which Joe Hill considered his best song, and "Workers of the World, Awaken," despite a tendency to slip into the unfortunate fustian that is the one great defect of the Wobblies' serious songs, are quite good; it is a pity that there are not more of this quality. But most, in a literary sense, are contemptible. It is very difficult, for example, to say anything favorable about a song that begins, as does "The Tramp," with

> *If you all will shut your trap*
> *I will tell you 'bout a chap*

or which has a refrain like

> *Oh, Mr. Block, you were born by mistake*
> *You take the cake*
> *You make me ache.*
> *Tie a rock on your block and then jump in the lake,*
> *Kindly do that for Liberty's sake.*

or

> *Scissor Bill, he is a little dippy*
> *Scissor Bill, he has a funny face*
> *Scissor Bill, he should drown in Mississippi*
> *He is the missing link that Darwin tried to trace.*

But "Preacher and the Slave" is a classic, and nearly good enough to expiate all of Joe Hill's sins as a man and as a composer.

THE MAKING OF A FOLKSONG:
"HALLELUJAH, I'M A BUM"

A half-century ago, while rattling through the Midwest in a boxcar, a young "busker"[9] composed an impious parody on

---

[9] busker: tramp entertainer   hobo: migratory worker
jocker: experienced tramp   tramp: professional unemployed
preshun: apprentice tramp

a gospel hymn he had once sung as a boy soprano in his church choir. The first tentative refrain ran,

> *Hallelulia, on the bum bum,*
> *Hallelulia, bum again;*
> *Hallelulia, give us a handout*
> *To revive us again.*

He liked the song, and so did the tramps to whom he sang it for pennies or a share of a handout, and in the years that followed he improvised stanzas, some of which became permanent, and broadcast the song through the country from boxcars, saloons, and jungles. He lent the song to the people. Thirty years later he tried to get it back, but discovered the folk were a very tenacious bunch of people.

Harry McClintock first realized that he had lost ownership of the song in 1926, shortly after he had recorded "Hallelujah, I'm a Bum" and "The Bum Song (No. 1)" for the Victor Record Company. When he learned that sixteen New York music publishers had printed sheet music of the song and that many more were turning out broadsides, he charged the pirates with infringement of copyright, but found that his claim of ownership had been challenged. At that time he had a radio program on San Francisco's Station KFRC, and he broadcast an appeal for those who still had copies of broadsides he had sold in 1906 to lend them to substantiate his claim. Several of these were returned to him, and also two copies of the first IWW songsheet which had been published in 1907. With this evidence he established his authorship to the satisfaction of the legal authorities, had the pirates suppressed, and settled down to enjoy the royalties.

In 1932, while reading George Milburn's *Hobo's Hornbook,* he found that the folk had got hold of his song again, but this time their grip was strengthened by an even more acquisitive group, the folklorists. Milburn had printed two versions of "Hallelulia" and had appended to them this note:

It is hardly safe to classify the following widely-sung ballad as a Wobbly song. There is some dispute as to its origin. Budd L. McKillips, who has himself written some first rate hobo poetry, has given me the following notes on "Hallelujah, Bum Again's" history: "A member of the I.W.W. is credited with having written the words to 'Hallelujah, I'm a Bum.' The question of authorship isn't worth an argument, but if anybody will take the trouble to do some investigating, he will find that 'Hallelujah, I'm a Bum' was a lilting, carefree song at least eight years before the I.W.W. came squalling into the world. . . . The song was found scribbled on the wall of a Kansas City jail cell where an old hobo, known as 'One-Finger Ellis,' had spent the night, recovering from an overdose of rotgut whiskey."

—George Milburn, *Hobo's Hornbook*,
New York, 1930, p. 97.

Aside from such quodlibetical questions as which Kansas City Ellis was in, what connection he had with the scribbled text (witness, informant, or scribbler?) the date of "One-Finger's" repose in the sneezer, and the method whereby McKillips came into possession of this hazy information, McClintock raises the objection that the testimony does not obviate the authenticity of his authorship. Against Milburn's attribution of the song to the prolific *Anon* which has been accepted by all subsequent editors of "Hallelujah, I'm a Bum," Mac McClintock offered his version of its origin, which has at least the virtue of being first-hand and coherent:

As a kid I was a boy soprano in a church choir in my home town, Knoxville, Tennessee. My voice started changing when I was thirteen and by the time I ran away with a circus, which was in the following year, I had almost conquered the adolescent squeaks and could give with the baritone or low tenor.

The Gentry Brothers' Dog and Pony Show played its last date of the season on a muddy lot in Anniston, Alabama, in 1896, paid off its help, which was unusual with a circus of that period, and headed for winter quarters. I was a "road kid" and strictly on my own.

Some forty or fifty canvasmen and razorbacks had been paid off in Anniston. About half of them grabbed the first rattler out of town; the rest found a hobo jungle on the edge of town and went into camp. Corn whiskey of the "white lightning" variety could be bought for forty or fifty cents per quart; and the boys gave it quite a play. I had never tasted anything stronger than a sip of beer before, and my first— and last—swallow of corn squeezin's was plenty. Even a kid could see Trouble coming, so I latched onto a west bound freight and so missed the battle when the Anniston police raided the jungles, beat the b'jeezuz out of the boozers and tossed them all into the clink. I also missed the roundup of the other gang; there were too many of them

in one bunch and they were summarily hauled off the train at some
other town and probably made the chain gang. I had learned my first
valuable lesson—from then on I traveled alone. I was only a kid and
looked even younger than I was. So the brakemen on the trains and
the coppers in the towns ignored me and let me go my way unmolested.

Eating, regularly and well, was no trouble at all. I had only to
choose a house, massage the back door with my knuckles, and a feed
would be forthcoming. Mostly it would be a matronly colored woman
who answered my knock and seldom did one of them fail to seat me
at the kitchen table and shake up a hot meal for me. Sometimes I got
a "handout" of cold victuals, wrapped in newspaper, but when that
happened there would be enough to feed two or three men.

It was in New Orleans that I found that singing in saloons could
be profitable. There were plenty of grog shops in the Paris of America;
Bourbon Street, for instance, was just about nothing else but. Musicians
worked for whatever the customers tossed into the kitty and any joint
that didn't have a band had at least a piano and a Negro to play it.
One night I walked into a "can joint," a species of saloon that has
long been extinct. There was a bar, but most customers, coming in
parties, were seated at tables. Glasses were provided and the beer was
served in tin containers holding a gallon—at two bits per can. A bunch
of Limey sailors were having a bit of a singsong and I ventured to
join in one of the choruses. I was immediately invited to grab a glass
and sit in.

Somehow I dropped the information that I had hoboed into New
Orleans and expected to resume my wanderings as soon as the weather
got warmer. Their interest was flattering and I am afraid that I loaded
them with some pretty tall tales about hobo life. They kept dropping
coins into my pockets at odd intervals and I woke up next morning
with nearly four bucks in small change. So when I hit the road again
I was no longer a moocher of poke-outs at back doors; well, anyway,
not exclusively. In a strange town I searched for sounds of "revelry
by night" and there were few saloon crowds that would refuse to listen
to a kid who wanted to sing.

But my new trade of singing for my supper brought new dangers,
on the road and in the jungles. Most of the vagrants were mechanics
or laborers, uprooted and set adrift by hard times, and they were
decent men. All any of them needed for respectable citizenship was
a shave, a clean shirt, and a job. But there were others, "blowed-in-the-
glass-stiffs," who boasted that they had never worked and never would,
who soaked themselves in booze when they could get it and who were
always out to snare a kid to do their begging and pander to their
perversions. The luckless punk who fell into the clutches of one of

these gents was treated with unbelievable brutality, and I wanted no part of such a life. As a "producer" I was a shining mark; a kid who could not only beg handouts but who could bring in money for alcohol was a valuable piece of property for any jocker who could snare him. The decent hoboes were protective as long as they were around, but there were times when I fought like a wildcat or ran like a deer to preserve my independence and my virginity. I whittled my way out of two or three jams with a big barlow knife, and on one occasion I jumped into the darkness from a boxcar door—from a train that must have been doing better than thirty miles per hour. I lay in the ditch where I landed until picked up by a section gang next morning. They took me to a private hospital and the Doc found contusions, concussion, a fractured collarbone and several cracked ribs. That was in Girard, Kansas, and those big hearted folks kept me around until my bones had knit and I was as good as new.

My wanderings that year covered most of the Middle West; I got as far west at Pueblo, visited St. Louis and Chicago, and landed in Cincinnati late in the fall. Somewhere along the line I was humming the old gospel hymn "Revive Us Again," and I put new words to it and called it "Hallelulia, on the Bum."

> *I went to a bar and I asked for a drink*
> *He gave me a glass and said "There is the sink"*
>
> *Hallelulia, on the bum bum . . .*
>
> *Rejoice and be glad, for the springtime has come;*
> *We can throw down our shovels and go on the bum.*

There were only two or three verses at first but new ones practically wrote themselves. The jungle stiffs liked the song and so did the saloon audiences, most of whom had hit the road at one time or another, and the rollicking, devil-may-care lilt of the thing appealed to them. Occasionally the name of a popular local beer was used in the chorus. Instead of "Hallelulia give us a handout," it became "Hallelulia give us a Pilsener."

The Spanish American War came along in the spring of 1898 and one of the biggest training camps in the United States was set up in Chicamauga Park, near Chattanooga, Tennessee. I was too young and too skinny to get into the Army but I did establish a newspaper route and built it up until I had to cover it on horseback. More than 80,000 men were encamped there that summer and there were literally hundreds of kids hustling newspapers. By that time I had acquired a five-string banjo and learned to plunk a few chords as accompaniment to my songs. There were no USO units in those days, no movies, and no radio. No one ever thought of asking the stage folk, proverbially generous in such matters, to give the boys in camp a tumble. Whatever entertainment there was came right out of the ranks or was provided by guys like myself.

"Hallelulia, on the Bum" became a popular camp song. Verses in dispraise of unpopular officers were catchy and easy to write.

> *Our own Captain Jones, he sure likes to strut*
> *All Captain Jones needs is a kick in the butt.*

> *Hallelulia he's a bum bum,*
> *Hallelulia sing it again;*
> *Hallelulia, give him a kickout (dishonorable discharge)*
> *Send him back home again.*

There were lots more verses, mostly unprintable, and only a few were contributed by me. The soldiers sang about the grub, the mosquitoes, the pay (thirteen dollars a month), the moonshine corn, the provost guard in Chattanooga and any other topic that suggested itself.

After the war the soldiers carried the song back to their widely scattered home towns, and the song rapidly was assumed into the great songbag of the people. Mac McClintock, being only an individual, had lost his identity with the song. Later, when he joined the burgeoning IWW as one of its first singers, "Hallelujah, I'm a Bum" became its unofficial anthem, and McClintock's claim of authorship was met with considerable incredulousness. As the years pass, it is to be hoped that Mac has found some compensation, real and psychic, in the realization that he has written a durable song which he has lost to tradition, for the folk have a firm hold on it now, and they are not going to give it back to him.[10]

The hobo song as folk material is a rich territory, but one that has veen virtually untouched. The only important study done in the field is that of Milburn, but since his book lost money for its publisher, it is unlikely that any future ambitious investigation will be made—commercially at least.

The songs produced by the hobo possess a unity unapproached by other cultural areas in American folk music. All hobo songs treat of the same subject—life on the road. Of course there are various phases which show a surface differentiation—songs of the handout, the train, the "town clown and harness bull" for example—but basically they are one. And all of them, with only a

---

[10] Several protest songs have been made up to the tune of "Hallelujah, I'm a Bum," e.g., "Hallelujah, I'm a Travelin'" and "Hallelujah, I'm a Ku Klux."

few exceptions, are expressions of sublimated protest.[11] The stage of conscious complaint had been by-passed. It is a subject that will reward deep probing.

Some indication of what a competent investigator may turn up in the matter of buried significance of the conscious sort is in "The Big Rock Candy Mountains," a song that has been accepted for decades into the bosoms of American families as a delightful fantasy, a child's dream of heaven, a song to be printed in gay colors on the nursery wall. But George Milburn has shown the distasteful significance of this apparently innocent song:

> "The Big Rock Candy Mountains," a tramp song, provides some excellent samples of tramp fantasy. In many small cities and villages the children of poor whites use the railroad yards as their playgrounds. From these urchins the jockers sometimes recruit their preshuns, and to entice them they tell them roseate tales of tramp life. These fabrications are known as ghost stories. To the Home Guards, "The Big Rock Candy Mountains" may appear a nonsense song, but to all pied pipers in on the know it is an amusing exaggeration of the ghost stories used in recruiting kids.

Mac McClintock claims also the authorship of this song, and in addition to virtually the same substantiation advanced to support his authorship of "Hallelujah, I'm a Bum," he offers his original version of the song, which, despite the necessary expurgation, retains enough of the original significance to certify its precedence over versions now current on family radio programs:

> *One summer day in the month of May*
> *A jocker he came hiking.*
> *He came to a tree and "Ah," says he,*
> *"This is just to my liking."*
> *In the very same month on the very same day*
> *A Hoosier boy came hiking.*
> *Said the bum to the son, "Oh will you come*
> *To the Big Rock Candy Mountains?"*
>
> REFRAIN: *I'll show you the bees in the cigarette trees,*
> *And the soda water fountain*
> *And the lemonade springs where the blue bird sings.*
> *In the Big Rock Candy Mountains.*

[11] The largest number of exceptions is that comprising the IWW parodies, which represent the product of an external agitation stirring up the great sedimentary protest which lay heavy beneath the surface layer of good-natured complaints against uncharitable housewives, brutal railroad police, and the general hell of it all.

So they started away on the very same day,
The bum and the kid together,
To romp and to rove in the cigarette grove
In the land of the sunny weather.
They danced and they hiked for many a day,
The mile posts they were counting;
But they never arrived at the lemonade tide
Or the Big Rock Candy Mountains.

The punk rolled up his big blue eyes
And said to the jocker, "Sandy,
I've hiked and hiked and wandered too,
But I ain't seen any candy.
I've hiked and hiked till my feet are sore
I'll be God damned if I hike any more
To be   *   *   *   *   *   *   *
In the Big Rock Candy Mountains."

THE MIGRANTS

Since the Dust Bowl days a new type of homeless unemployed has come into existence on a wide scale, and no longer
can all migratory workers be called hoboes. When the Joads piled
their pitiful belongings into their ancient truck and headed west,
they created a social class heretofore unknown—the American
nomad. The Second World War and its resultant false prosperity
and the planting of broomcorn in the Dust Bowl have not cor-
rected the conditions that produced the Okies, nor have the Okies
gone back to the Middle West with the profits of their labors in
war plants.[12] An hour's drive from Los Angeles into the rich San
Joaquin Valley will take the observer several centuries back
through civilization. He will see entire families (except for the
smallest babies who lie between the rows in the merciless California sun) grubbing at weeds among the potatoes or at excess
cotton shoots in fields on the other side of the highway with their
fingers or crude implements, like twelfth-century peasants.

The substantial citizens of Fresno, and Bakersfield, and Visalia,
and Tulare want to help them, of course, but "What are you

---

[12] The migrants are not all Dust Bowl refugees, nor is abused Nature the only
force driving once independent farmers into the migrant stream. The big corpora-
tion-type farms, timber companies, and other combinative exploiters of the land
share responsibility with the Dust Bowl for the estimated 2½ million homeless crop
gatherers in America today.

going to do with them? As soon as they get their wages they go spend it all on liquor and then sit in their shacks drinking and playing that dreadful hillbilly music of theirs till the booze is all gone and then they go out in the fields again. What are you going to do with them?"

It is incredible to see how fast futility can be ground into a people and their fine impulses so completely frustrated that they no longer think of looking for a way out. These victims of human erosion have even acquired a grim sense of humor based on despair. Down in Los Angeles they gather in Pershing Square and sing of the hilarious disappointment awaiting their kinfolk who have yet to come west to the Golden State:

> *Hey, Okie, if you see Arkie,*
> *Tell 'im Tex has got a job for 'im*
> *Out in Californie—*
> *Pickin' up gold—*
> *All he needs is a shovel.*

Woody Guthrie, the voice of the migrants, caught the terrible humor of it long ago:

SO LONG, IT'S BEEN GOOD TO KNOW YOU

I've sung this song but I'll sing it again
Of the place that I lived on the wild windy plain
In the month called April, the county called Clay,
Here's what all of the people there say—

REFRAIN: *So long, it's been good to know you*
　　　　So long, it's been good to know you
　　　　So long, it's been good to know you
　　　　This dusty old dust is a-gittin' my home,
　　　　And I've got to be drifting along.

A dust storm it hit and it hit like thunder
It dusted us over, it dusted us under,
It blocked out the traffic, it blocked out the sun
And straight for home all the people did run,
　　　　　　　　　　　　　　singing—

The sweethearts they set in the dark and sparked,
They hugged and kissed in that dusty old dark,
They sighed and cried, and hugged and kissed,
Instead of marriage they talked like this,
　　　　　　　　　　　　"Honey—

The telephone rang and it jumped off the wall,
And that was the preacher a-making his call
He said, "Kind friend, this might be the end,
You got your last chance at salvation from sin—

The churches was jammed, the churches was packed,
That dusty old dust storm blowed so black
That the preacher could not read a word of his text,
So he folded his specks, and he took up collection,
　　　　　　　　　　　　　　said—

While directing the filming of *The Grapes of Wrath* John Ford needed background music for a group scene. He asked the Okies whom he had recruited as character extras to sing something that was known to every Okie, Arkie, and Mizoo. Without hesitation, they began singing "Goin' Down the Road Feelin' Bad."[13]

GOIN' DOWN THE ROAD FEELIN' BAD

I'm goin' down this road feelin' bad;
I'm goin' down this road feelin' bad;
I'm goin' down this road feelin' bad, Lord God,
'Cause I ain't goin' be treated thisaway.

[13] See the section on Woody Guthrie for additional migrant songs.

My kids need three meals a day;
My kids need three meals a day;
My kids need three meals a day, Lord God,
And I ain't goin' be treated thisaway.

I'm goin' where the climate suits my clothes;
I'm goin' where the climate suits my clothes;
I'm goin' where the climate suits my clothes, Lord God,
And I ain't goin' be treated thisaway.

These two-dollar shoes hurt my feet;
These two-dollar shoes hurt my feet;
These two-dollar shoes hurt my feet, Lord God,
And I ain't goin' be treated thisaway.

To quote Lawrence Gellert, in *Me and My Captain,*

The migratory Negro "just a-lookin' for work" suffers most. A "vag." No white folks to intercede for him. He falls as easily as small change into the pocket of the Constable. This dignitary collects no fixed salary, but one computed on the number of arrests made. Then County and State mete out justice, each according to its needs. A sliding scale of "costs" is added to the usual sentence. It is based on the law of supply and demand for convict labor.[14]

TWO HOBOES

Railroad look so pretty,
Box car on the track.
Here come two hoboes,
Grip sack on their back.

REFRAIN: *Oh, babes,*
Oh, no-home babes.

One is my brother,
'Nother my brother-in-law,
Hike all the way from N'Orleans
Back to Arkansas.

Back where you ought to be
Instead of being at home;
Instead of being at home, babes,
You're on the road like me.

[14] Copyright 1936, Lawrence Gellert. Page 2.

Clothes are all torn to pieces,
Shoes are all worn out,
Rolling 'round an unfriendly world,
Always roaming about.

Where you gwine, you hoboes?
Where you gwine to stay?
Chain gang link is waiting—
Can't make your getaway.

6. Songs of the farmers[1]

It's a hard,
It's a hard,
It's a hard on we poor farmers,
It's a hard.

So far as his songs indicate, the land-owning American farmer has been a good deal less "embattled" than the history of articulate discontent in other fields of labor would lead us to expect. He has produced more songs (judging by the number of farmers' songbooks) than any other laborer, and has suffered more from predatory exploitation than any other laborer, but the number of songs of social and economic protest that he has written is negligible.

Perhaps this is because the farmer has rarely thought of himself as a laborer. Certainly he has never identified himself, on a scale large enough to produce any tangible results, with the cause of labor as a whole. If he has been aware of any class distinctions

[1] See also Migrants.

in American society, it has not been apparent that he saw himself as belonging to the same stratum as that of the worker who labored for a regular wage under a visible employer. He has traditionally been the rugged individualist, nurturing the illusion of his independence, and organizing with other farmers only to realize limited objectives. It is true that the farmer was prominent in the struggles which led to the emergence of American democracy in the early part of the nineteenth century, but it must be remembered that agriculture at that time dominated the economy of the United States, and most of the population lived in rural areas. The farmer had not yet begun to think of himself as a farmer—he was still the people.

These two characteristics of the farmer's economic philosophy—his reluctance to identify himself as a member of the working class and to unite in a strong, permanent union with other farmers—are facets of a more fundamental defect: his inability to see his problems in their larger significance, a defect which foredoomed all the nineteenth-century attempts to make himself a political force. There have been persistent attempts of farm leaders of broader vision to ally the farmer with labor as a whole, but such combinations collapsed quickly because of the basic instability of the alliance. The farmers made demands which affected their own temporary welfare only, and thus alienated labor, which felt that any party which took no interest in the welfare of any laboring group forfeited the support of all workers.

The People's Party, founded in 1892 as the culmination of a quarter-century of farmers' protest against their exploitation by the railroads, was such a failure. The deterioration of the parties which preceded it—the Greenback, Greenback-Labor, and the Alliances—impressed upon some of its leaders the necessity of gaining the support of labor to realize its end, but the fundamental weaknesses of the farmer as an organizer could not be overcome. Strong factions of the Southern branch of the party opposed Negro participation; other elements of the party collaborated with the Republicans, and still others declared for fusion with the Democrats.

Labor, whose aid the party solicited, was given no active support in return, except resolutions of "sympathy" for its objectives. In the face of such disunity and confusion of purpose, the collapse of the People's Party was inevitable.[2]

The relation of the farmer and the wage worker has never been one of close association; and, more often than not, it has been one of mutual toleration if not downright antipathy.[3] The latter animosity is reflected in a number of labor songs. Pat Brennan, a Wobbly migratory worker, versified a common discontent among the crop pickers.

THE HARVEST WAR SONG

(Tune: "Tipperary")

We are coming home, John Farmer, we are coming back to stay.
For nigh on fifty years or more, we've gathered up your hay.
We have slept out in your hayfields, we have heard your morning
shouts;
We've heard you wondering where in Hell's them pesky go-abouts.

REFRAIN: *It's a long way, now understand me; it's a long way to town;*
It's a long way across the prairie, and to hell with Farmer
John.
Here goes for better wages, and the hours must come down
For we're out for a winter's stake this summer, and we
want no scabs around.

You've paid the going wages, that's what's kept us on the bum;
You say you've done your duty, you chin-whiskered son-of-a-gun;
We have sent your kids to college, but still you rave and shout,
And call us tramps and hoboes, and pesky go-abouts.

But now the wintry winds are a-shaking our poor frames
And the long-drawn days of hunger try to drive us bo's insane.
It is driving us to action—we are organized today,
Us pesky tramps and hoboes are coming back to stay.

The farmer's traditional aloofness is probably the chief reason for his reluctance to sing about his misfortunes. A Mid-Western

[2] This characteristic disunity was responsible for the impotence of the New York Anti-Rent Association, which denounced an affiliation with agrarianism or the Free Soil movement. Thomas Devyr, the greatest of the Anti-Rent leaders, was repudiated because of his efforts to identify the local problem with those of a larger significance. He later saw his warnings fulfilled when the Anti-Rent party wisped away like a summer cloud.

[3] The textile workers have never forgotten that it was a farmer jury that convicted their leaders in the Aderholt case.

observer, puzzled by the scarcity of songs of discontent in that area during the Depression, concluded:

> The chances are that the depression—in the Corn Belt at least—will run its course without having got itself into song. . . . As for singing, neither religion nor rocky times seem to fetch any music out of him (the farmer).
>
> —Lowry Charles Wimberly, "Hard Times Singing,"
> *American Mercury*, June, 1934, p. 197.

But the independent farmer is not utterly inarticulate about hard times; he has written a few songs of discontent during his long years of tilling a soil that was not always amenable. The better songs in this category turn the lash of his anger against the inanimate land and the people foolish enough to farm it. The various "Arkansas Travelers" are well-known examples. A less familiar variant of this type which dates from the latter part of the nineteenth century carries the protest over to Kansas:

IN KANSAS

They chaw tobacco thin
In Kansas.
They chaw tobacco thin
In Kansas.
They chaw tobacco thin
And they spit it on their chin
And they lap it up agin
In Kansas.

Oh they churn the butter well
In Kansas.
Oh they churn the butter well
In Kansas.
Oh they churn the butter well
And the buttermilk they sell
And they git lean as hell
In Kansas.

Oh potatoes they grow small
In Kansas.
Oh potatoes they grow small
In Kansas.
Oh potatoes they grow small
And they dig 'em in the fall
And they eat 'em hides and all
In Kansas.

Oh they say that drink's a sin
In Kansas.
Oh they say that drink's a sin
In Kansas.
Oh they say that drink's a sin
So they guzzle all they kin
And they throw it up agin
In Kansas.

Come all who want to roam
In Kansas.
Come all who want to roam
In Kansas.
Come all who want to roam
And seek yourself a home
And be happy with your doom
In Kansas.

When the farmer protests against a less immediate enemy, he is likely to exhibit the self-interest which estranges him from the cause of labor as a whole, and weakens his songs.

He has produced a flood of songs on the theme, "the farmer is the man that feeds them all." One of the more successful songs in this vein dates from the post-Civil-War era:

THE FARMER IS THE MAN

When the lawyer hangs around while the butcher cuts a pound,
Oh, the farmer is the man who feeds them all.
If you'll only look and see, I think you will agree
That the farmer is the man who feeds them all.

REFRAIN: *The farmer is the man, the farmer is the man,*
    Lives on credit till the fall;
    Then they take him by the hand, and they lead him
        from the land,
    And the middleman's the one who gets it all.

When the lawyer hangs around while the butcher cuts a pound,
Oh, the farmer is the man who feeds them all,
And the preacher and the cook go a-strolling by the brook,
Oh, the farmer is the man who feeds them all.

REFRAIN: *The farmer is the man, the farmer is the man,*
    Lives on credit till the fall;
    With the int'rest rate so high, it's a wonder he don't die,
    For the mortgage man's the one who gets it all.

Farmers' union songs are usually the least successful of all. Often they are rhetorically saccharine:

> *Work on, O Farmers' Union!*
> *For thy mission is divine*
> *Never vessel plough'd life's ocean*
> *With more royal work than thine.*
>
> *Then let us be right loyal*
> *To our leaders brave and true*
> *Never doubting that their wisdom*
> *Will lead us safely through.*
>
> *Thousands rise to call thee blessed*
> *Will you help them as they sing?*
> *Oh, the grand old Farmers' Union*
> *And the happiness it brings.*
> *—etc.*

Or they are distressingly simple:

> *Work together for each other,*
> *Onward we go*
> *Onward we go, work together*
> *Onward we go, for each other*
> *Onward we go, work together*
> *Onward we go.*

Not many farmers' songs are like this one, sung during the 1939 milk strike in New York:

MISTER FARMER

Mister Farmer, Mister Farmer, come go along with me,
Mister Farmer, Mister Farmer, come go along with me,
Come hitch up with the Milk Trust and we'll keep the system free.

So they followed the Milk Trust stooges, and what did they find?
So they followed the Milk Trust stooges, and what did they find?
Nothing in their pockets and a knife from behind.

Classification, classification, you'll be the death of me;
Classification, classification, you'll be the death of me;
I never can figure what my milk check's gonna be.

Mr. Borden, Mr. Sheffield, you've treated us unfair;
Mr. Borden, Mr. Sheffield, you've treated us unfair;
Now our barns are unpainted and our cupboards are bare.

Well, some began to grumble and some began to moan,
Well, some began to grumble and some began to moan,
Up came the mortgage men and took away their homes.

Come all you dairy farmers and listen to me
Come all you dairy farmers and listen to me
Don't trust the Milk Trust or you'll stay in poverty.

Any survey of farmers' songs must lead to the conclusion that the independent farmer has produced very little of value in the way of songs of protest. However, the farmer who has had the illusion of independence crushed out of him by the loss of his land or who works the farm of another man—the migrant, the sharecropper, the tenant farmer, and the prison worker—is an entirely different type of worker. His songs are full of bitter protest which, ironically enough, shows him to have a better developed sense of social consciousness and economic orientation than his more prosperous and better educated fellow farmer.

Sharecroppers and tenant farmers, as we know them today, came into existence just after the Civil War. The plantation owners, deprived of their slave labor and impoverished by the war, desperately tried to hold on to their land by giving it out on shares or for a specified rental to the poor whites or freed slaves. Some land they were forced by circumstances to sell, and much of this fell into the hands of merchants and speculative landowners who became a new economic class in the South, and who likewise rented out their farms.

The plight of these hired Southern farmers has always been

pitiful. There seems to be no corrective for their circumstances other than large-scale combinative farming, which unfortunately drives many of them into the widening stream of homeless migrants.

The following songs of the penurious Southern farmer, the tenant and the sharecropper, are representative of a large body of similar pieces.

DOWN ON ROBERTS' FARM

Come ladies and gentlemen, listen to my song
I'll sing it to you now but you might think it wrong;
It might make you mad, but I mean no harm;
Just about the renters on Roberts' farm.
It's hard times in the country, out on Roberts' farm.

You move out to Mr. Roberts' farm,
Plant a big crop o' cotton and a little crop o' corn,
He'll come round to plan and to plot,
Till he gets a chattel mortgage on everything you got.
It's hard times in the country, down on Roberts' farm.

Yonder comes Paul Roberts with a flattering mouth;
He moves you to the country in a little log house.
You got no window but the cracks in the wall;
He'll work you all summer and rob you in the fall.
It's hard times in the country, down on Roberts' farm.

I moved down to Mr. Roberts' farm,
I worked on a dairy, I worked on a farm.
I milked old Brindle and she had one horn,
It's hell to be a renter on Roberts' farm.
It's hard times in the country, down on Roberts' farm.

You go to the field and you work all day,
Till way after dark, and you get no pay;
Just a little piece of meat and a little turn of corn,
It's hell to be a renter on Roberts' farm,
It's hard times in the country, down on Roberts' farm.

Roberts' renters, they'll go down town
With their hands in their pockets, and their head hung down.
We'll go in the store, and the merchant will say,
"Your mortgage is due and I'm a lookin' for my pay."
It's hard times in the country, down on Roberts' farm.

I went down to my pocket with a trembling hand,
"I can't pay you all but I'll do what I can."
The merchant jumped to the telephone call:
"I'm going to put you in jail if you don't pay it all."
It's hard times in the country, down on Roberts' farm.

Mr. Paul Roberts with a big Overland!
He's a little tough luck, you don't give a damn.
He'll run you in the mud like a train on the track;
He'll haul you to the mountains but he won't bring you back.
It's hard times in the country, down on Roberts' farm.

> —As sung by Bascom Lunsford, who learned it from
> Claude Reeves of Little River, Transylvania County,
> North Carolina, who wrote the song from personal
> experience. *ca.* 1935

THESE OLD CUMBERLAND MOUNTAIN FARMS

It's hard to be bound down in prison,
But it's worse on these Cumberland Mountain farms;
Ruther be in some old penitentiary,
Or up in old iron Tennessee.

How wearily I've climbed them old mountains
Through the rain and the sleet and the snow;
Tip yo' hat when you meet Mr. Ridges,
Bow yo' head when you meet Mr. Ross.

Young Warner he run a commissary,
Mister, you bet he was a thief;
He sold apples at fifty cents a dozen,
And potatoes at fifty cents apiece.

When the Coffee County boys came to the mountain
They expected to get a lot to eat;
But when they called them in to dinner,
They got salmon, corn dodgers, and meat.

It's seventy miles to Chattanooga,
It's a hundred and twenty to Basell;
It's a thousand miles from here to civilization,
But it's only a few steps from here to hell.

Young people, you've heard all my story,
And I hope you don't think it all wrong;
If you doubt the words I have told you,
See Red Campbell, for he composed this song.

> —From People's Songs Library.

"There Are Mean Things Happening in This Land" was composed by John Handcox, Negro organizer, sharecropper, and songwriter for the Southern Tenant Farmers' Union during its early days. Of his composition Handcox says:

When the planters in East Arkansas saw that the people were joining the union they told them to git off the land. They didn't wait for some of them to git—they threw them off. It was a cold winter. The hungry people had no place to go. When they held union meetings the laws clubbed them till they lay like dead on the ground. It didn't make no difference if they was men or women. They killed some union members and threw some others in jail. This was in the winter, in 1936.

In the spring, at cotton chopping time, it didn't make much difference if we was working or not—our young ones was still hungry. So we began to talk about a strike. Most of us was workin' from sun up to sun down and making less than 70 cents a day. We wanted $1.50 a day for ten hours' work. We made handbills and posters and signs telling what we wanted, and plastered them up all over the place. There was about 4000 altogether who said they would go out on strike.

The planters got scared. The laws arrested every man they could get ahold of and took them back to work at the point of guns. They beat up men and women, and they shot some, and tried to scare us. They ran a lot of folks out. But they couldn't break the strike. We had marches. We all lined up, sometimes more than a hundred of us on a line, and marched through the plantations, cross country. In lots of places where we marched the choppers stopped work and went on strike with us. At one plantation the scabs they had brought from other places dropped their hoes and run like rabbits for cover when they saw us comin'.

As we were marching, we were asking, like somebody asked in the Bible, "What you mean that you crush my people and grind the face of the poor?"

THERE ARE MEAN THINGS HAPPENING IN THIS LAND

On the 18th day of May
The union called a strike,
But the planters and the bosses
Throwed the people out of their shacks.

REFRAIN: *There are mean things happening in this land,*
There are mean things happening in this land,
But the union's going on, and the union's
growing strong,
There are mean things happening in this land.

The planters throwed the people off the land,
Where many years they spent,
And in the hard cold winter,
They had to live in tents.

The planters throwed the people out,
Without a bite to eat;
They cursed them and they kicked them,
And some with axe-handles beat.

The people got tired of working for nothing,
And that from sun to sun;
But the planters forced them out to work
At the point of guns.

—People's Songs Library.

Alan Lomax says "Raggedy Raggedy" had a tremendous emotional effect on the sharecroppers to whom John Handcox, the composer, sang it.

RAGGEDY RAGGEDY

Raggedy raggedy are we (oh Lawdy),
Just as raggedy as raggedy can be;
We don't get nothing for our labor—
So raggedy, raggedy are we.

So hungry, hungry are we,
Just as hungry as hungry can be;
We don't get nothing for our labor—
So hungry, hungry are we.

So homeless, homeless are we,
Just as homeless as homeless can be;
We don't get nothing for our labor,
So homeless, homeless are we.

So landless, landless are we.
Just as landless as landless can be;
We don't get nothing for our labor,
So landless, landless are we.

So cowless, cowless are we,
Just as cowless as cowless can be;
The planters don't 'low us to raise them
So cowless, cowless are we.

So hogless, hogless are we,
Just as hogless as hogless can be;
The planters don't 'low us to raise them,
So hogless, hogless are we.

So cornless, cornless are we,
Just as cornless as cornless can be;
The planters don't 'low us to raise 'em,
So cornless, cornless are we.

So pitiful, pitiful are we,
Just as pitiful as pitiful can be;
We don't get nothing for our labor,
So pitiful, pitiful are we.

—People's Songs Library. Recorded by
Grace Blackstone at Highlander Folk
School, Monteagle, Tennessee.

John Handcox tells the story of "The Man Frank Weems":

On the eighth day of June we had another march. Jim Reese was leadin' it, and Frank Weems, one of the Negro farm hands, was walkin' along next to him. We was singin' union songs when a fellow come up and says the planters was comin'. Frank Weems and Jim Reese said, "Keep marchin' boys, you ain't breakin' no law."

Pretty soon a bunch of planters and riders and town bums ride up to us in their automobiles. We stay in line, lookin' at them, wonderin' what they're a-goin' to do. When they git out of their automobiles we see they all got guns and baseball bats. We don't say anything. "Where you goin'?" one of 'em says. "Down the road," says Jim. Then they begin sluggin' us with those guns and bats. A lot of men run for their lives. A lot of us fall down and can't git up again. Then pretty soon they git back in their automobiles an' ride away.

Jim Reese, he lays there on the road for maybe four hours. Then he looks around and he sees Frank Weems layin' there beside him. He looks bad. "Are you all right, Frank?" he asks. But Frank Weems doesn't answer him. Then Jim gits worried and gits to go for help. When he comes back Frank Weems is gone. No man in Earle ever saw Frank Weems again. We keep askin' "Where is Frank Weems?" We keep askin' is he in the swamp or in Blackfish Lake or rottin' in a ditch somewhere? We keep askin' it. Where is Frank Weems?

In April, 1937, Frank Weems appeared. He went to the Workers' Defense League in Chicago and told his story. When he had regained consciousness he had dragged himself into a ditch and rested. He then spent a week in a hobo jungle and from there made his way to the North.

THE MAN FRANK WEEMS

He was a poor sharecropper
Worked hard every day
To make an honest living
And his multiplied accounts to pay.

REFRAIN: *Now I want somebody to tell me, tell me,*
And tell me right;
Yes I want somebody to tell me
Where is the man Frank Weems.

He was a farmer of Crittenden County,
A county just east of Cross,
Where they call them out with farm bells
And work under a riding boss.

Frank heard about the union,
Then he sought to show its aims.
And when he had well understood,
He sure did sign his name.

I'm sure he told his companions
What a grand thing the union would be;
And if we gave it our brave support,
Some day it would make us free.

It was in nineteen hundred and thirty six
And on the ninth of June,
When the STF union pulled a strike
That troubled the planters on their thrones.

The planters they all became troubled,
Not knowing what 'twas all about;
But they said, "One thing I'm sure we can do,
That's scare the niggers out."

Frank Weems was one among many,
That stood out true and brave;
Although he was taken by cruel hands,
Now he sleeps in an unknown grave.

Sleep on, Frank, if you are sleeping,
Rest in your unknown grave,
Ten thousand union brothers to mourn your loss
And to give your children bread.

—Recorded by Grace Blackstone, at the
Highlander Folk School, Monteagle, Tennessee.

Samson Pittman, a sharecropper bard, tells how he composed the "Cotton Farmer Blues":

This song was composed in 19 and 27 by Samson Pittman at the condition of the farmer being treated and at the shortness of their cotton. I thought it was very necessary to put out a record of these things. I composed them of the necessity of the farmers. It was very popular among everyone that heard it and it became to be a true fact everywhere well known. Well, the town merchants laughed to think of such a song being composed.

COTTON FARMER BLUES

Farmer went to the merchant
Just to get his meat and meal
Farmer went to the merchant
Just to get his meat and meal,
But the merchant told the farmer,
You've got boll weevils in your field.

You've got a good cotton crop
But it's just shooting dice
You've got a good cotton crop
But's just shooting dice
Now you will work the whole year round, buddy,
Yet the cotton won't be no price.

Now you go to the commissary
He'll give you plenty of meal and meat
Now you go to the commissary
He'll give you plenty of meal and meat
(Just anything you want)
Well, he'll give you half a price for your cotton
Not a doggone thing for your feed.
(That's too bad, too bad)

Yes, boys, if I could get 50 cents a day
And if they'd raise me to a dollar,
Yes, boys, if I could get 50 cents a day
And if they'd raise me to a dollar,
Don't you know I'd give that cotton crop away.

(I know these farmers. That's the reason
I'm telling you like I said, boys; now there
ain't but the one thing, boys, that made
me begin to sing.)

When they mistreat me every time
It looks like I got to have another drink
Yes boys, I'm going away to stay,
Because I ain't goin' to let this merchant
Try to screw me this a-way.

—Library of Congress Reference Records.
Archive of American Folk Song.
(For music, see "Little David Blues," p. 163.)

Taken over by other labor groups, this adaptation of the gospel hymn, "Roll the Chariot On," has become one of the most widely used picket line songs, rivaling even "We Shall Not Be Moved" and "Solidarity Forever." It is a good example of the "zipper" song—one which permits instant adaptation to a particular dispute by allowing the name of an employer or antipathetic congressman to be "zipped" in.

ROLL THE UNION ON

REFRAIN: *We're gonna roll, we're gonna roll,*
We're gonna roll the union on;
We're gonna roll, we're gonna roll,
We're gonna roll the union on.

If the planter's in the way,
We're gonna roll it over him,
Gonna roll it over him,
Gonna roll it over him,
Gonna roll the union on.

If the merchant's in the way

If the banker's in the way

If the preacher's in the way

If Futrell's in the way

If Wall Street's in the way, etc.

—People's Songs Library. Taken from a Bulletin of the original Southern Tenants Farmers Union; made up in 1937 by a Negro woman in Little Rock, Arkansas, a student in the New Era Schools.

7. A labor miscellany

Songs of the Automobile Workers, Steel Workers, Seamen, Longshoremen, and Lumber Workers

If they ask you what's my union,
It's the CIO,
It's the CIO.

In labor these days everybody sings, from the teacher* to the domestic worker. In the Southern hills, the aluminum plant strikers sing their ventriloquistic song of ridicule to the plant-locked scabs:

Send me some beans, love, send them by mail,
Send them in care of Powder Mill "jail."

---

* "But remember, a teacher has prestige;
He can feed his kids that old *noblesse oblige.*"

In the city the subway workers pour out their grief to the mayor:

> *It's hard times on the subway lines,*
> *It's hard times, Little Flower.*

Even the baker, the most sequestrated of public servants, gets out on the picket line occasionally and exhorts the public:

> *U don't need a biscuit,*
> *Don't buy Uneeda!*

With so much singing being done, it is impossible to represent adequately in a survey of protest song more than two or three occupations out of the hundreds that are regularly turning out versified plaints; the few that are represented must therefore stand as examples of the groups less prolific. The several labor groups which follow are among the most important which spatial limitations prevent treating in detail, yet there are others which cannot even be mentioned. The International Ladies' Garment Workers' Union, for example, has at least fifty songs of its own in more than a dozen songbooks, yet not one has been included here. All these songs, vigorous in determination to make the worker respected, prove that there is growing in the United States a new folk community that, as Woody Guthrie says, is "bound for glory."

THE AUTOMOBILE WORKERS

The United Automobile Workers CIO has been called in an apt description "the most volcanic union in the country."[1] Its ebullience has been manifested in a number of ways, and one of the most expressive has been its songs, which exceed in number those of any other labor organization during a comparable period of time. The following selections have been chosen almost at random from more than fifty songs of some stability written by union members during the last ten years.

The most popular and most famous song to proceed from the International Union, United Automobile, Aircraft, and Agricultural Implement Workers of America, to give the UAW its full name, is titled simply "UAW-CIO":

[1] John Gunther, *Inside U.S.A.*, New York, 1947, p. 409.

UAW-CIO

I was standing down on Gratiot Street one day
When I thought I overheard a soldier say:
"Every jeep in our camp has that UAW stamp,
And I'm UAW too, I'm proud to say."

REFRAIN: *It's that UAW-CIO*
          Makes the army roll and go,
          Turning out the jeeps and tanks,
          The airplanes every day;
          It's that UAW-CIO
          Makes the army roll and go,
          Puts wheels on the U.S.A.

I was there when the union came to town;
I was there when old Henry Ford went down;
I was standing by Gate Four when I heard the people roar,
"Ain't nobody keeps us union workers down."

I was there on that cold December day
When we heard about Pearl Harbor far away;
I was down at Cadillac Square when the union rallied there
To put those plans for pleasure cars away.

There'll be a union label in Berlin
When the union boys in uniform march in;
And rolling in the ranks there'll be UAW tanks,
To roll Hitler out and roll the union in.

THE BALLAD OF HENRY FORD

Across the board sat Henry Ford
And his face was full of woe;
Oh, he bit his nails and his face grew pale,
But he talked with the CIO.

REFRAIN: *Oh, he talked, yes, he talked,*
Oh, he talked with the CIO;
Though he balked, still he talked,
Oh, he talked with the CIO.

Oh, the flivver king tried everything
To prevent a union crew;
He used labor spies, and those trigger guys,
And a stooge named Bennett,[2] too.

Oh, the pay was low, and you slaved for the dough,
'Cause the speedup was a crime;
And heaven help the man who would go to the can
Upon the bosses' time.

Oh, the union guys tried to organize
And it was an uphill fight;
But they did pull through, and the union grew,
And a strike was called one night.

Oh, you know the rest, Henry tried his best,
Pitting black against the white;
But when the scabs found out what the strike was about,
They walked out and joined the fight.

Old Henry felt he could run his belt
Any damn way he pleased;
And he did it too, till the union grew,
And brought him to his knees.

Then he talked, yes, he talked,
Oh, he talked with the union men.
Though he balked, still he talked,
And by God, he'll do it again.

The most effective songs of any union are its picketline chants, despite their extreme simplicity. Here are two from the UAW disputes; the first, "Go Tell Young Henry," was hardly necessary, for young Henry Ford was responsible for the death of the old

[2] Harry Bennett, head of the Ford company police.

Ford system; the second song carries the vituperation over to General Motors.

GO TELL YOUNG HENRY

(Tune: "Go Tell Aunt Nancy")

Go tell young Henry,
Go tell young Henry,
Go tell young Henry,
The Old Ford system's dead.

KNUTS TO KNUDSEN

Knuts to Knudsen,
Slush to Sloan,
Boo's for Boysen,
The union's our own!

THE STEEL WORKERS

The organization of the steel workers in 1936 depended in part at least on the successful battle waged on the automobile industry by the UAW. Before John L. Lewis built his Steel Workers' Organizing Committee into an organization strong enough to force Steel to recognize the union, the steel workers had never been able to contend with their employers, despite the realization of union men that "we have to organize steel before we organize any plant manufacturing fishhooks."[3] There was a great need for a workers' bargaining agency in the foundries, for the suffering of the steel workers was as bitter as that of the miners. The only difference between the steel town and the mine patch was that the one was urban and the other rural; the deprivations were the same.

After the Homestead strike of 1892, in which steel workers routed with cannon and blazing oil an army of Pinkerton "punks," the steel companies ruthlessly extirpated the union movement. Andrew Carnegie sanctimoniously deplored the action of his manager in inciting bloodshed, but at the same time gave full approval to the company's handling of the strike. The policies of the steel industry were the policies of Andrew Carnegie, and the degrada-

[3] Mary Heaton Vorse, *Labor's New Millions*, New York, 1938, p. 47.

tion of the steel worker for two generations must be taken as a tarnish on the reputation of the most lavish of all philanthropists.

THE BALLAD OF JOHN CATCHINS

Come gather round and I will sing
A song you'll know is true;
About a brother working man,
A man that's union through and through.

John Catchins is a union man,
He joined on charter day;
He did not like a company town,
Where they used clacker* instead of pay.

The furnace where he made his time
Is Thomas mill in Birmingham.
Republic Steel they owned that plant,
And they're the roughest in the land.

In thirty-three the eagle came
He brought the NRA;
John Catchins said, "Our time has come,
We'll organize this very day."

And then they had election day
To vote the union straight;
And when the vote was counted up,
Republic got a measly sight.

Those rich men's hearts are harder still
Than steel made in their mill;
Republic would not be content
To obey the law of the government.

Tom Girdler called his board around
A frame-up for to plan;
"We're goin' to drive that union out,
And we will use what means we can."

They sent for Thomas Carpenter;
The superintendent scratched his head.
They gave him a drink from a silver cup,
And this is what he said:

"The man that's union through and through
John Catchins is his name;
He leads the men on the picket line
And he's the one we've got to frame.

* Clacker: scrip.

*"When we reduce the wages down
Or double up a job or two,
Or when the price of the rent goes up,
He criticizes me and you.*

*"He's taught his family union ways,
His wife and children all;
He tells them they must organize
Because divided they will fall.*

*"So he's the man we've got to frame
No matter what it will entail;
We'll put him surely underneath
The sheriff's hard rock jail.*

*"We'll call in that detective guy,
The one named Milt McDuff;
We'll tell him what we're paying for,
And make him do his dirty stuff."*

*They put John Catchins in the jail;
The lies that they did tell
Would close the roads to heaven up
And send their lousy souls to hell.*

*Come gather round us, brothers all,
Together, let us shout:
"If we must take that jailhouse down,
We're goin' to get John Catchins out.*

*"When brother John is free again,
He'll have a big surprise;
We'll all be in the CIO
Republic Steel will organize."*

—Recorded in Chicago from the singing
of Mr. and Mrs. Joe Gelders.

The CIO had peacefully but dramatically won its fight for company recognition from United States Steel Corporation in March 1937, but Little Steel—Youngstown Sheet and Tube Company, Republic Steel Corporation, and Inland Steel Company—fought bitterly to keep the union out of their plants, and the biggest and worst strike since 1919 was the result. Tom Girdler of Republic was especially determined and bitterly scourged United States Steel for its defection; he insisted on trying to keep the mill in Chicago running, and this precipitated what became known as the Chicago or Memorial Day Massacre. On May 30, 1937, some fifteen hundred strikers with wives and children assembled in a hall near the Republic mill. Aroused by two union organizers, about three hundred of the crowd started for the mill to protest its continued operation, but some two hundred police headed by Captain James L. Mooney charged the strikers, clubbed, retreated, and charged again. Suddenly a pistol shot rang out, and the police first shot into the air and then into the crowd. When the shooting and clubbing subsided, ten demonstrators lay dead or dying and 78 others were treated for injuries in hospitals or jails. Although the police alleged some of the strikers had guns, the officers were forced to admit that they found no lethal weapons on the strikers they arrested, and it is of course significant that the dead were strikers and not police. Afterwards, careful study of motion picture films clearly revealed that the strikers had not provoked the attack. Such wanton brutality aroused the American public's sympathy for the strikers. The union lost this battle but won the final contention four years later when by government intervention Little Steel was forced to recognize the union.

BALLAD OF THE CHICAGO STEEL MASSACRE

On dark Republic's bloody ground
The thirtieth day of May
Oh, brothers, let your voices sound
For them that died that day.

The men who make our country's steel,
The toilers of the mill,
They said, "Our union is our strength,
And justice is our will."

"We will not be Tom Girdler's slaves,
But freemen will we be."
Hear those voices from the new-made graves,
"We died to set you free."

In ordered ranks they all marched down
To picket Girdler's mill;
They did not know that Girdler's cops
Had orders, "Shoot to kill."

As they marched on there so peacefully,
Old Glory waving high,
Girdler's gunmen took their deadly aim,
And the bullets began to fly.

Oh that deep, deep red will never fade
From Republic's bloody ground;
Oh, workers they will not forget
They will sing this song around.

They will not forget Tom Girdler's name,
Nor Girdler's bloody hands;
He will be a sign for tyranny
In all the world's broad lands.

Men and women of the working class,
And you little children too,
Remember that Memorial Day
And the men that died for you.

—Copyright 1939 by Earl Robinson.

SEAMEN

Workers who engage in characteristically hard occupations by choice rather than by necessity cannot be expected to do much protesting against either the occupation or the way in which it is administered. For this reason as much as any other, the protest songs emanating from the sailors are fewer than one might expect from such a large body of song that this ancient profession has produced. The hauling and capstan shanties that comprise the greater part of the sailormen's songs had some complaint against labor administration and social conditions in them, but not impressively much. Despite the medieval labor relations and brutal work that existed in the marine until the middle of the nineteenth century, the only protest is something like "Leave Her, Johnny."

I thought I heard the old man say,
Leave her, Johnny, leave her!
You can go ashore and draw your pay.
It's time for us to leave her.

The winds were foul, the work was hard,
From Liverpool docks to the Brooklyn yard.

She shipped it green and made us curse,
The mate is a devil and the old man worse.

The winds were foul, the ship was slow,
The grub was bad, the wages low.

We'll sing, oh, may we never be
On a hungry bitch the like of she.

The foc's'le songs were likely to be the land songs that had undergone but a slight sea-change; a little protest in ballads like "Andrew Rose," but still nothing of any overt, sharp protest.

When, after the middle of the century, steam replaced sail, the shanties died and the sailors' folksong lost its distinctiveness. Modern songs sung by sailormen are hardly different from land songs, and their songs of protest are scarcely distinguishable from those of shore-bound industrial workers, except that the best ones are unprintable. The sailor's life is still a hard life, and his songs reflect that toughness; what we can offer as typical of his protest is therefore pitifully emasculated.

DON'T TURN AROUND

Don't let anybody turn you around,
Turn you around, turn you around;
Don't let anybody turn you around,
Keep on the union way.

I went down to the union hall,
The meeting it was begun;
A stooge got up to lead us astray,
But he didn't get nary a one.

The AFL goes by water,
The CIO by land;
But when we get to where we're going,
We'll shake each other by the hand.

The NMU has traveled long,
For sailors like to roam;
But now we're going to City Hall,
We want to bring our sailors home.

A folk memory—little more than that—is recalled by a few union songs sung to the tunes of almost forgotten shanties. "What Shall We Do with the Drunken Sailor" provides the melodic vehicle for this strike song, "What Shall We Do for the Striking Seamen?"

What shall we do for the striking seamen?   (3)
Help them win their battle.

REFRAIN: *Oho! and all together,*
Oho! and all together,
Oho! and all together,
Help them win their battle.

Turn in food for the striking seamen. . . .   *(3)*

Share our homes with the striking seamen. . . .   *(3)*

Send a wire to President Truman. . . .   *(3)*

March on the line for the striking seamen. . . .   *(3)*

SAILING THE UNION WAY

Sailing, sailing,
Sailing the union way;
We're making the trip in a union ship
And we'll get union pay.

Sailing, sailing,
What do the seamen say?
Thirty per cent for food and rent
Or no ship sails today.

Sailing, sailing,
What do the firemen shout?
Thirty per cent for food and rent,
Or not a ship goes out.

Sailing, sailing,
Telling the company
We're dropping the hook in a cozy nook
As long as it may be.

Sailing, sailing,
Nothing is ailing here.
We're sad as can be for the company
We're crying in our beer.

Sailing, sailing,
What does a union prove?
Thirty per cent for food and rent
Or not a ship will move

One indication of how closely allied land industries have become with the maritime trades is to be found in the songs of the longshoremen. Instead of turning to the seamen for inspiration, the longshoreman sets his songs of protest to cowboy melodies; the following three songs, typical of what has been emanating from the longshoremen, are in order sung to the tunes of "Roving Gambler," "Home on the Range," and "The Streets of Laredo." The first song, "Longshoreman's Strike," shows that the trend is not recent.

LONGSHOREMAN'S STRIKE

I am a decent laboring man who works along the shore
To keep the hungry wolf away from the poor longshoreman's door;
I work all day in the broiling sun on ships that come from sea,
From broad daylight till late at night for the poor man's family.

REFRAIN: *Give us good pay for every day,*
    That's all we ask of you;
    Our cause is right, we're out on strike,
    For the poor man's family.

The rich man's gilded carriages with horses swift and strong;
If a poor man asks for a bite to eat they'll tell him he is wrong.
Go take your shovel in your hand and come and work for me,
But die or live, they've nothing to give to the poor man's family.

They bring over their 'talians, and Naygurs from the South,
Thinking they can do the work, take beans from out our mouth,
The poor man's children they must starve, but we will not agree,
To be put down like a worm in the ground and starve our families.

    —From broadside in Harris Collection, Brown University.

FRISCO STRIKE SAGA

'Twas the month of July,
In the hot sun we did fry,
On the docks of old Frisco Bay.
We were rolling our trucks
For a few lousy bucks,
And the bosses held out half our pay.

REFRAIN: *Oh, hold that picket line,*
    We're fighting for our jobs and more pay;
    For the longshoremen's right,
    To picket and fight,
    And to organize in our own way.

Then we went to Fink Hall
For the strawbosses' call,
And he gave us the six months' run around;
And we begged for a job
From a pot-bellied slob
Who'd run us clear down to the ground.

But the longshoreman swore
He would stand it no more,
And he called to his fellow workingmen;
And the boys all heard him say
Under Section 7 A
The bosses are gypping us again!

Then there came on the scene
With his liver full of spleen
Joe Ryan, big shot of ILA.[4]
And in language so polite,
Warned us, "Boys, now don't you fight,
Just take your troubles to the NRA."

But those stevedores yelled "Boo!
With scab herders we are through;
We'll see who's running this here ILA.
Now we're out to win this strike,
And your tactics we don't like,
The rank and file have learned a better way."

THE BALLAD OF BLOODY THURSDAY

As I was a-walking one day down in Frisco,
As I was a-walking in Frisco one day;
I spied a longshoreman all dressed in white linen
Dressed in white linen and cold as the clay.

"I see by your outfit that you are a worker,"
These words he did say as I slowly passed by;
"Sit down beside me and hear my sad story,
For I'm shot in the breast and I know I must die.

"It was down on the Front where I worked on the cargoes,
Worked on the cargoes ten hours a day;
I lost my right fingers because of the speedup,
The speedup that killed many a man in my day.

"With too much of a sling load on old rusty cable
The boss saved ten dollars, ten dollars, I say;
That old rusty sling broke and fell on my buddy;
Ten lousy bucks carried Jimmie away.

"Those were the days when the Boss owned the union,
We poor working stiffs—we had nothing to say;
Ours was to work and to keep our big traps shut;
We stood in the shape-up for a dollar a day.

"But our children were hungry, their clothing was tattered;
It's then that we workers began to get wise;
We tore up our fink books and listened to Bridges,
Saying, 'Look at your kids, brother, let's organize.'

[4] ILA: International Longshoremen's Association. Ryan has been doubtfully commemorated in several other songs and ballads.

"Strong and united we went to the bosses
For better conditions and a decent day's pay;
The bosses just laughed—we all had a meeting,
That's why we're hitting the bricks here today.

"Our struggles were many, our struggles were bloody,
We fought the shipowners with all that we had;
With thousands of dollars they tempted our leaders
But our guys were honest—they couldn't be had.

"It was there on the line that I marched with my brothers,
It was there on the line as we proudly passed by;
The cops and the soldiers they brought up their rifles,
I'm shot in the breast and I know I must die.

"Four hundred strikers were brutally wounded;
Four hundred workers and I left there to die;
Remember the day, sir, to all of your children,
This bloody Thursday—the fifth of July.

"Don't beat the drums slowly, don't play the pipes lowly;
Don't play the dead march as they carry me along;
There's wrongs that need righting, so keep right on fighting
And lift your proud voices in proud union songs."

Fight on together, you organized workers,
Fight on together, there's nothing to fear;
Remember the martyrs of this bloody Thursday,
Let nothing divide you, and victory is near.

—From People's Songs Library.

THE LUMBER WORKERS

Unlike the seamen, the lumber workers have managed
in spite of technological changes to preserve the savor of the old
songs. Except for an occasional verse like, "Go strike your blow
for the CIO and Local 29," the modern lumberman's song might
be a contemporary of "The Little Brown Bulls" or "The Jam at
Gerry's Rocks."

OLD SAWBUCKS

Old Sawbucks was a logger in the mighty days of old;
His word was law to all the jacks and when he yelled they jumped.
The logs went down the skidway at an awful pace, I'm told,
The jacks were straining every nerve, from morn to night they
humped.

Full sixteen hours he drove them, for he said, "It's plain to see
If they have any idle time they may begin to think;
And the harder the jacks labor, the better off I'll be."
He kept the men in terror; his roar would scare them pink.

All night the jacks were busy, for the bedbugs and the lice
Kept every worker scratching all the time he was in bed.
The smells disturbed his slumber and a few stray rats and mice;
The only hope Jack had for rest was after he was dead.

He fed his men on liver and a little Irish stew;
The pancakes were like rubber and the biscuits were like lead;
Said he, "That chuck is good enough for any logging crew;
And some sawdust in the sausage will make filling for the head."

The midnight dining chamber was a vast and grand affair.
The men ate in the forest and the chuck froze on their plate.
The jacks were used to all of this and they didn't seem to care;
But the union came along and there's been a change of late.

Bedding now is decent and the jacks can get some rest;
Chuck has been improved a lot, it's really fit to eat.
We're going to keep fighting till we finally get the best,
Of fruits and eggs and butter and the choicest cuts of meat.

Sometimes you meet a goofy guy who fails to do his part
In the ever present struggle for an ever rising wage;
It seems the ignorant fellow simply doesn't have the heart
To aid his fellow workers in the battle of the age.

A few stray stools were with us but we quickly got their number
We high-tailed all those out of camps; we're rid of them of late.
We found when we examined them their heads were made of leather
It's due to the sawdust sausage the stupid devils ate.

So let's battle on, my brothers, each one helping out his neighbor;
Let's rid the earth of parasites and all their mangy crew.
Remember that the future of the world belongs to labor,
The battle is a hard one and the fighters are too few.

—From the North Star Lumber Camp, Minnesota.

THE BUZZARDAREE

There's a buzzardaree on the North Shore
With a beak like a philagazoo;
With small piggish eyes and a grin of disguise
When he hires a man for his crew.

REFRAIN: This ornery skunk with a head like a monk
And a beak like a philagazoo.

Now jacks, take a tip, if you want to get gypped
Just work for this Gillagaboo;
When it comes to the payoff he always is short
And will try his bluffing on you.

Then when you show him the time you have kept
The wind blows through his bazoo;
Not all of you know him but some of you do,
For he's tried the same trick on you.

Now while in the land of the cedar and spruce
Above other things I crave
To bury him under a whatchamacall
And place a thingumabob on his grave.

—By "Pine Cone." In People's Songs Library.

THE BALLAD OF VOIGHT'S CAMP

From Highway 65 it's quite a tramp
To Little Fork River to Ed Voight's camp,
Where we're giving a lot of thought
To how to improve the gyppo's lot.
In his bunk our steward seems nice and cozy,
But when he gets home things ain't so rosy;
The grocery bill goes up so high
When the steward gets home it hits the sky;
Though the kids are sick, their shoes worn out,
You never see those youngsters pout.
They know their dad has not been shirking,
For believe you, men, he's sure been working.

In these woods it's work, not glory.
Every day, the same old story;
The cedar looks good, but lo! it's rotten,
A post from the top is all I've gotten.
We're sending our steward to the union meeting,
And hope he'll remember to send our greeting.
We hope that he won't be a flop;
We want better pay when we cut the crop.
We know that our union would have more power
If we'd all cut timber by the hour.
Let's give the timber barons a taste
Of paying for their own rotten waste.

We say up here at Little Fork
We're through delivering charity work.
They used to have horses to do all the dragging,
But now they use men, and I'm not bragging,
Some of those logs, I'll bet my socks,
Would be too heavy for Paul Bunyan's ox.
Says a pretty tired fellow with a sickly smile,
"Do you think the union is really worth while?"
Well, look at those truckers who carry no book,
As you watch them each morning more peaked they look.
We know it's wrong and bad union manners
To load such pulp by pancake jammers;
We don't want the gyppos to take such a beating,
That's why the union called this meeting.

Said the boss to the steward, "All these new regulations
Sure raise the expense in the operations;
This crew believes in long vacations,
Every week end they go see their relations.
A forty-hour week, one man in each bunk,
If this timber won't move soon, I'll be sunk.
We're bucking the weather, no frost in the bog,
This doggone season's the last I'll log."
Says the steward to the boss, "Get busy, get wise
It's time for you jobbers to organize."

8. The song-makers

If anybody asks you who composed this song,
If anybody asks you who composed this song,
Tell him 'twas I, and I sing it all day long.

Ella May Wiggins, Aunt Molly Jackson,
Woody Guthrie, and Joe Glazer

"In the ballad," wrote one of the most distinguished American literary authorities, ". . . the author is of no account. He is not even present. We do not feel sure that he ever existed."[1] When the comparatively few ballads that have come down to us are put over against the seven centuries and more of English folksong-making, it is not surprising that such a statement could be made. Of the 305 ballads in Francis Child's monumental collection, only one was the work of a known composer. But all of

[1] Kittredge, *op. cit.*, p. xi.

Child's ballads, and all of the hundreds that he did not consider, English and American, had composers who lived, and worked, and put into song the stories their community wanted to hear. As the articulate members of the folk who in the aggregate have been credited with the authorship of genuine folksong, these anonymous people are of the greatest interest to anyone who wishes to understand the origin of balladry; but it remains the tragic fact that they are more ephemeral than the scraps of song they put together in a moment of leisure taken from work that at the time seemed more important. Their songs may live for generations, even centuries, but they themselves have seldom had even a tombstone to prove that they walked the earth.

If we live in an age of declining balladry, we are compensated by our opportunity to know the people who compose folksong. The following section is an introduction to a small but representative group of these unsung ballad makers: a textile worker, a miner's wife, a migrant, and a union song writer. The first three are unquestionably members of the folk; the fourth is a member of that peripheral class whose songs, written with conscious artistry, have again and again been taken by the folk as their own. These are the people who have made our folksongs.

Ella May Wiggins

There was nothing in Ella May Wiggins' appearance to distinguish her from the other women among the five hundred textile workers at the union "speakin'" as she exhorted them to join the union, just three weeks before she was to die with a bullet in her breast. Small, brown-haired, good-featured, not yet thirty, in another age and another environment she would have been an attractive young woman just beginning life, but in Gastonia, North Carolina, in August 1929, she was an economic slave, prematurely aged, her face pinched and wrinkled by the lifetime of undernourishment, degrading labor, and childbearing behind her.

Those who remembered Ella May when she was a girl said she had been pretty, doll-like; but beauty is an ephemeral thing at the level of poverty.

"I never made no more than nine dollars a week," she told the assembled mill hands, "and you can't do for a family on such money. I'm the mother of nine. Four died with the whooping cough. I was working nights, and I asked the super to put me on days, so's I could tend 'em when they had their bad spells. But he wouldn't. He's the sorriest man alive, I reckon. So I had to quit, and then there wasn't no money for medicine, and they just died. I couldn't do for my children any more than you women on the money we got. That's why I came out for the union, and why we all got to stand for the union, so's we can do better for our children, and they won't have lives like we got."[1]

Like the other textile workers in the Southern mills, Ella May came from the American peasantry. When she was ten years old, the Mays' farm in the back-country Great Smokies ceased to produce even poverty's staple—"taters"—and they moved down to the logging camps around Andres, North Carolina. While her father moved about, working in the neighboring lumber camps, Ella May and her mother took in washing for the bachelor loggers, scrubbing the grimy clothes in wooden tubs outside their flat-car shanty.

Not only physical nutriment but mental nutriment was also hard to come by in such an environment. Schools had little to offer; terms often lasted only six months a year, teachers were few and inferior, classes were unmanageably large, and the ignorance imbedded by centuries of deprivation exuded an atmosphere hostile to learning; but Ella learned to read and write before marrying John Wiggins at the age of sixteen. Her first child was born a year later; before the birth of her second baby a heavy log fell on her husband, crippling him for life, and Ella inherited the responsibility of providing for the family.

The Wigginses moved over to cotton mill country, where Ella worked sixty hours a week for ten years as a spinner—thirty thousand hours of debilitating labor, with nothing to show at the

[1] Quoted in Margaret Larkin, "Ella May," *New Masses*, vol. 5, no. 6 (November 1929).

end but nine children. Sedentary life in the rural South offers few diversions of a wholesome nature, and John Wiggins quickly became a drunkard. When he finally deserted his family, Ella reclaimed her maiden name and moved her emaciated brood to Bessemer City, taking a spinner's job in the American Mills. Shortly after her arrival the National Textile Workers' Union organized the mill workers, and she joined with enthusiasm, becoming a committee worker. Her greatest value to the union, however, was her ability to " 'pose" and sing "song ballets." As a child she had gained a local reputation as a singer because of her clear voice and innate sense of rhythm; these talents she joined to the rich tradition of mountain song composition that she had inherited, and made up songs about the workers' plight, their hopes, and their determination to remedy intolerable conditions.

But if she had made herself famous among the mill workers, she had made herself infamous among the operators, and she was early marked for reprisal. Her death came at the height of the appalling anarchy which attended the National Textile Workers' Union strike at Gastonia.[2] The Gastonia *Gazette* had set afire the destructive prejudices of the Southern fundamentalist farmers, prejudices that needed but little additional ignition where Communists, atheists, labor organizers, and discontented workers combined to disrupt their complacent feudalism, and by the beginning of September all semblance of law and order had vanished. On September 9, immediately after the mistrial in the Aderholt case had temporarily saved the sixteen men accused of his murder, a mob composed of from three to five hundred men surged through the strike area assaulting union members, destroying union property, and gathering incentive for more effective measures for extirpating the union. Led by a motorcycle policeman, a horn-blowing cavalcade of one hundred automobiles roared to the Loray mill and raided the union headquarters to the battle cry "We're all 100% Americans and anybody that don't like it can go back to Russia. . . . Long live 100% Americanism!"[3] Similar raids and demonstrations were carried on at nearby Bessemer City and Charlotte.

[2] See above, pp. 133-39.
[3] Nell Battle Lewis, "Anarchy vs. Communism in Gastonia," *The Nation*, vol. 129 (September 25, 1929), p. 321.

Conditions worsened during the next few days, and it was an open secret that the infamous Committee of One Hundred—the "Black Hundred"—allegedly sponsored by the owners of the Loray mill, would prevent the mass meeting scheduled for September 14 at Gastonia.

But the strikers were not to be deterred by threats. On the afternoon of September 14 a truckload of union members left Bessemer City bound for the "speakin'" grounds at South Gastonia. Shortly after leaving Bessemer the truck was halted by a mob which had stationed itself on the highways to intercept union delegates. The truck was wrecked, and as the helpless and unarmed occupants spilled out on to the highway, several shots were fired by the mob, one of which lodged in the breast of Ella May Wiggins, killing her almost instantly. Her fellow workers were convinced that she had been deliberately singled out for death because of her song-making.

During the perfunctory hearing (at which the same grand jury that earlier had indicted sixteen men and women for first-degree murder in the death of Chief Aderholt released without an indictment men widely known as members of the mob that had killed Ella May) L. C. Carter, one of Ella May Wiggins' companions, testified:

"A lot of them in the truck began jumping out and them that called themselves the law yelled, 'Halt them damn Russian Reds,' and they began shooting at them."

"Did you run?" the solicitor asked.

"No. I don't come from a sellin-out country."

"Folks where you come from don't run?"

"No, they hain't apt to."[4]

See the story of the Gastonia strike, above, p. 133. "Vera" is Vera Buch, who gave up English teaching to organize the textile workers. One of the sixteen originally held for the killing of police chief O. F. Aderholt, she was released after the mistrial which ended the first phase of the case. Manville Jenckes was the owner of the Loray mill, and allegedly was the instigator of Ella May Wiggins' murder.

4 New York *World*, September 25, 1929.

CHIEF ADERHOLT

Come all of you good people, and listen while I tell;
The story of Chief Aderholt, the man you all knew well.
It was on one Friday evening, the seventh day of June,
He went down to the union ground and met his fatal doom.

They locked up our leaders, they put them into jail,
They shoved them into prison, refused to give them bail.
The workers joined together, and this was their reply,
"We'll never, no, we'll never, let our leaders die."

They moved the trial to Charlotte, got lawyers from every town;
I'm sure we'll hear them speak again upon the union ground.
While Vera, she's in prison, Manville Jenckes is in pain.
Come join the Textile Union, and show them you are game.

We're going to have a union all over the South,
Where we can wear good clothes, and live in a better house;
No we must stand together, and to the boss reply,
"We'll never, no, we'll never, let our leaders die."

—People's Songs Library.

It is difficult for residents of more civilized areas to understand the terror inspired by "the Law" in people among whom it is administered by deputized thugs. "The Law" becomes an amorphous, omnipresent, pervasive oppression against which there is no defense. Imagine then the jubilation that the workers feel for the champion who will contend with this monster in their behalf!

Such a champion was the International Labor Defense, which sent down the most competent lawyers available to defend the union leaders accused of the Aderholt murder. Many non-union members joined the ILD in an expression of unbounded admiration for its working in fighting for the underdog.

ILD SONG

Toiling on life's pilgrim pathway,
Wheresoever you may be.
It will help you, fellow workers,
If you will join the ILD.

REFRAIN: *Come and join the ILD*
Come and join the ILD
It will help to win the victory,
If you will join the ILD.

When the bosses cut your wages,
And you toil and labor free,
Come and join the textile union,
Also join the ILD.

Now our leaders are in prison,
But I hope they'll soon be free.
Come and join the textile union,
Also join the ILD.

Now the South is hedged in darkness,
Though they begin to see.
Come and join the textile union,
Also join the ILD.

—Library of Congress, Archive of American Folksong.

Cutting away all the irrelevancies of the story in the manner of the true folk composer, Ella May states the basis of the conflict which cost her her life. Fred Beal, the somewhat ineffectual union leader, was the "red-headed bastard" the mob tried to lynch several days before Ella May was murdered.

THE BIG FAT BOSS AND THE WORKERS

(Tune: "Polly Wolly Doodle")

The boss man wants our labor, and money to packaway,
The workers wants a union and the eight hour day.

The boss man hates the workers, the workers hates the boss,
The bossman rides in a big fine car, and the workers has to walk.

The boss man sleeps in a big fine bed, and dreams of his silver and
gold,
The workers sleeps in an old straw bed and shivers from the cold.

Fred Beal he is in prison, a-sleeping on the floor,
But he will soon be free again, and speak to us some more.

The union is growing, the ILD is strong,
We're going to show the bosses that we have starved too long.

—People's Songs Library.

ALL AROUND THE JAILHOUSE

All around the jailhouse
Waiting for a trial;
One mile from the union
*   hall*
Sleeping in the jail.
I walked up to the policeman
To show him I had no fear;
He said, "If you've got money
I'll see that you don't stay here."

"I haven't got a nickel,
Not a penny can I show."
"Lock her up in the cell," he
*   said,*
As he slammed the jailhouse door.
He let me out in July,
The month I dearly love;
The wide open spaces all around
*   me,*
The moon and stars above.

Everybody seems to want me,
Everybody but the scabs.
I'm on my way from the jail-
*   house,*
I'm going back to the union hall.
Though my tent now is empty
My heart is full of joy;
I'm a mile away from the union
*   hall,*
Just a-waiting for a strike.

Two hundred of her fellow workers slodged through the mud behind Ella May's coffin the gray, rainy morning she was buried. All along the route other workers and sympathizers stood to honor her as she passed. As her body was let down into a ten-dollar grave one of her friends sang "The Mill Mother's Lament," her most beautiul song.

THE MILL MOTHER'S LAMENT

We leave our homes in the morning,
We kiss our children good bye
While we slave for the bosses
Our children scream and cry.

And when we draw our money
Our grocery bills to pay,
Not a cent to spend for clothing,
Not a cent to lay away.

And on that very evening,
Our little son will say:
"I need some shoes, Mother,
And so does sister May."

How it grieves the heart of a mother,
You everyone must know,
But we can't buy for our children
Our wages are too low.

It is for our little children,
That seem to us so dear,
But for us nor them, dear workers,
The bosses do not care.

But understand, all workers,
Our union they do fear;
Let's stand together, workers,
And have a union here.

—People's Songs Library.

Aunt Molly Jackson

"Since I was a little girl I have composed songs and sung them to pass my sorrows away. Some people think my stories are too sad to be true and other folks say they are not interested in the songs I write because they are so sorrowful they cannot be true. But I have never written one word that has not been the truth, and I believe I have had more troubles than any other poor woman who has ever been born."

Aunt Molly, as she says, has had a hard cross to bear: her mother died of tuberculosis; her father was blinded in a coal mine; her brother was killed in a coal mine; her husband was killed in a coal mine; her son was killed in a coal mine; her sister's child starved to death; another brother was blinded; and she herself was crippled in a bus accident. But there were many other women who mourned fathers, husbands, sons, and brothers among the seventy thousand men killed in the coal mines during Aunt Molly's adulthood in Kentucky, and many other women saw children starve to death. Aunt Molly is exceptional only because she was articulate, and she was articulate because the seeds of social consciousness disseminated by her father found fertile ground in her physical strength and fierce pugnacity—characteristics strong in her today. She is seventy-three now (she has looked that old for ten years), stone gray, and crippled, but a certain "smart alax" of a folklorist still has cause to fear her sharp eyes and powerful worker's hands for "messing up" her songs in transcription.

Aunt Molly's combativeness and strength came from a long line of hardy pioneer stock. Her mother's people—the Robinsons—and her father's family—the Garlands—had been in Clay County for seven generations. Aunt Molly speaks with pride of the resourcefulness of her Scottish and Irish ancestors:

> They cut down trees and built their own log cabins; they cleared their own land; they built their own fences and split their own rails; they built their own church houses and their own schools out of logs; they raised their own corn that fattened their own hogs; they caught possums and coons with their own dogs; they owned the stuff that they all worked and raised—I still say them were the good old days.
>
> I can still remember the old armchair I used to set in and watch my grandmother card and spin. I can remember when we had sheep by the hundreds; sheep by the hundreds on my grandmother's farm, sheep that gave blankets that kept us all warm; they knit socks and stockings to put on our feet; in fact they raised all we wore and all we eat, till the coal operators began to swindle and cheat.[5]

She is proud too of the miscegenation of her intrepid great-grandfather, who stole her great-grandmother, a full-blooded Indian, from a Cherokee chief and brought her from Oklahoma to Clay County, where he married her. In her ballad about Frank Little, a martyred IWW organizer, Aunt Molly says,

> *Frank Little was an Indian*
> *A brave Cherokee;*
> *He had the same fighting blood in him*
> *That I have in me.*

[5] Something of the ease with which Aunt Molly composes her songs can be seen in her conversations and correspondence, which lapse almost effortlessly into ballad metre if they are sustained beyond a few sentences.

Like most mountain folk in the last century, her parents married young. At the time of her marriage to seventeen-year-old Oliver Perry Garland, Deborah Robinson was fifteen, but they had already attained a maturity that most urban people never reach. At sixteen Oliver Garland built a log cabin in anticipation of his marriage, while working his own farm, and at nineteen he was ordained a Baptist minister, a profession he was to exercise Saturdays and Sundays for forty-four years until death at sixty-three. In 1880, when she was sixteen, Deborah bore Mary Magdalene Garland, who was to become the famous Aunt Molly Jackson.

When she was three years old her father sold his farm and moved to adjoining Laurel County, where he opened a general store, selling groceries, dry goods, and meat on credit to the miners until he "went broke" two years later. Like other unfortunates before him, his failure at individual enterprise forced him down into the mines, and for the rest of his active life he mined coal six days a week, preached one sermon on Saturdays and two on Sundays, and at night organized the miners. "My dad was a strong union man and a good minister," Aunt Molly says, "so he taught me to be a strong union woman." From the age of five she accompanied her father to union meetings, led picket lines, carried messages, and helped "teach uniting" to the miners. "Just before he died my father asked me to carry on after he was gone, so if I live to be one hundred I will teach unity all of my days—one for all and all for one."

At the age of four, Aunt Molly composed her first song, inspired by her mother's reading of the Bible.

> *My friends and relations, listen if you will;*
> *The Bible plainly tells us we shall not kill.*
>
> *If you love your neighbor, he will love you;*
> *Do unto others what you want them to do to you.*
>
> *If I love you, and you love me,*
> *Oh, how happy we all would be!*
>
> *But if I hit you and you will fall,*
> *Then you won't answer me when I call,*

Because you will be so mad at me
You will not want to play under my walnut tree.

So I want to be good to you so you will be good to me,
Then we can all be happy—don't you see?

This walnut tree I was singing about was a big white walnut tree that was in our front yard. I still remember what my mother done for me for my reward. She made me a doll house out of a big dry goods box and then she took corn stalks and made me two doll beds. She made two oat straw pillows to put under my dolls' heads; then she made me two bed ticks and filled them up with soft silk weeds. She said she had done this for my good deed—for composing a song that was good advice to others—and she often sung my song to other mothers.

Her mother died when Aunt Molly was six, leaving four children. As Deborah had predicted just before her death, Oliver married again within a year—eleven months, to be precise—to a woman who was to bear him eleven more children. As Aunt Molly remarks in one of her songs,

> *These Lost Creek miners*
> *Claim they love their wives so dear*
> *That they can't keep from giving them*
> *A baby or two every year.*

My stepmother's first baby was born before she and my daddy had been married a year, and then eleven months later her second baby came along. Now I had two babies to nurse and I had to chop wood and carry water from Farmer Nelson's well. My own dear mother's brother told me that I would grow up to be a fool if my stepmother kept me home to work all the time and would not let me go to school. But I went to school for three months after my mother died and I learned to read and write.

What her uncle said made a frightening impression on her, and she vowed that she would not "grow up to be a fool," and so she studied her books while rocking the babies to sleep.

Aunt Molly's first jail sentence came at the age of ten.

I was visiting my Granddad Garland who lived on a farm in Clay County. I played a Christmas joke on a family of children by the name of Lewis without meaning any harm, but I was framed up by

some meddlesome spies, and they had me indicted for a disguise. My
Granddad took me away, and three weeks later when I came back to
Clay County the deputy sheriff arrested me. Then I wrote a song
which tells the true story:

MR. CUNDIFF, WON'T YOU TURN ME LOOSE?

The day before Christmas I had some fun;
I went up to Bill Lewis's and made the children run.

REFRAIN: *Mister Cundiff, won't you turn me loose?*

The next Monday morning old Bill Lewis took out a writ;
When I found it out, the wind I sure did split.

It was just three weeks till I came back to Clay,
Old Alphus Cotton arrested me the very next day.

Then I thought my case would be light,
For Cotton took me before Judge Wright.

Judge Wright told me I had done wrong
For blacking my face and putting breeches on.

He listened to me till I told my tale,
Then he gave me ten days in Mister Cundiff's jail.

When they put me in jail they thought I was a fool;
They didn't even give me as much as a stool.

But the jailer's wife, she treated me kind
Because she thought I had no mind.

Now, what she thought I did not care;
I knew I was as smart as her.

I meant no harm, the only thing I done
Was to black my face and take grand-dad's big old rifle gun.

And play like I was a little black boy
I was just having a little fun.

But Judge Wright told me I had done wrong
For blacking my face and putting breeches on.

The jailer told me I had turned pale
When the judge told him to put me in jail.

But there's no use to cry and snub
While I am eating old Mister Cundiff's grub.

Though very much better I would do
If old Cundiff would furnish me some 'backer to chew.

But I am healthy, young, and stout,
And if I can't get any 'backer I can do without.

Mister Cundiff, if you will open up your jailhouse door,
I will not put my grand-dad's breeches on no more.

Now your old hymn book lies on your shelf;
If you want any more song, sing it yourself.

All the folks in Clay County thought the judge had treated me all wrong, so when they came in town they would come over to the jail and hear me sing my song. Some would give me money and some of them would give me big plugs of Cup Greenville[6] 'backer (in them days everybody's children chewed " 'backer," as they called it). So I stayed in jail ten days till my kinfolks paid my $25 fine, but I come out with $38 in money and 27 plugs of Cup Greenville.

Aunt Molly was to have many more experiences with a Law that sent ten-year-old children to jail.

At fourteen she married Jim Stewart, a young coal miner. Before she was seventeen she had borne him two sons, and had completed a course of training as a registered nurse and midwife. At eighteen she began a practice in a Clay County hospital that was to last ten years, following which she set up her own "head-quarters" in Harlan County, out of which she worked until she had her crippling accident in 1932. In thirty-four years as a nurse and midwife she delivered 884 babies—babies who were to grow up to live on "lentil beans and corn bread, and live in log cabins full of cracks so big you could throw big cats and dogs through."

Jim Stewart's susceptible constitution began to fail under the hard life in the mines, and in 1912 he and Aunt Molly went to Florida in an effort to recover his health. During the winter they

[6] "We called it Cup Greenville because there was a tincup-like on every plug."

spent in Pomona Aunt Molly had her first contact with racial discrimination.

I found out how the colored race is treated in the deep South. Three or four days after I was in Pomona I went to the post office. I saw an old colored man coming on the same side of the street and when he saw me he crossed over to the other side. I said, "How do you do," and he said, "What are you trying to do to me, have me lynched?" and he acted like he was afraid of me, so I asked a rich white lady if the colored folks in Florida thought they was too good to speak to poor white folks, and she told me a colored man could be lynched for speaking to a white woman.

One morning I went to a big wholesale company store and a little Negro boy came in to sweep the floor and his white boss began to curse him for a black son of a B. Then he kicked the boy in the back and knocked him down on his face and broke his nose, and the blood poured out of that child's nose and the boss kept kicking him, and I called him a low-down dog. I told him if I had a pistol I would blow his stinking brains all over the floor. He ran to the phone and called the police. "Come out here and arrest a white woman for taking sides with the niggers," he said, so I ran out the back way and ran home before they caught me. The little Negro boy could not have been more than ten years old.

A rock fall killed Jim Stewart after he had been married to Aunt Molly twenty-three years. During those years other coal-mine tragedies had struck her family. A piece of slate had fallen on her father's head and had destroyed his optic nerves; a huge boulder crushed the life out of her brother, Richard Garland; a rock and slate slide killed her son. In one family three men died in an industry which paid them barely enough to keep alive, and sometimes not that much. "I still hear hungry children cry," Aunt Molly remembers. "I held them in my arms and saw them die with the diseases of poverty—T.B., pellagra, and the bloody flux. I saw my own sister's little fourteen-month-old baby girl starve to death for milk while the coal operators was riding around in fine cars with their wives and children all dressed up in diamonds and silks, paid for by the blood and sweat of the coal miners. Oh, how can I forgive when I can never forget?"

For forty-seven years, from the age of five until her exile from the mine country in 1931, she was the life and spirit of the Kentucky miners, not only as a nurse and midwife, but as a union organizer. These forty-seven years saw a great many troubles, tragedies, struggles, and victories, all of which she chronicled in song, so that the other miners and miners' wives would neither forgive nor forget. In the black days of the Kentucky miners during the first years of the Depression, Aunt Molly carried on a bitter struggle against the operators, undaunted by the sight of her fellow organizers being shot down in cold blood. "I have often wondered why they have not killed me—they have beat me and tear-gassed me and had me thrown in jail. Ah yes, they tried to get rid of me but somehow they failed."

In 1931 her second husband, a miner named Bill Jackson, divorced her to free himself from reprisals made against her because of her union activities,[7] and shortly afterward she was forced to leave the state together with other blacklisted organizers. But her oppressor succeeded only in making epidemic a protest which had been endemic. She toured thirty-eight states singing the troubles of the miners, and begging funds for their relief.

Her first appeal outside Kentucky was made in New York's Coliseum before an estimated twenty-one thousand people. To introduce herself to the throng, Aunt Molly composed this song:

> I was born and raised in old Kentucky;
> Molly Jackson is my name.
> I came up here to New York city,
> And I'm truly glad I came.
>
> I am soliciting for the poor Kentucky miners,
> For their children and their wives,
> Because the miners are all blacklisted
> I am compelled to save their lives.
>
> The miners in Bell and Harlan counties organized a union;
> This is all the poor coal miners done,
> Because the coal operators cut down their wages
> To 33 cents and less a ton.
>
> All this summer we have had to listen
> To our hungry children's cries;
> Through the hot part of the summer
> Our little babies died like flies.
>
> While the coal operators and their wives
> All went dressed in jewels and silk,
> The poor coal miners' babies
> Starved to death for bread and milk.

[7] See the fourth stanza of "I Am a Union Woman."

Now I appeal to you in tender mercy
To give us all you have to give,
Because I love my people dearly
And I want them all to live.

I collected hatfuls of bills that night, and my youngest brother, Jim Garland, pulled off his two socks and filled them full of silver, and next morning we sent over $900 to the starving miners and their families. The songs that I composed of the true conditions of the miners in Kentucky in 1931 and 1932 helped me to collect thousands of dollars that saved hundreds of lives and helped them to build the strong coal miners' union that they have today.

At the end of 1932, while making appeals in Ohio, she was seriously injured when the bus in which she was riding turned over. She instituted a damage suit against the Toledo Silver Express Company, but while the case crawled through the courts, the company went bankrupt. Then, like many a folk ballad-maker before her, she eked out a living composing songs, until she married her present husband, Gustavos Stamos.[8]

Outside the mine country she found the forces of oppression just as strong as they were in Kentucky. When she came to live in New York in 1936 she carried over her fighting philosophy of "one for all and all for one" to the unemployed industrial workers, gaining a new reputation thereby. While applying for home relief herself in 1941, she was asked for her birth certificate. In the argument that followed Aunt Molly's expressed indignation that she had to have a birth certificate before being eligible to eat, the clerk said to her, "You talk like a radical. I believe you are a red."

"This is what a young American learned girl said to me in this land of the free. Oh, how foolish some people can be! You see, we did not have any births registered till 1912—a man just came around taking names; then we knew we was borned, but we didn't know when."[9]

Crippled now and nearly destitute, Aunt Molly fears that such

---

[8] Properly, Aunt Molly's surname is now Stamos, but since the miners still remember her as Aunt Molly Jackson, I have elected to call her by that name.

[9] Reticence was never one of Aunt Molly's virtues. When she arrived in New York in 1936 it was Christmas time, and the utility companies would not make installations. Typically militant, she marched down to the electric company and gave them what for. "Just because Jesus Christ was born nineteen hundred and thirty-six years ago I can't get no electric today?"

thoughtless accusations will jeopardize her precarious living. She is most concerned about the palpable Communist ideology taken on by some of her songs that have undergone considerable folk transmission and alteration. For example, the second stanza of "The Murder of Harry Simms" as it was written by Aunt Molly is

> Harry Simms was a pal of mine,
> We labored side by side,
> Expecting to be shot on sight
> Or taken for a ride
> By some life-stealing gun thug
> That roams from town to town
> To shoot and kill our union men
> Wherever they may be found.

When it came back to Aunt Molly years later it had become

> Harry Simms was a pal of mine,
> We labored side by side,
> Expecting to be shot on sight
> Or taken for a ride
> By the dirty capitalist gun thugs
> That roam from town to town,
> Shooting and killing our Comrades
> Wherever they may be found.

and the song itself had grown another concluding stanza:

> Comrades, we must vow today,
> This one thing we must do;
> We must organize the miners,
> In the dear old NMU;
> And get a million volunteers
> Into the YCL
> And sink this rotten system
> In the deepest pits of hell.

She becomes annoyed at any gratuitous changes in her songs; when the changes imply a foreign source for her independent thinking, she becomes incensed.

I've been framed up and accused of being a Red when I did not understand what they meant. I never heard tell of a Communist until after I left Kentucky—then I had passed fifty—but they called me a

Red. I got all of my progressive ideas from my hard tough struggles, and nowhere else.

Some of these hard tough struggles are told in the following songs. Wherever possible, I have let Aunt Molly make her own introductions.[10]

HARD TIMES IN COLMAN'S MINES

"This is a song I composed in 19 and 10 at a mining company in Bell County, Kentucky, when I was trying to get the miners to come out on strike for eight hours and better pay, and for decent homes to live in. I would sing this song and then I would make a long speech, and this way I organized that group of miners while they was in my reach. Colman was the name of the coal operator. He was working over 400 men in this way in 19 and 10. This song will tell you the awful condition the miners was in."

Come out on strike, boys, it's all you can do;
Old Colman gets rich making slaves out of you.

REFRAIN: *It's a hard time in Colman's mines,*
A hard time we know.

Take my advice, boys, I'll tell you what to do,
If you will stand by me, I'll see you through.

You get up in the morning, all you got to eat
Is corn bread and water gravy without any meat.

[10] Aunt Molly Jackson has recorded 204 songs for the Library of Congress Archive of American Folk Song, many of which are available, though at a prohibitive cost. However, her recording of "The Little Dove" and "Ten Thousand Miles" may be had at a reasonable price.

We're cold and hungry, no shoes on our feet,
Corn bread and wild greens is all we got to eat.

The best we got to live in is small one-room shacks,
Kin throw your dogs and cats through the cracks.

When you're asked about moving, all you can say,
"We're so poor and hungry, we can't get away."

Unite and stick together, boys, it's all that can be done,
Throw down your tools, walk out in the sun.

If we all get together, one for all and all for one,
We can put these hard times on the run.

So come out on strike, boys, it's all you can do,
Old Colman gets rich making fools out of you.

POOR MINER'S FAREWELL

"I composed this song one day while I was walking along thinking of how soon a coal miner is forgotten after he is dead. The day I composed this song I never will forget; it was about three weeks after my own dear brother was killed. I found my brother's three oldest children out on the street. They told me they had been over to a store to try to get some food. They said, 'We are out of money, and we have been all over town trying to get some groceries on time, but everyone has turned us down.' Then my brother's little blue-eyed boy looked up at me so sweet and said to me, 'Aunt Molly, will you get us some food to eat?' So I walked along back home that evening, feeling so sad, and thinking of my brother's dear children left without a dad. So I composed this song."

They leave their dear wives and little ones too,
To earn them a living as miners all do;
Poor hard-working miners, their troubles are great
So often while mining they meet their sad fate.

REFRAIN: *Only a miner killed under the ground,*
Only a miner and one more is found;
Killed by some accident, there's no one can tell
Your mining's all over, poor miner, farewell.

Poor orphaned children, thrown out on the street
Ragged and hungry, with nothing to eat.
Their mothers are jobless and their fathers are dead;
Poor fatherless children, left a-crying for bread.

When I'm in Kentucky so often I meet
Poor coal miners' children out on the street.
"How are you doing?" to them I said.
"We're hungry, Aunt Molly, we're begging for bread."

T-BONE SLIM

This is the story of T-Bone Slim.[11] He told me how he got put in jail for a year and a day. He said he had tried to get a job for two months, and had been picked up as a vagrant different times till he had become desperate. He had not eat a bite in two days, he said, and it had been ten weeks since he had lain in a bed. He was so cold and hungry he said he was desperate. When he saw this old "big shot," as he called him, he just knocked the big shot down, and took his suit of clothes, watch, money and all. Just as he was taking off the old man's shoes he saw some men coming and he ran off with the fine suit on and a high top hat, and when they saw him with his old ragged shoes and that high silk hat and that fine suit of clothes, they grabbed him and pulled him before the judge. He said when they turned him out he did not have a *cent* and he could not get a job for food and *rent*. He said he did not want to steal and *rob;* he said he began to wonder how he could find a *job*. He said he was almost out of his *mind* when he went down on the water front and joined the seamen's picket *line*. I was leading the picket line and I met him there. In the seamen's union hall he told me this story. I remembered it all, and a few days later I composed this *song*. Old T-Bone Slim got sunk in a ship when World World II come *along*. He was a good union seaman, but he is dead and *gone*.[12]

As I went walking down Peacock Street,
No clothes on my back, no shoes on my feet,
I was hungry and cold, it was late in the fall,
I knocked down some old big shot, took his clothes, money,
and all.

REFRAIN: *Oh, tell me how long must I wait for a job?*
I don't like to steal, I don't like to have to rob.

When I took everything this old big shot had,
They called me a robber, yes, they called me bad.
They called me a robber, yes, they called me bad,
Because misery and starvation drove me mad.

They locked me up for a year and a day
For taking that old big shot's money away.
Now they turned me out about an hour ago
To walk the streets in the rain and the snow.

[11] T-Bone Slim was the famous IWW columnist who coined the term "Brisbanality." He was the author of the great IWW song, "The Popular Wobbly," and others.
[12] Note the rime slipping into Aunt Molly's prose.

No clothes on my back, no shoes on my feet;
Now a man can't live just walkin' the street.
I'd no money for room rent, no place to sleep;
Now a man can't live just walkin' the street.

Now a man can't live with no food to eat,
I'll be sorry to my heart if I have to repeat.
If I knocked down some old big shot, and took all his kale,
Then they'll put me back in that lousy jail.

MY DISGUSTED BLUES

This is one of my blues. I made this up in 19 and 41, when I was out of a job and out of cash, just leading a picket line for them unemployed friends of mine. Just think of your Aunt Molly *Jackson,* with great satis*faction,* leading a picket line full of sorrow and *pity,* in 19 and 41, in New York *city.*

I get up every morning
Feeling so disgusted and blue,
Because I have no money
And I can't get no work to do.

REFRAIN: *Trouble, trouble, is all I ever see*
Because I met so many people that tries to make
a slave out of me.
Trouble, trouble, I worry all day long
Because everything I do something goes on wrong.

When you have a lot of money
You have a lot of friends come around;
But when you are broke and disgusted
Not one friend can be found.

Yes, trouble and disappointments
Is all I ever find;
I believe that trouble and disappointments
Will destroy my worried mind.

LONESOME JAILHOUSE BLUES

It originated from a bunch of 'em a-gettin' mad at me because I took part in a strike, and they framed me and had me put in jail. This was in Clay County, three miles above Manchester, up on Horse Creek. This happened in '31. I picked the melody and then composed the words to fit the melody.

Listen, friends and workers,
I have some very sad news;
Your Aunt Molly's locked up in prison
With the lonesome jailhouse blues.

You may find some one will tell you
The jailhouse blues ain't bad;
They're the worst kind of blues
Your Aunt Molly ever had.

I joined the miner's union,
That made them mad at me.
Now I am locked up in prison
Just as lonesome as I can be.

I am locked up in prison
Walking on the concrete floor.
When I leave here this time,
I don't want to be here no more.

Because I joined the union
They framed up a lot of lies on me;
They had me put in prison
I am just as lonesome as I can be.

I am locked up in prison,
Just as lonesome as I can be;
I want you to write me a letter
To the dear old ILD.

Tell them that I am in prison
Then they will know what to do.
The bosses had me put in jail
For joining the NMU.

This NMU means union
Many thousand strong;
And if you will come and join us
We will teach you right from wrong.

HUNGRY RAGGED BLUES

On the seventh day of May, 19 and 30, during the strike, the miners built a soup kitchen out of slabs over in a meadow. When it was finished I told all of the wives to bring everything we had from our mining shacks and put it all together, and go around and collect vegetables from the farmers to make soup as long as the farmers had anything to give. By the middle of October we was desperate; we did not see how we was going to live. For two or three days we did not have anything to make soup out of. On the 17th morning in October my sister's little girl waked me up early. She had 15 little ragged children and she was taking them around to the soup kitchen to try to get them a bowl of soup. She told me some of them children had not eat anything in two days. It was a cold rainy morning; the little children was all bare-footed, and the blood was running out of the tops of their little feet and dripping down between their little toes onto the ground. You could track them to the soup kitchen by the blood. After they had passed by I just set down by the table and began to wonder what to try to do next. Then I began to sing out my blues to express my feeling. This song comes from the heart and not just from the point of a pen.

I'm sad and weary, I got those hungry ragged blues;
I'm sad and weary, I got those hungry ragged blues;
Not a penny in my pocket to buy one thing I need to use.

I woke up this morning with the worst blues I ever had in my life;
I woke up this morning with the worst blues I ever had in my life;
Not a bite to cook for breakfast, poor coal miner's wife.

When my husband works in the coal mine he loads a car most
    every trip;
When my husband works in the coal mine he loads a car most
    every trip;
Then he goes to the office that evening and gets denied his scrip.

Just because it took all he made that day to pay his mine expense;
Just because it took all he made that day to pay his mine expense;
A man that'll work for coalite and carbide ain't got a lick of sense.

All the women in the coal camp are sitting with bowed-down heads;
All the women in the coal camp are sitting with bowed-down heads;
Ragged and barefooted and their children a-crying for bread.

This mining town I live in is a dead and lonely place;
This mining town I live in is a dead and lonely place;
Where pity and starvation are pictured on every face.

Oh, don't go under that mountain with the slate a-hanging over
*   your head;*
Oh, don't go under that mountain with the slate a-hanging over
*   your head;*
And work for just coalite and carbide and your children a-crying
*   for bread.*

Oh, listen, friends and workers, please take a friend's advice;
Oh, listen, friends and workers, please take a friend's advice;
Don't load no more, don't pull no more, till you get a living price.

FARE YE WELL, OLD ELY BRANCH

Old Hughes, the coal operator up at Ely Branch, had been expect-ing a strike for two weeks' back pay, so he didn't order nothing for the commissary. There was nothing left but dried beef and canned tomatoes. Now my husband liked a lot to eat, and since you can't buy food nowhere else excepting at the commissary, he decided we got to leave. He was a machinist and was missed more than any other one of the men. Also we had just moved into our first new house. It was all nice and wallpapered up, and golly, I felt sorry to leave. So I com-posed this piece and went down and dropped it by the spring where all the women had to go to get water, so that it would get around without no one knowing who wrote it. But Mrs. Burrow, she saw me, and said, "What's that you dropping down? A love letter?" So I showed it to her and told her, "Don't you say nothing about who wrote it." But Jack Welsh's wife, she knew my handwriting 'cause I'd writ some letters for her, and pretty soon to my house come John Yager, the bookkeeper down at the store. He says, "I'll give you $5.00 if you make up a tune to that." So I sat right down and sang out a tune right off. Later, after we moved, old Hughes met me and said, "You didn't do me no harm by that song. I printed it up and made fifty dollars selling copies at twenty cents apiece to the men."

(Tune: "Old Joe Clark")

Fare ye well, old Ely Branch,
Fare ye well, I say;
I'm tired of living on dried beef and tomatoes
And I'm a-goin' away.

When we had a strike in Ely this spring
These words old Hughes did say:
"Come along boys, go back to work,
We'll give you the two weeks' pay."

When they put on their mining clothes
Hard work again they tried,
And when old pay day rolled around
They found old Hughes had lied.

When Hughes thinks his mines was going to stop,
A sight to see him frown;
There's gas enough in old Hughes
To blow these mountains down.

Oh, take your children out of Ely Branch
Before they cry for bread;
For when old Hughes' debts are paid,
He won't be worth a thread.

Hughes claims he owns more mines than these;
He says he's got money to lend.
And when old pay day rolls around
He can't pay off his men.

I'd rather be in Pineville jail
With my back all covered with lice,
Than to be here in old Hughes' coal mines
Digging coal at Hughes' price.

I think John Yager's a very nice man
He's the same old John every day;
But a man can't live on dried beef and tomatoes,
So I'm a goin' away.

Fare ye well, old Ely Branch,
Fare ye well, I say;
I'm tired of living on dried beef and tomatoes
And I'm a-goin' away.

I AM A UNION WOMAN

When I was organizing the miners around Bell and Harlan counties in 19 and 31 I sang this song. I used it in my organizational work; I always sang this song before giving my speech.

(For music, see "Which Side Are You on?" p. 170.)

I am a union woman,
As brave as I can be;
I do not like the bosses,
And the bosses don't like me.

REFRAIN: *Join the NMU,*
Come join the NMU.

I was raised in old Kentucky,
In Kentucky borned and bred;
And when I joined the union
They called me a Rooshian Red.

When my husband asked the boss for a job
These is the words he said:
"Bill Jackson, I can't work you sir,
Your wife's a Rooshian Red."

This is the worst time on earth
That I have ever saw;
To get shot down by gun thugs
And framed up by the law.

If you want to join a union
As strong as one can be,
Join the dear old NMU
And come along with me.

We are many thousand strong
And I am glad to say,
We are getting stronger
And stronger every day.

The bosses ride fine horses
While we walk in the mud;
Their banner is a dollar sign
While ours is striped with blood.

EAST OHIO MINERS' STRIKE

This was composed in 19 and 32 to explain what condition the miners was in at that time, to make an appeal for money.

Come all you fellow workers,
Listen to what I have to say.
The East Ohio miners
They're standing on the picket line today.

They're fighting starvation wage cuts;
Listen to what the operators done:
They cut the poor miner's wages down
To twenty-three cents a ton.

Then the miners told them
Just what they aimed to do.
"We'll fight starvation wage cuts
By joining the NMU."

The NMU is a miners' union;
They're fighting hand in hand
Against starvation wage cuts.
"Bread and freedom is our demand."

Oh, these operators' wives,
They wear their diamond rings;
The miners' wives and children
They wear just any old thing.
Yes, we wear just any old thing.

While the miners are striking
They're struggling hand in hand;
It is our duty, fellow workers,
To help them all we can.

Their children are all hungry,
And oh! How sad I feel.
Will you help us, fellow workers,
And hear our loud appeal?

THE DEATH OF HARRY SIMMS

My brother Jim was the district organizer in 19 and 31 when Harry Simms was sent to Bell County to help him with the miners' union. Harry Simms was staying at Jim's house, and when he left the house at 5:00 the morning he was killed, he told Jim, "It's my job to lead the miners to Pineville, and gun thugs or no gun thugs, I'm going. If they pop me off, don't waste no time grieving after me, keep right on going. We'll win." You see, Jim told him that the Brush Creek coal operators had offered any gun thug one thousand dollars to kill Jim or Harry Simms. So he met this gun thug on the railroad track, and the thug shot him in the stomach. They took him and another union man who was with him to town, and put the other fellow into jail. They left Harry Simms sitting on a rock in front of the town hospital with a bullet in his stomach. He sat there on the rock an hour or more with his hands on his stomach, bleeding to death. He was sitting there because the hospital wouldn't take him in till somebody guaranteed to pay his bill. After awhile a man said he would pay the bill, so they took Harry in, but it was too late.

The gun thug got away and hid in the caves for six months, and one night he started to cross the road and someone shot him six times with a Colt .45 pistol all around his heart, then whoever it was shot him, cut off his head and throwed it on the other side of the road.

Harry Simms was shot, as Aunt Molly tells, on his way to Pineville. His mission was to lead the Brush Creek miners to the town, where they were to collect five truckloads of food and clothing sent to them from outside the state. Feeling ran high in Bell County during the trial of the two implicated gun thugs. When they were summarily acquitted, they had to be taken out of the area under the protection of over a thousand troopers and special police.

Come and listen to my story,
Come and listen to my song.
I'll tell you of a hero
That is now dead and gone;
I'll tell you of a young boy,
His age it was nineteen;
He was the bravest union man
That ever I have seen.

Harry Simms was a pal of mine,
We labored side by side,
Expecting to be shot on sight
Or taken for a ride
By some life-stealing gun thug
That roams from town to town
To shoot and kill our union men
Where e'er they may be found.

Harry Simms and I was parted
At five o'clock that day.
"Be careful, my dear brother,"
To Harry I did say.
"Now I must do my duty,"
Was his reply to me;
"If I get killed by gun thugs
Don't grieve after me."

Harry Simms was walking up the track
That bright sunshiny day.
He was a youth of courage,
His steps was light and gay;
He did not know the gun thugs
Was hiding on the way
To kill our brave young hero
That bright sunshiny day.

Harry Simms was killed on Brush Creek
In nineteen thirty-two;
He organized the miners
Into the NMU;
He gave his life in struggle
'Twas all that he could do;
He died for the union,
He died for me and you.

The thugs can kill our leaders
And cause us to shed tears,
But they cannot kill our spirit
If they try a million years.
We have learned our lesson
Now we all realize
A union struggle must go on
Till we are organized.

DREADFUL MEMORIES

In 19 and 31 the Kentucky coal miners was asked to dig coal for 33 cents a ton and they had to pay the company for the carbide to make a light and coalite to shock the coal. And they had to pay for their picks and augers to be sharpened—the coal company took one dollar from each man's wages every month for having their picks and augers sharpened. And each man paid two dollars a month for a company doctor even if he did not have to call the doctor once. All we had to make a light in our shacks was kerosene lamps, and after the miners was blacklisted for joining the union March 5, 1931, the company doctor refused to come to any one of the coal miner's families unless he was paid in advance. So I had to nurse all the little children till the last breath left them, and all the light I had was a string in a can lid with a little bacon grease in it. Kerosene was five cents a quart, and I could not get five cents. Thirty-seven babies died in my arms in the last three months of 1931. Their little stomach busted open; they was mortified inside. Oh, what an awful way for a baby to die. Not a thing to give our babies to eat but the strong soup from soup beans, and that took the lining from their little stomachs, so that they bled inside and mortified, and died. And died so hard that before we got help from other states my nerves was so stirred up for four years afterward by the memory of them babies suffering and dying in my arms, and me sitting by their little dead bodies three or four hours before daylight in the dark to keep some hungry dog or cat from eating up their little dead bodies. Then four years later I still had such sad memories of these babies that I wrote this song.

Dreadful memories! How they linger;
How they pain my precious soul.
Little children, sick and hungry,
Sick and hungry, weak and cold.

Little children, cold and hungry,
Without any food at all to eat.
They had no clothes to put on their bodies;
They had no shoes to put on their feet.

REFRAIN: *Dreadful memories! How they linger;*
How they fill my heart with pain.
Oh, how hard I've tried to forget them
But I find it all in vain.

I can't forget them, little babies,
With golden hair as soft as silk;
Slowly dying from starvation,
Their parents could not give them milk.

...rget them, coal miners' children,
...ved to death without one drop of milk,
...coal operators and their wives and children
dressed in jewels and silk.

Dreadful memories! How they haunt me
As the lonely moments fly.
Oh, how them little babies suffered!
I saw them starve to death and die.

Woody ...ie

They just ...nake em no honerier than me. It looks like Im a doing everyt... can to make a hobo out of me. I get good chances to get on th... and make a little money and get a start up the old ladder, b... that honery streak comes out and I ruin the whole thing. I kick... f in the britches pretty hard some times. You dont hate me any... than I do. You dont bawl me out any more than I do. Oh we... n it all anyhow, I never really set my head on a being a public figure. Its all what you mean when you say success. Most of the time success ain't much fun. Lots of times it takes a lot of posing and pretending.

In these words, scribbled in a moment of depression on the back of the manuscript of his "Jailhouse Blues," Woody Guthrie tries to explain why he is a failure. "Everybody tells me how good I am," he says, "but I can't make a living for my wife and kids." This general praise of which Guthrie speaks has come not only from workers who have been inspired by his union songs or from dilettantes who find his unusual method of delivery for the moment quaint, but from eminent folklorists and musicologists as well. The Library of Congress called him "our best contemporary ballad composer"[13]; Alan Lomax goes further to say Guthrie is "the best folk ballad composer whose identity has ever been known"; Elie Siegmeister calls him a "rusty-voiced Homer."[14]

Guthrie's self-recrimination is not, as he believes it is, an ex-

[13] Prefatory notes to Guthrie's recording of "The Gypsy Davy," in the Archive of American Folk Song Album I.
[14] Elie Siegmeister, *A Treasury of American Folk Song*, New York, 1943.

planation for his failure—as the world defines failure; his "honeri-ness" is an effect rather than a cause, an expression of frustration born of many injuries, physical and psychological. His tragic boyhood; his inability to understand why his fight against the oppression of the poor by the rich should make him the object of official surveillance; his childhood companions' accusation that his birth had driven his mother insane; the death of his sister through fire and the repetition of the tragedy years later when his little daughter was burned to death; the shocking discovery that his children by a former marriage had grown to represent the racial bigotry he had dedicated his life against—all these and many more psychological traumata left deep scars of which his extreme self-consciousness—in itself fatal to a public entertainer—is only the most obvious.

Nor can this "honeriness," even in the superficial significance given to it by Guthrie, be condemned as reprehensible, for it consists of his shyness acting upon an innate, inexpressed integrity which prevents him from pandering, as some of his old companions have done, to "what the public wants." So disillusioned has he become through the defections of these friends that he uses even the term "folk music" with noticeable hesitation, explaining that he usually hears the words from the mouths of "silk-stocking balladeers." His definition of "silk-stocking balladeers" moves on the borders of the unquotable, but in its expurgated essence, it describes those inferior tenors whom competition in the popular field has driven into swank night clubs and parlors of society matrons, where they pass off forgotten Scottish ballads and watered-down versions of lusty frontier songs as living folk music.

"I won't say that my guitar playing or singing is anything fancy on a stick," Guthrie once wrote. "I'd rather sound like the cab drivers cursing at each other, like the longshoremen yelling, like the cowhands whooping and the lone wolf barking—like anything in this big green universe than to sound slick, smooth-tongued, oily-lipped."

Too many of the "good chances to get on the radio" which he has been offered are like his audition in Rockefeller Center's Rainbow Room, where the "shrimps are boiled in Standard Oil."

"They offered me a job at $75 a week," Guthrie relates. "That was about $70 more than I'd ever got for regular singing before,

so I said to myself, 'Boy, you got you a job.' But when they tried
to rig me up in whiskers and a hillbilly clown suit, I ducked into
the elevator and rode the 65 stories back down to the U.S.A.
Made up a song about it as I was going down, went,

> *Never comin' back to this man's town again;*
> *Never comin' back to this man's town again;*
> *Ain't never comin' back to this man's town again,*
> *Singin' "Hey, hey, hey, hey."*

Like all the composers of the better songs of protest, Guthrie
has had a life of almost continuous hardship. Only the earliest
years, spent in Okemah, Oklahoma, where he was born in 1912,
were in any measure happy. Before the first World War Okemah
was, as Guthrie puts it, the "singingest, dancingest, walkingest,
talkingest, laughingest, yellingest, preachingest, cryingest, drink-
ingest, gamblingest, fist-fightingest, shootingest, bleedingest, gun-,
club-, and razor-carryingest of the oil boom towns." Ominously,
it was also in the heart of what was later to become the Dust Bowl.
There young Guthrie sold newspapers, danced street jigs, and
sang for pennies the traditional songs that were the heritage of
the old Indian territory residents.

His father was the embodied spirit of the oil boom. A big,
lusty, expansive Texan, a trained pugilist and professional guitarist, Charles Edward Guthrie could have made an adequate living
at a number of trades, but chose instead to live by his wits. Seeing
the opportunities open to the intrepid in land speculation, he
plunged into the oil and money rush, dragging his wife Nora,
and his children Roy, Woody, and Clara behind him. There was
time for relaxation in the Guthrie household only at night, when
the children gathered around the fire and listened to their Aunt
Lottie, her nose stuffed with "nerve tightener," sing the old songs.

Perhaps it was this frantic pace that first unsettled his mother's
reason, but after their new six-room house burned down and her
husband lost "a farm a day for thirty days" in the collapse of the
land boom, her spells of violent insanity became more frequent.
When little Clara was burned to death in an oil-stove explosion,
the family disintegrated. Nora was sent to the Norman State
Asylum, and Charles, the last vestige of his spirit burned out of

him in a third house fire, went back to Texas to be taken care of by his sister.

So Woody went into his teens a virtual orphan. His last few years as a child were spent finding bare and unwholesome subsistence as a "junkie," shoe-shine boy, spittoon cleaner, and bus boy. At sixteen he took the road to the South, working where work was to be found, and singing and playing his harmonica for nickels when there was no work to do.

In Pampa, Texas, he met his uncle Jeff, an itinerant musician, who gave him his first guitar and a semi-professional job in his band as a sit-in guitarist. Between dances Woody learned to play the mandolin and fiddle.

After several years of barnstorming through the South, Guthrie married a girl named Mary Jennings, and "lived in the ricketiest of the oil town shacks long enough to have no clothes, no money, no groceries, and two children." [15]

The years between Guthrie's marriage and the War can be reduced to a simple pattern, endlessly repeated: Unable to find steady work where he settled his little family, he would trek off alone to new hunting grounds, accumulate enough money to send for his wife and children, and gradually slip back into poverty again. His first absence from his wife took him to Los Angeles, where he got a job singing more or less regularly on Station KFVD. He augmented the small salary with quick trips through the state, singing for migratory workers, and incidentally acquiring a hatred for the injustice which had spawned their pitiful economic status. When he had amassed enough money, he sent for his family. Eventually severing his relations with KFVD, Guthrie gravitated more and more toward singing for labor groups, until his savings, sustained only by irregular contributions from the migrants and other workers in a similar state of insolvency, ran out. The family, now grown to five, piled into an old car and set out across the two thousand miles of desert to their shack in Texas, where Woody deposited his wife and children and set out alone for New York with $35 in his pocket borrowed from his brother Roy.

[15] Both girls, named Sue and Teeny. In his first published record in the Library of Congress albums (AAFS 2A) Guthrie can be heard interrupting his song to whisper "Hello, Sue" to his little daughter.

In New York he stayed for a while with Will Geer[16] and then moved to the Bowery. Alan Lomax discovered him, took him to Washington, and recorded all the songs he "could remember on a pint of pretty cheap whiskey." He made two albums of Dust Bowl ballads for Victor Records, saw *The Grapes of Wrath*, met Pete Seeger, a former Harvard student turned folk singer, and set off with him through the Middle West. Eventually he found himself back in New York and for the moment a successful purveyor of folk songs on several big radio shows. He sent for his family again, but soon after their arrival he became disgusted with the "whole sissified and nervous rules of censorship on all of my songs and ballads," and, like the Joads, loaded his family in a car and set out once more for California. He was given a job by the Bonneville Power Administration to work along with the great dam builders and chronicle their achievement in song; this he did, writing and recording twenty-six ballads which now repose in the Oregon Department of the Interior. He also acquired a hatred for the monopolistic cupidity of the private power owners, which, like his contempt for the citrus barons, was reflected in his compositions. And then back to New York, and back to California, and back to New York, until his marriage cracked under the peripatetic strain.

In 1943 his name appeared somewhat incongruously as the author of a book which its publishers, E. P. Dutton and Company, described as "an autobiography written in the national idiom with a sort of national grasp . . . perhaps the strongest picture yet written of America's will to win." Condensed from a Thomas Wolfeian spate of a million words to 428 pages, but still retaining words that were sometimes not words, redundances which were woven into surprisingly effective English, extravagantly picturesque phrases typical of the new Heroic Age of which he sings, *Bound for Glory* was a powerful but distressing book—powerful in its picture of the millions of little people whom Guthrie saw making the America that was "bound for glory," but conversely depressing in its recounting of the injustices and oppression that made their task so difficult.

After he and Mary had been divorced, Woody took a job in

[16] Before attaining success as an actor, Will Geer had toured the Western migrant camps with Guthrie, singing for the Okies, Arkies, and Mizoos.

the Merchant Marine, shipping out with Cisco Houston, a guitar player who came from a town in California "so small that 'Come Again' was painted on the back of the 'Welcome' sign." Their first ship was torpedoed off the coast of Sicily, but staggered into Bizerte, where he and Houston caught an empty Liberty ship back to the United States. They immediately shipped out again for Africa.

Back in the United States after this trip, Guthrie met Moses Asch, son of Sholem Asch and the man largely responsible for the current renascence of folk music on records. Asch recorded 120 of Guthrie's songs, and published his second book, a forty-eight-page collection of reminiscences and songs, entitled *American Folk Song*.

Upon his return to the United States after a second torpedoing, Guthrie was drafted into the army, which sent him West again, through Texas to Las Vegas (pronounced "Lost Wages" by Guthrie), where he was given a dependency discharge, having by that time acquired another wife and daughter.

Once more in New York, Guthrie became associated with the Almanac Singers, and through them with People's Songs, an organization in which his individuality was quickly submerged. Before any harm was done to his style, however, People's Songs began to use for its purposes union and topical songs on a much higher level of conscious art than the nearly pure folk material that Guthrie was producing, and he gradually dissociated himself from the group. At the present time Guthrie's home is officially in Beach Haven, New York, but his actual whereabouts cannot be stated with any assurance. The last time I visited his home his wife told me that several months before he had gone down to the corner store for a newspaper, and that was the last she heard of him for three weeks, when he sent her a letter from California.

When I first visited Guthrie in 1946 he was living in a crowded apartment in Coney Island with his wife and four-year-old daughter, Cathy Ann,[17] whom he nicknamed "Stackabones." I found him, a little weather-worn man with incredibly bushy, wiry hair, sitting before a typewriter in a hollowed-out space in the middle of a tiny room filled with guitars, fiddles, harmonicas, mandolins, tambourines, children's toys, record albums, books, pictures, and scat-

17 Cathy Ann was the child who later died in an electrical fire.

tered manuscripts. Remembering his musical declaration that he was "never comin' back to this man's town again," I asked him why he had changed his mind about this city of "rich men, preachers, and slaves."

"Everything's moved to the city," he answered with a great sweep of his arm, and speaking to the world. "Big business brought the workers, the workers brought the music, and the music brought me."

I asked if he agreed with a more famous contemporary who said that folksongs were gaining popularity in the cities because city people were bored with screen glamour and soap operas, and wanted instead "something real."

He did not. "The unions started the boom," he insisted. "The workers wanted to sing about their fight, but they couldn't borrow popular tunes because the money men who own the big monopoly on music would sock them with the copyright laws. They had to go where they should have gone in the first place—to the old songs made by workers years ago in the woods and on the plains and on the oceans."

He pushed a two-inch thick book of bound typewriter paper toward me. "Look," he said, "there's more than three hundred songs I've written, most of them to the old tunes. You won't hear the night club orgasm gals singing these songs, but I've sung them on picket lines, in union halls, in foc's'les, in river-bottom peach camps—everywhere—and I've never once seen them fail. Folks sweat under the collar, throw their coats in the corner, stamp their feet, clap, and sing these songs. Our songs are singing history."

Since that meeting, Guthrie has been exceptionally prolific in song writing, and probably his stack of compositions now is three or four times as thick. The most important reason for this sudden increase in production is that since his more or less permanent settlement in New York Guthrie's sources have changed from living to literary material. In his earlier days—in the days when the Dust Bowl ballads and his famous strike and picket-line songs were written, his compositions were spontaneously generated to relieve an expanding feeling of protest; the inspiration came from within. Today his songs are likely to be perfunctory versified paraphrases of newspaper accounts of injustices perpetrated on individuals or groups with whom he has no personal acquaintance. The inspiration and feeling of protest are still there in sufficient quantity to lift his compositions well above the level of the average contemporary labor-protest song, but both suffer through diffusion, and the "dissociation of sensibility" which inevitably results from the utilization of secondary sources is everywhere evident. This does not mean that Guthrie no longer writes songs that approach the quality of "Pretty Boy Floyd" and "Tom Joad," but merely that the percentage of songs of first quality is smaller. Everything is grist for Guthrie's mill now. Some months ago, when the newspapers reported a corollary of Einstein's theory which seemed to indicate that it was impossible to determine the direction of a body's movement, Guthrie translated its meaning to him in a song whose refrain was,

> *Well I can't go east or west,*
> *And I can't go up or down,*
> *And I can't go north or south,*
> *But I can still go round and round.*

Not all of Guthrie's compositions are songs of overt protest. Of an estimated thousand songs in his manuscript collection, I found only about 140 whose basic theme was one of protest; the remainder fell into conventional folksong categories—love, humor, crime, ballads of disaster, tragedies, and war, non-protest labor songs, and even nursery songs.

Many of these attain the quality of the best of his protest songs, but since their themes lie outside the scope of this work, their examination must await another study. It may, however, be mentioned as an illustration of the inherent quality of his work, that many of these less controversial songs have had extraordinary success in view of the fact that songs of nearly pure folk origin are denied the usual channels of commercial distribution. His "Oklahoma Hills" made a small fortune for his cousin, a cowboy singer to whom its composition was erroneously attributed; his "Philadelphia Lawyer," a humorous ballad of first quality, attained an astounding popularity on the West Coast during the latter part of 1949; his "So Long, It's Been Good to Know You" in a version lamentably divested of all its earlier significance, is currently among the sheet music and record best sellers.[18]

The "Philadelphia Lawyer," in the economical way in which the substitution of an occasional line produces a completely different story in a completely different mood, is a fine example of Guthrie's skill at the sort of adaptation that has characterized folk composition. Taking the sentimental ballad "The Jealous Lover," and discarding the tragic theme, Guthrie makes of an undistinguished story of unhappy love a distinguished story of irresponsible love and its consequences, while incidentally ridiculing a profession for which he has only despite.

Way out in Reno, Nevada,
Where romances bloom and fade,
A great Philadelphia lawyer
Fell in love with a Hollywood maid.

"Your face is so lovely and pretty,
Your form so fair and divine;
Come with me to the big city,
And leave this wild cowboy behind."

Wild Bill was a gun-toting cowboy;
Six notches were carved on his gun.
All the boys around Reno, Nevada,
Left Wild Bill's sweetheart alone.

One night when Bill was returning
Out from the desert so cold,
He dreamed of his Hollywood sweetheart,
Whose love was as lasting as gold.

As he drew near to her window,
Two shadows he saw on the shade;
'Twas the great Philadelphia lawyer,
Making love to his Hollywood maid.

[18] It is a source of constant distress to Guthrie's friends that the profits from these songs have gone to other persons. Like the IWW, which never copyrighted their songbooks, Guthrie in spite of his complaint that his songs have never made him any money, seems content to let them fall into the public domain. During the height of the "Philadelphia Lawyer's" popularity, George Wilhelm, a West Coast radio announcer, took it upon himself to institute a suit for infringement of copyright in Guthrie's name, but dropped the action when Guthrie exhibited no interest in the proceedings.

The night was as still as the desert,
With the moon hanging high overhead.
He listened awhile to the lawyer,
He could hear every word that he said.

"Come, love, and we will wander
Down where the lights are so bright.
I'll win you a divorce from your husband
And we can get married tonight."

Tonight in old Pennsylvania
Beneath the whispering pines
There's one less Philadelphia lawyer
In old Philadelphia tonight.

In songs of more serious intent such heavy dependence on traditional material has greatly impaired the quality of Guthrie's songs. "Gotta Get to Boston" is representative of perhaps a score of songs in which the incompatible combination of dissimilar origins obviates the effect which Guthrie tries to achieve. "Root Hog or Die," of which this is but a slight adaptation, is hardly the kind of song one would associate in theme with the Sacco-Vanzetti tragedy.

Train wheels can roll me
Cushions can ride;
Ships on the oceans,
Planes in the skies;
Storms they can come, love,
Flood waters rise,
But I gotta get to Boston
Or two men will die.

Root hog or die, friend,
Root hog or die;
I gotta get to Boston
Root hog or die.
Sacco and Vanzetti die at sundown tonight
So I gotta get to Boston
Root hog or die.

But Guthrie's use of tangible[19] folk material is rarely so heavy handed. Usually his borrowing extends only to the utilization,

[19] By this qualification I exclude the technique, style, and mood of American folksong, the characteristics of Guthrie's compositions which inextricably bind him with the folk.

with little adaptation, of the tunes of traditional folk songs. A common notation on his manuscripts is something like "This goes good to the tune of 'Blue Eyes' with a little of 'Wildwood Flower' mixed in." Unlike most writers of union songs and topical parodies, Guthrie never uses the tune of a popular song for his compositions.

This characteristic folk purity of his tunes can be extended not only to his compositions as a whole, but to his personality also. Despite his intermittent residence in New York, the economic and social orientation he has gained through acquaintance with college-educated organizers and political workers, and the voracious reading of heavy books, Guthrie has retained unspoiled his folk origins. Dr. Charles Seeger, in determining Guthrie's cultural evolution, says that he has not yet attained cb.[20] But with the most sincere deference to Dr. Seeger's profound knowledge, I submit that Guthrie has remained consistently close to f, making only sporadic and temporary excursions to the borders of hb.

In the matter of accompaniment Guthrie has gone further to the right. Those familiar with the music of the Carter family, the most respected of hillbilly singing groups, can detect vestigial traces of Maybelle Carter's "picking" in Guthrie's guitar style.[21] When, after Guthrie made his first coast-to-coast radio appearance he received a grimy postcard from West Virginia signed "The Carters" and saying "You're doing fine, boy," he proudly acknowledged his debt. Guthrie deplores the practice of "folk singers" learning the guitar either from books or under the guidance of a professional teacher.

I can't play any chord by looking at any book and never could. . . . I'll bet you the chording books that Leadbelly has used in his greening and grey years wouldn't make a pile big enough for you to find on your floor. Leadbelly learnt how to play the guitar the same way that

20 In a review of several commercial albums of American folksongs (JAFL vol. 31) Dr. Seeger set up a very useful formula by which the relative authenticity of "folk singers" can be evaluated: $f - hb - cb - c$, in which f = folk, hb = hillbilly, cb = citybilly, c = concert. Most folk singers move from f to c, sometimes with such rapidity that their integrity is quickly lost in the process; a very few, among whom is Dr. Seeger's son Pete, move in the opposite direction.

21 As indeed her influence can be detected also in Leadbelly, a supposedly pure folk singer; compare the Carter family's "Worried Man Blues" (Victor 27497) and Leadbelly's "Poor Howard" (Musicraft 225) for similarity in guitar style.

I did, by "ear," by "touch," by "feel," by "bluff," by "gessin," by "fakin," and by a great crave and drive to keep on playing.

If I'm sort of lazing it around, I leave out a few of the extrays. If I'm scattering wild oats for my goats, I lay in a few more just to keep my string finger oily and limber. If I play with one other instrument, I do this way. If it's two others, I play some other way. If it's at a sixteen guitar hoot, I am forced by the laws of nature and averages, to naturally find some 17th lost part nobody else is using and tickle around with that. . . .

I've pounded out "Ida Red," "Old Joe Clark," "Old Judge Parker Take Your Shackles Offa Me," for as high as thirty or forty minutes with no more than two chords, D to A, D to A, and D to A ten blue jillion times through a square dance. Lots of the old fullblood fiddlers will toss you down off from his platform if you go to getting too fancy with your chording.[22]

Some idea of the inspired carelessness which above all else is responsible for his nearly original guitar style is evident in this reply to my request for information concerning the chords used in several of his records:

I only used straight C chord all the way down the line on the "Buffalo Skinners," just C C C C C C C C C and right down to Birmingham and then on down to Jacksboro and then out past El Paso and then on up into New Mexico. CCCCCCCCCCCCCCCCCCCCC picking finger style.

On "Sally Don't You Grieve" it was E natural A natural, with no sevenths that I know of. Maybe so. Could of been. Works either way. You get down your gitbox and try it and you will see.

You are right about the "Song of the Gypsy Dave" but I used no sevenths here that I especially knew about. Maybe I don't know when I do use a seventh. I learned all I know by watching and never could tell you what the letter and the number was anyhow. You try it several ways and let your fingers just sort of feel the way they want to go and follow them and you will usually come across something that was better than you thought.

This lack of system precludes his playing the same song the same way twice, but rarely can a listener say with any assurance that the second repetition was better than the first, or vice versa. Supreme ease is the most characteristic feature of his playing; his

[22] From a letter printed in *People's Songs*, September 1948, p. 6.

fingers seem to run uncontrolled over the frets, eliciting subtle effects of which he seems not to be aware. Watching him, one has the impression that he could take his guitar by the neck, shake it, and the chords and runs would fall out in abject obedience to his mastery.

In the matter of language and imagery Guthrie's style, when not obviously adapted from an existing song or lifted consciously from the great body of folk idiom, is unique; I have not been able to detect any influences such as are to be found in his guitar playing. He is a logophile, but his hypnosis with words does not manifest itself, as it does with others who have this affliction, in polysyllables. Guthrie rarely strays far from the Anglo-Saxon word-hoard, but the curious associations which he finds between simple terms lead him into fantastic flights of imagery. Metrical restrictions fetter these flights in his songs, but in his prose they are completely unrestrained. In reply to a somewhat ill-considered criticism of the psychology he uses to convey his political philosophy, Guthrie wrote me:

I fall on the rim of my table of grief and cry because you have ripped aside the cloudy blanket of my soul and shown me that I am too far to the left of the center, too radical in my political views, and, sad to tell, too unpleasant even in my class relationships. No, it is not my class relationships but my outlook upon them that deals the cinders in the stew. Well, how else could I view our class relationships? Is there a friendlier way? Maybe there is. I will ask my wife or my baby or somebody when they come back. But the baby is asleep tonight and the wife is prancing somewhere out West and I am here in my kitchen all by myself. Since nobody else but me is here I cannot take any fast action on my outlooks about the class relations. I think that I will listen in at my daughter's door and see if she is asleep, then if she is and so are all of my neighbors, I am going to set in quiet study and deep thought for one whole hour and vision every picture and sight and smell of pleasant nature that I can in regard to class relationships.

His diction is filled with picturesque expressions which we, who can merely write grammatical correctness, may envy: Of a broken watch: "It ticks like hell but won't keep time." Of a small boy: "He ain't old enough to be of any age." Of an obvious fact which an obtuse person cannot apprehend: "A blind man could feel that with a stick." Of Missouri mosquitoes: "So thick you couldn't stir 'em with a stick." Of a little man battling furiously against overwhelming opposition: "He was fightin' like a bee in under a horse's tail." Of despair: "I been troubled so long I forgot how to worry." Of incomprehension: "All I know is I add up all I know and I still don't know."

A characteristic of Guthrie's songs not possible to detect in examinations of the texts is their extreme speed of composition. This fact was indelibly impressed on me several years ago in an incident memorable for a coincidence which would pale the most egregious of Thomas Hardy's into insignificance. I had booked air passage from Torrance, California, to Philadelphia, Pennsylvania, and after boarding the plane, found in the adjoining seat Woody Guthrie, whom I had met only once before, and then some three thousand miles away. While we were flying across Oklahoma next day, I prodded Guthrie awake and pointed below to Oklahoma, covered by an unbroken bank of clouds. "There's your old home," I said. He looked soberly at the clouds for a moment and then asked me if I had a pen. I handed him a particularly fluid ball-pointer and in a matter of seconds he had written a song beginning "I want to lay my head tonight on a bed of Oklahoma clouds." Amazed, I asked, "Do you always write a song that fast?" "No," he drawled in his expansive, impersonal way, "only when I got a good pen."

One could recite endless anecdotes illustrating Guthrie's colorful personality, but in so doing one might easily lose sight of his real importance as a man and as a symbol, aspects of Guthrie's character which John Steinbeck, himself a chronicler of the American nomads, expressed in a preface to Guthrie's first Asch record album:

Woody is just Woody. Thousands of people do not know he had any other name. He is just a voice and a guitar. He sings the songs of a people and I suspect that he is, in a way, that people. Harsh voiced and nasal, his guitar hanging like a tire iron on a rusty rim, there is nothing sweet about Woody, and there is nothing sweet about the songs he sings. But there is something more important for those who will listen. There is the will of a people to endure and fight against oppression. I think we call this the American spirit.

But Woody Guthrie sees himself in a less imposing way; he says merely, "Let me be known as the man who told you something you already know."

Guthrie composed this fine ballad after seeing the motion picture version of John Steinbeck's *The Grapes of Wrath*. "I wrote this song," he says, "because the people back in Oklahoma haven't got two bucks to buy the book, or even thirty-five cents to see the movie, but the song will get back to them and tell them what Preacher Casy said."

TOM JOAD

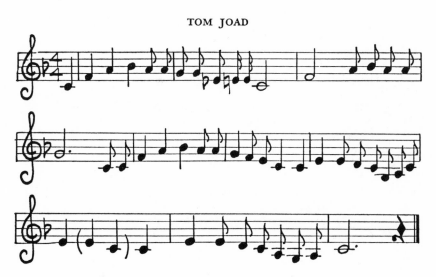

Tom Joad got out of the old McAlester pen;
There he got his parole.
After four long years on a man-killing charge
Tom Joad come walking down the road, (poor boy)
Tom Joad come walking down the road.

Tom Joad, he met a truck-driving man;
There he caught him a ride.
He said, "I just got loose from McAlester pen
On a charge called homicide, (killin')
A charge called homicide."

That truck rolled away in a cloud of dust;
Tom, he turned his face toward home.
He met Preacher Casy and they had a little drink,
And he found that his family, they was gone,
He found that his family, they was gone.

He found his mother's old-fashioned shoe,
He found his daddy's hat;
And he found little Muley and Muley said,
"They've been tractored out by the cats,
They've been tractored out by the cats."

Tom Joad walked down to the neighbor's farm;
Found his family;
They took Preacher Casy and they loaded in a car,
And his mother said, "We've got to get away,"
His mother said, "We've got to get away."

Now the twelve of the Joads made a mighty heavy load,
And Grandpa Joad did cry;
He picked up a handfulla land in his hand,
Said, "I'll stay with the farm till I die;
Yes, I'll stay with the farm till I die."

They fed him short-ribs, and coffee, and soothing syrup,
But Grandpa Joad did die.
They buried Grandpa Joad by the side of the road;
Grandma on the California side,
They buried Grandma on the California side.

Well, they come to a mountain and they looked to the West,
And it looked like the Promised Land.
That bright green valley with the river running through,
There was work for every single hand, (they thought)
There was work for every single hand.

The Joads rolled away to a jungle camp,
There they cooked a stew.
All the hungry little kids in the jungle camp
Said, "We'd like to have some too;"
Said, "We'd like to have some too."

Ma Joad she says, "Go get you a stick,
And come and get some stew;
But, mind you children, you're a gonna have to wait,
Till my men folks gets through,
Till my men folks gets through."

Well, a dep'ty sheriff fired loose at a man,
Shot a woman in the back.
Before he could take his aim again
Preacher Casy dropped him in his tracks, (poor boy)
Preacher Casy dropped him in his tracks.

They handcuffed Casy and they took him to jail,
But then he got away;
And he met Tom Joad by the old river bridge,
And these few words he did say, (poor boy)
These few words he did say:

"Well, I preached for the Lord a mighty long time;
Preached about the rich and the poor.
Us workin' folks is got to get together,
Cause we ain't got a chance anymore;
We ain't got a chance anymore."

The vigilantes come and Tom and Casy run
To the bridge where the water run down,
But a vigilante thug hit Casy with a club.
They laid Preacher Casy on the ground, (poor Casy)
They laid Preacher Casy on the ground.

Tom Joad he grabbed that deputy's club,
Hit him over the head.
Tom Joad took flight in the dark rainy night
With a deputy and a preacher laying dead, (two men)
A deputy and a preacher laying dead.

Tom Joad run back where his mother was asleep,
He woke her up out of bed,
And he kissed goodbye to the mother that he loved,
Said what Preacher Casy said, (Tom Joad)
He said what Preacher Casy said.

"All the world might be justa one big soul;
Well, it looks thataway to me;
Everywhere that you look in the day or night,
That's where I'm a-gonna be, (Maw)
That's where I'm a-gonna be."

"Wherever little children are hungry and crying,
Wherever people ain't free,
Wherever men are fighting for their rights
That's where I'm a-gonna be, (Maw)
That's where I'm a-gonna be."

COULEE DAM

I saw the Columbia River and the big Grand Coulee Dam from just about every cliff, mountain, tree, post, and every other angle from which it can be seen. I made up 26 songs about the Columbia and about the dam and about the men, and these songs were recorded by the Department of Interior, Bonneville Power Administration, Port-

land, Oregon. The records were played at all sorts and sizes of meetings where the people bought bonds to bring the power lines over
the fields and hills to their own little places.

But there were reactionary congressmen in back of the people that
owned those little private dams and power houses out there, that didn't
want to see the Grand Coulee built, because it would make electricity
dirt cheap and cut down on their profits. (They fought to try to keep
the TVA out of the State of Tennessee, too.) They can always think
up a million nice good excellent reasons why it is better for you to
go ragged and hungry and down and out and even in the dark, as
long as it makes them a profit. But lots of people made speeches on
both sides. Movie stars flew up in big airplanes and told the folks
how nice it was not to have no electricity, and not to have no Coulee
Dam at all. But we made speeches on our side, and we played the
records over the loud speakers there in those little towns, and the
people shelled out the money and bought the bonds and brought
the electricity over the hill to milk the cows, shoe the old mare, light
up the saloon, the chili joint window, the ladies' dresses and hats in
windows, the schools and the churches along the way, to run the factories turning out manganese, chrome, bauxite, aluminum, steel, and
flying fortresses by the hundreds to bomb the Japs out of this war with.
That's how things get done. Just people doing it. People can get more
done that way than anybody else I ever seen, and I'm a man that's
seen a lot of them.

—Record Prefaces "Woody Guthrie" Album, Asch 347.

(Tune: "Wabash Cannonball")

Well the world has seven wonders,
So the travelers always tell;
Some gardens and some towers,
I guess you know them well.
But now the greatest wonder,
Is in Uncle Sam's fair land;
It's that King Columbia River,
And the Big Grand Coulee Dam.

She heads up the Canadian Rockies,
Where the rippling waters glide;
Comes a-rumbling down the canyon,
To meet that salty tide,
Of the wide Pacific Ocean,
Where the sun sets in the west;
And the Big Grand Coulee country,
In the land I love the best.

In the misty crystal glitter
Of that wild and windward spray,
Men have fought the pounding waters,
And met a watery grave.
Well she tore their boats to splinters,
But she gave men dreams to dream;
Of the day the Coulee Dam
Would cross that wild and wasted stream.

Uncle Sam took up the challenge
In the year of thirty-three,
For the farmers and the factory,
And all of you and me.
He said Roll along, Columbia,
You can ramble to the sea;
But River, while you're rambling,
You can do some work for me.

Now in Washington and Oregon,
You hear the factories hum;
Making chrome and making manganese
And light aluminum.
And there roars a Flying Fortress,
Now to fight for Uncle Sam;
Spawned upon the King Columbia
By the Big Grand Coulee Dam.

In the misty crystal glitter
Of that wild and windward spray;
Men have fought the pounding waters,
And met a watery grave.
Well she tore their boats to splinters,
But she gave men dreams to dream;
Of the day the Coulee Dam
Would cross that wild and wasted stream.

Another of Guthrie's songs about the migrant workers:

PASTURES OF PLENTY

It's a mighty hard row that my poor hands has hoed
And my poor feet has traveled a hot dusty road
Out of your dustbowl and westward we rolled,
Lord, your desert is hot and your mountains are cold.

I work in your orchards of peaches and prunes,
And I sleep on the ground 'neath the light of your moon.
On the edge of your city you'll see us and then
We come with the dust and we go with the wind.

California, Arizona, I make all your crops,
Then it's north up to Oregon to gather your hops;
Dig beets from your ground, cut the grapes from your vine
To set on your table your light sparkling wine.

Green Pastures of Plenty from dry desert ground,
From the Grand Coulee Dam where the waters run down;
Every state in this union us migrants has been
We'll work in your fight and we'll fight till we win.

It's always we ramble, that river and I,
All along your green valley I'll work till I die;
My land I'll defend with my life if needs be,
'Cause my Pastures of Plenty must always be free.

Guthrie's sympathy for the migratory worker is international. In this ballad he tells of the death of twenty-eight Mexican migrant deportees in an airplane crash near Coalinga, California, on January 28, 1948.

PLANE WRECK AT LOS GATOS

The crops are all in and the peaches are rottening
The oranges are piled in their creosote dumps;
You're flying them back to the Mexico border
To pay all their money to wade back again.

REFRAIN: *Goodbye to my Juan, Goodbye Rosalita;*
Adios muy amigo, Jesus and Marie,
You won't have a name when you ride the big airplane
All they will call you will be deportees.

My father's own father he waded that river;
They took all the money he made in his life;
My brothers and sisters come working the fruit trees
And they rode the truck till they took down and died.

Some of us are illegal and some are not wanted,
Our work contract's out and we have to move on;
Six hundred miles to that Mexico border,
They chase us like outlaws, like rustlers, like thieves.

We died in your hills, we died in your deserts,
We died in your valleys and died on your plains;
We died neath your trees and we died in your bushes,
Both sides of this river we died just the same.

The sky plane caught fire over Los Gatos Canyon,
A fireball of lightning and shook all our hills.
Who are all these friends all scattered like dry leaves?
The radio says they are just deportees.

Is this the best way we can grow our big orchards?
Is this the best way we can grow our good fruit?
To fall like dry leaves to rot on my top soil
And be called by no name except deportees?

—Composed February 3, 1948.

DEAD FROM THE DUST

Next to the migratory crop pickers, the miner has been the worker closest to Guthrie's heart, perhaps because there were lead, zinc, and soft coal mines within twenty miles of his birthplace.

My kinfolks and friends that hold the brass handle,
As we stand round her grave I see tears in your eyes.
My mother's cold clay is wrapped in this pine box—
She is dead from the dust that blows from the mine.

One short year ago we carried my father
To lower him down and to weep and to cry;
These mountains he loved and he dug in the slate rock;
He was wrecked by the dust that blows from the mine.

Four small graves you see, you helped me to dig them,
To hold my two sisters and brothers knee high;
Two lived a few years to cough blood on the pillow,
Two dead at birth from the dust of the mine.

I can't stand here now around these cold grave mounds;
I've prayed and I've cried till my tears have run dry.
I've got to go ask that coal operator
Why he lets my folks die from that dust from his mine.

When that policeman sees me he'll think that I'm crazy,
Running wild down the street with fire in my eyes.
No, that trooper won't know about my folks in this grave hill
Killed by that dust that blows from the mine.

You can build a machine for a few silver dollars
That would clean all this dust as it flies in the skies;
I'd rather dig coal than to stand digging grave holes
For my people choked dead from that dust of the mines.

If the dicks cut me down on my way to his office,
My good union sistren and brethren, don't cry;
Make him put you to work and build that big cleaner
So you will not die, choked by dust from the mines.

—Composed September 21, 1949.

In interpreting the character of the notorious Oklahoma bad man as that of a modern Robin Hood, Guthrie merely versifies the opinion of Floyd which may still be heard around McAlester today. John Steinbeck, in *The Grapes of Wrath* (Chapter 8) reflects this view in the words of indomitable Ma Joad:

"I knowed Purty Boy Floyd. I knowed his ma. They was good folks. He was full a hell, sure, like a good boy oughta be." She paused and then her words poured out. "I don' know all like this—but I know it. He done a little bad thing a' they hurt 'im, caught 'im an' hurt him so he was mad, an' the nex' bad thing he done was mad, an' they hurt 'im again. An' purty soon he was mean-mad. They shot at him like a varmint, an' he shot back, an' then they run him like a coyote, an' him a-snappin' an' a-snarlin', mean as a lobo. An' he was mad. He wasn't no boy or no man no more, he was jus' a walkin' chunk a mean-mad. But the folks that knowed him didn't hurt 'im. He wasn' mad at them. . . ."

PRETTY BOY FLOYD

If you'll gather 'round me, children,
A story I will tell
Of Pretty Boy Floyd, an outlaw,
Oklahoma knew him well.

It was in the town of Shawnee,
It was Saturday afternoon;
His wife beside him in his wagon,
As into town they rode.

There a deputy sheriff approached him
In a manner rather rude,
Using vulgar words of language,
And his wife she overheard.

Pretty Boy grabbed a log chain,
And the deputy grabbed a gun;
And in the fight that followed,
He laid that deputy down.

He took to the trees and timbers
And he lived a life of shame;
Every crime in Oklahoma
Was added to his name.

Yes, he took to the trees and timbers
On that Canadian River's shore;
And Pretty Boy found a welcome
At a many a farmer's door.

There's a many a starving farmer
The same old story told,
How this outlaw paid their mortgage
And saved their little home.

Others tell you 'bout a stranger
That come to beg a meal,
And underneath his napkin
Left a thousand dollar bill.

It was in Oklahoma City,
It was on a Christmas Day,
There come a whole car load of groceries
With a letter that did say:

"You say that I'm an outlaw,
You say that I'm a thief;
Here's a Christmas dinner
For the families on relief."

Now as through this world I ramble,
I see lots of funny men;
Some will rob you with a six gun,
And some with a fountain pen.

But as through your life you travel,
As through your life you roam,
You won't never see an outlaw
Drive a family from their home.

AIN'T GOT NO HOME IN THIS WORLD ANYMORE

A slight adaptation of the sentimental-sacred song, "Heaven Will Be My Home."

I ain't got no home,
I'm just a-roaming round;
Just a wandering worker,
I go from town to town.
The police make it hard
Wherever I go,
And I ain't got no home in this world anymore.

My brothers and my sisters
Are stranded on this road—
It's a hot and dusty road
That a million feet have trod—
Rich man took my home
And drove me from my door,
And I ain't got no home in this world anymore.

Was a-farming on the shares,
And always I was poor,
My crops I lay
Into the banker's store,
My wife took down and died,
Upon the cabin floor,
And I ain't got no home in this world anymore.

Now as I look around,
It's very plain to see
This world is such a great
And funny place to be,
The gambling man is rich,
The working man is poor;
And I ain't got no home in this world anymore.

THE MOUND OF YOUR GRAVE

Guthrie composed this song after reading in a life of Abraham Lincoln that the President used to visit the grave of Ann Rutledge alone.

I'm down on my knees in this dark stormy midnight,
Down on my knees in this cold windy rain;
I walked half the night and I've come to your graveside,
To cry on your breast, yes, to weep on your grave.

REFRAIN: *The ground it doth moan and the earth it's a trembling;*
Our trees and our flowers they dance in our winds;
The flowers they whine, and the wild wind is whistling
As I kiss this ground on the mound of your grave.

Well, what brings me here? I know you are asking.
I know they did watch down this trail I have come;
I've come several trips on bright nights of moonlight,
And other nights come in the rains and the storms.

I've wrastled with dogs, I've wrastled my handaxe,
I jostled rail fences, I've tumbled with men.
I'm strongest of men, but I'm the weakest of weaklings,
As I walk through this rain to fall down on your grave.

I rafted my raft down that big Mississippi,
It was barrels of molasses to old New Orleans;
When I saw those slaves sold, I felt just as weak, Ann,
As I feel tonight here, down by your grave.

Your letters I've brought, they're here in my pocket,
I hear all your words blowing down 'mongst my trees;
I hope your sweet words will guide all my works, Ann,
As you guided me down to weep on your grave.

I must rise up and go, my people are calling,
They'll see all this mud on my face and my hands;
When questions they ask me, I'll come for my answers
And fall down again on this mound of your grave.

UNION MAID

While he and Pete Seeger were singing for a union meeting in
Oklahoma City in 1940, Guthrie was impressed by the number
of women who accompanied the men. The next morning Pete
Seeger found stuck in the typewriter the words to this most famous
of Guthrie's union songs. This is one of the few topical parodies
which have threatened to displace the original songs whose tunes
they borrowed. I have seen at least a half-dozen union songs written
to the tune of "Redwing," but all of them have the notation,
"Sung to the tune of Union Maid."

There are many stories about the effectiveness of the "Union
Maid." During a strike in a small Philadelphia factory in 1946 a
member of the union was arrested for alleged violence on the
picket line. After his acquittal, the members of his union marched
out of the courtroom singing, "Oh, you can't scare me, I'm stick-

ing to the union." After the strike was won, a diner across the street changed its name to "The Union Maid Restaurant."

Perhaps no incident can attest more strongly to the popularity of the "Union Maid" than that which occurred during Senator Robert Taft's 1947 meet-the-people tour. Several passengers who recognized him on the train began singing the "Union Maid." In a rather strained and obvious effort to demonstrate his close ties with the people, Taft joined in the chorus. As Shaemas O'Sheel remarked later, "Can't say it did much good, though."

(Tune: "Redwing")

There once was a union maid,
She never was afraid
Of goons and ginks and company finks
And the deputy sheriffs that made the raids;
She went to the union hall
When a meeting it was called,
And when the legion boys come 'round,
She always stood her ground.

REFRAIN: *O, you can't scare me,*
I'm stickin' to the union,
I'm stickin' to the union,
I'm stickin' to the union,
O, you can't scare me,
I'm stickin' to the union,
I'm stickin' to the union,
Till the day I die.

This union maid was wise
To the tricks of company spies;
She couldn't be fooled by a company stool,
She'd always organize the guys.
She'd always get her way
When she asked for better pay;
She'd show her card to the company guard
And this is what she'd say:

Now you gals who want to be free
Just take a little tip from me;
Get you a man who's a union man
And fight together for liberty.
Married life ain't hard
When you got a union card;
And a union man leads a happy life
When he's got a union wife.

JESUS CHRIST

"I wrote this song looking out of a rooming house window in New York City in the winter of 1940. I saw how the poor folks lived, and then I saw how the rich folks lived, and the poor folks down and out and cold and hungry, and the rich ones out drinking good whiskey and celebrating and wasting handfuls of money at gambling and women, and I got to thinking about what Jesus said, and what if He was to walk into New York City and preach like He used to. They'd lock Him back in jail as sure as you're reading this. Even as you've done it unto the least of these little ones, you have done it unto me.'"

(Tune: "Jesse James")

Jesus Christ was a man that travelled through the land,
A carpenter true and brave;
He said to the Rich, "Give your goods to the poor,"
So they laid Jesus Christ in his grave.

REFRAIN: *Yes, Jesus was a man, a carpenter by hand,*
A carpenter true and brave;
And a dirty little coward called Judas Iscariot
Has laid Jesus Christ in His grave.

The people of the land took Jesus by the hand,
They followed him far and wide;
"I come not to bring you peace but a sword,"
So they killed Jesus Christ on the sly.

He went to the sick and he went to the poor,
He went to the hungry and the lame;
He said that the poor would win this world,
So they laid Jesus Christ in his grave.

One day Jesus stopped at a rich man's door,
"What must I do to be saved?"
"You must sell your goods and give it to the poor."
So they laid Jesus Christ in his grave.

They nailed him there to die on a cross in the sky,
In the lightning and thunder and rain;
And Judas Iscariot he committed suicide
When they laid Jesus Christ in his grave.

When the love of the poor shall turn into hate,
When the patience of the workers gives away,
"Twould be better for you rich if you'd never been born,
For you laid Jesus Christ in his grave."

This song was written in New York City,
Of rich men, preachers and slaves;
If Jesus was to preach like he preached in Galilee,
They would lay Jesus Christ in his grave.

Joe Glazer

Joe Glazer is a particularly talented representative of a group of composers who are contributing heavily to union song collections today. These men (almost all of whom are union educational directors) are either professional song writers or experienced amateurs who have not quite reached that elevated status of conscious artistry. They are of course not writers of folksongs (though a few of them entertain that pretension) nor is there any evidence that they have been received by the folk, but their songs are of such numerical importance in the contemporary union singing movement with which this study is so largely concerned that parenthetical mention at least should be made of them here.

Glazer is not one of the most prolific of these writers, for he has composed only about a dozen union songs, but he is one of the best. His recently published album of union records[23] is perhaps the best of its kind. The quality of these songs, their arrangements, and their rendition, is high enough to warrant their presence in the record cabinet of, say, a coal operator. In other words, they are of genuine worth purely as a source of entertainment.

A native of metropolitan New York, Glazer himself could not by any extension of definitive limits be classed as a member of the "folk." His closest association with folk music before being drawn into union activity was an abashed partiality for cowboy and hillbilly music of the more debased sort, an imperfection of his musical appreciativeness which he purged himself of while attending Brooklyn College. As an undergraduate he wrote a

[23] *Eight New Songs for Labor,* CIO Department of Education and Research Album.

number of college shows which featured novelty songs of an amateur and semi-professional nature. After graduation he tried to write songs professionally and, though he succeeded in getting one song published—a hot novelty number entitled "Yogi Yogi" which was subsequently performed with unbounded applause by one of the leading swing bands—he gave up this precarious vocation for a less glamorous but more substantial employment as an educational director for the Textile Workers Union of America.

During his seven years with TWUA he composed a few songs which more or less regularly appear in new union songbooks, but as he sees it, his most important accomplishment was his pioneering work in the field of union group singing. Appalled by the dullness and apathy that characterized most nonmilitant union meetings, he felt that only a strong group-singing program, relentlessly administered, would preserve in time of industrial peace that solidarity of purpose and warm camaraderie which seem spontaneously to appear during strikes and similar manifestations of labor unrest. His success with his program has led other union educational directors to adopt his ideas.

His association with the textile union and other labor groups has given Joe Glazer many opportunities to observe the workers as singers and composers. He has articulated a few of these impressions into generalizations which, since they coincide with my own observations, may be stated here:

1. 99 per cent of American industrial workers do not sing labor protest songs except during strikes.
2. Rural workers are by far the most productive in the matter of union songs and songs of social and economic protest.
3. Most songs of this nature come from the rural South.
4. Labor protest songs, except the very simple and the very good ones, have no chance to become traditional (for the reasons enumerated in the introduction to this study).

The question "How were these songs made?" hopefully but vainly asked of all informants by all collectors interested in formulating useful theories on the origin of folksong, demonstrated its usual sterility when submitted to Joe Glazer. Despite his high degree of literateness, the answers were different for most of his songs, and for all were discouragingly vague. The only defensible generalization which could be extracted from his various methods of composition was that a song starts with an idea.

The idea for "The Mill Was Made of Marble" allegedly derived from a verbose and declamatory poem of the same title which appeared "about three years ago" in the journal *Textile Labor,* but when Glazer checked back for copyright clearance, the editor of *Textile Labor* could find no poem by that title in his files. At any rate, the phrase "the mill was made of marble" impinged on his consciousness at some time and from some source, and later, after a period of mental gestation, reappeared as the idea for a song on the theme of a heavenly textile mill. It remained suspended in this stage of evolution for about a year until he mentioned the idea to (Margaret) Pat Knight at a Textile Education School session. Together they worked out the refrain and a tentative melody. With something tangible now to build upon, Glazer added lines, couplets, and stanzas to the nucleus, and revised the tune to fit the new words. When he had the song completed, he submitted it to Pat Knight for her ideas on final polishing, but she told him, "This is not the song we worked on together."

THE MILL WAS MADE OF MARBLE

I dreamed that I had died
And gone to my reward;
A job in heaven's textile plant,
On a golden boulevard.

REFRAIN: *Where the mill was made of marble*
The machines were made out of gold,
Where nobody ever got tired,
And nobody ever grew old.

The mill was built in a garden
No dust or lint could be found;
The air was so fresh and so fragrant,
With flowers and trees all around.

It was quiet and peaceful in heaven,
There was no clatter or boom;
You could hear the most beautiful music,
As you worked at the spindle or loom.

There was no unemployment in heaven,
We worked steady all through the year;
We always had food for the children,
We never were haunted by fear.

When I woke from this dream about heaven,
I knew that there never could be
A mill like that one down below here on earth
For workers like you and like me.

The inspired title and refrain line, "Too old to work and too young to die," which distinguishes the song Glazer wrote for the United Auto Workers' pension fight, is regrettably not his own. He confesses, "This line and—except for the meter-induced repetition—the whole refrain, comes from Walter Reuther's pension speech; and the first stanza fell naturally out of the refrain." After adapting Reuther's lines to fit the meter and rime of a rough melody, Glazer found that his inspiration had died, or rather, that it had gone into a dormant state, where it reposed for six months. Just before the Chrysler strike in 1950 he talked the incipient song over with several other union leaders and, working together under his general direction, these recruits produced the other three stanzas. The lack of unity and coherence which identifies communally produced song is evident in the almost perfect interchangeability of the rimed couplets in the second and third stanzas. Only in the first stanza, which Glazer wrote alone, and in the final stanza, which achieves continuity through its thematic recapitulation, is there any clear logical dependence between the four lines of the quatrain.

Recognizing the strong overtones of the ubiquitous "Villikins and His Dinah" in the music of the latter part of the stanzas, I commended him on his adaptation. But he denied any knowledge of "Villikins and His Dinah." "Do you know 'Sweet Betsy from Pike'?" I asked him. He said he didn't know that either, but when I sang a stanza or two of "Sweet Betsy" for him, he admitted having heard it somewhere before. With admirable objectivity, he agreed that there may have been some subconscious borrowing of this once-heard tune when he made up the music for "Too Old to Work."

TOO OLD TO WORK

You work in the factory all of your life,
Try to provide for your kids and your wife;
When you get too old to produce anymore
They hand you your hat and they show you the door.

REFRAIN: *Too old to work, too old to work,*
When you're too old to work and you're too young to die;
Who will take care of you? How'll you get by?
When you're too old to work and you're too young to die?

You don't ask for favors when your life is through,
You've got a right to what's coming to you;
Your boss gets a pension when he is too old,
You helped him retire—you're out in the cold.

They put horses to pasture, they feed them on hay,
Even machines get retired some day;
The bosses get pensions when their days are through,
Fat pensions for them, brother, nothing for you.

There's no easy answer, there's no easy cure;
Dreaming won't change it, that's one thing for sure;
But fighting together we'll get there some day,
And when we have won you will no longer say . . .

"That's All" is simply a union parody, like hundreds of others, of a semi-religious Negro song—in this case one popularized by the gospel singer, Sister Rosetta Tharpe. Glazer said that this is largely the product of group collaboration.

THAT'S ALL

REFRAIN: *That's all (that's all, that's all)*
I tell you that's all (that's all, that's all)
You got to be a union member, I tell you—
that's all (that's all, that's all)

You can go to college, you can go to school
But if you ain't a union man you're just an educated fool.

They're working you so hard that you're about to drop,
You straighten out the boss with a union shop.

If your congressman won't listen to what you have to say
Just tell him you'll remember on election day.

"I Ain't No Stranger Now," and "Shine on Me" are simplified adaptations of sacred songs which Glazer first heard sung by Negroes. The idea for the adaptation of both of these songs came from a group of textile workers whom he met at a North Carolina CIO union school in 1947.

I AIN'T NO STRANGER NOW

REFRAIN: *I ain't (no I ain't) no stranger now (no I ain't)*
I ain't (no I ain't) no stranger now (no I ain't)
Since I've been introducëd to the CIO
I ain't no stranger now.

Run scab (run to the boss) and hide your face (run to the boss)
Run scab (run to the boss) and hide your face (run to the boss)
Won't you run to the boss and hide your face
I ain't no stranger now.

I'm a union man (I feel so good) in a union town (I feel so good)
I'm a union man (I feel so good) in a union town (I feel so good)
I'm a union man in a union town
I ain't no stranger now.

Brother, sign (put your name down here) a card today (put your
name down here)
Brother, sign (put your name down here) a card today (put your
name down here)
Won't you come and sign a card today
You'll be no stranger now.

SHINE ON ME

REFRAIN: *Shine on me, shine on me,*
Let the light of the union—shine on me
Shine on me, shine on me,
Let the light of the union—shine on me.

Once I had no union but now I've got one
Since I joined the union I've got the blues on the run.
No starvation wages, no more misery
Since the light of the union has shined on me.

"Humblin' Back," a pleasingly facile parody on "St. James Infirmary," depends like "Too Old to Work" on an inspired thematic
line, and again the line is regrettably not original. In this case
it comes from a North Carolina organizer named Draper Wood,
who believed in consolidating his advances before he made them.
"Don't get yourself out on a limb," he frequently advised, " 'cause
you'll have to come a-humblin' back." The rest of the song, Glazer
says, was written with great deliberation and at one sitting.

HUMBLIN' BACK
(Tune: "St. James Infirmary" with variations)

I was workin' in a plant way down in Georgia
Conditions were bad that's a fact.
When I tried to do something about it
I always came a-humblin' back.
I went fishin' with the foreman on Sunday
I thought I had the inside track;
But he forgot me early on Monday
And I had to come a-humblin' back.

REFRAIN: *Humblin' (humblin')*
Humblin' (humblin')
I had to come a-humblin' back (that mornin')
Humblin' (humblin')
Humblin' (humblin')
I had to come a-humblin' back.

They asked me to join up with the union;
I said, "Nothin' doin' here, Mac."
The union man said "Brother, you'll be sorry;
Someday you'll come a-humblin' back."
So I went to the boss one mornin'
Just to try to get a little more jack;
But he was very dis-encouragin'
And I had to come a-humblin' back.

Now things was getting rough way down in Georgia
I was feelin' like a sad, sad, sack.
I was gettin' mighty tired and weary
Cause I always came a-humblin' back.
So I talked to the boys all around me;
I talked to Joe, I talked to Pete, I talked to Zack;
And we joined up, yes we joined up with the union,
So we'd never come a-humblin' back.

Now things are lookin' up way down in Georgia
We're rollin' on the union track;
You can do it like we did it in Georgia
And you'll never come a-humblin' back.

"And this was a song that wrote itself," says Glazer, after he hit upon the pun, S-L-Avery. The song derives of course from the Montgomery Ward strike famous in photographic history for the picture of S. L. Avery, Montgomery Ward's president, being carried out of the building by two soldiers.

MONKEY WARD[24] CAN'T MAKE A MONKEY OUT OF ME
Monkey Ward can't make a monkey out of me;
The union will protect me from S-L-Avery;
I'm not a slave and I won't behave
Just like a chimpanzee—
Monkey Ward can't make a monkey out of me.

Now if he breaks the union, here's how it's gonna be,
You'll be just like a monkey a-climbing in a tree.
You'll jump around and kiss the ground
For Sewell Avery—
Monkey Ward can't make a monkey out of me.

REFRAIN: *Get wise! Organize!*
It's your only chance for real democracy.
Get wise! Organize!
Will you be a man or a monkey?

We're gonna make a monkey out of Sewell Avery;
We'll feed him on bananas and we'll stick him in a tree;
We'll twist his tail around a nail
And then we'll shout with glee—
Monkey Ward can't make a monkey out of me.

"But Montgomery Ward won the strike and broke the union," adds Glazer, "and we sang 'Monkey Ward has made a monkey out of us.'"

[24] Monkey Ward: Montgomery Ward.

Appendix

Songs of Social and Economic Protest on Records

AIN'T IT HARD TO BE A RIGHT BLACK NIGGER? James (Iron Head) Baker, Central state farm, Sugarland, Tex. Library of Congress, Archive of American Folk Song* 202 B1, 617 B2, 721 B1 and B2.

AIN'T THIS A MEAN WORLD TO LIVE IN? Four unidentified Negroes, Belle Glade, Fla. L of C, AAFS 374 B.

AIN'T WORKIN' SONG. Charley Campbell, State docks, Mobile, Ala. L of C, AAFS 1336 B2.

ALL OUT AND DOWN. Huddie Ledbetter (Leadbelly). Melotone 0314.

ATOMIC ENERGY. Sir Lancelot. Charter 102.

BAD HOUSING BLUES. Josh White. Keynote album 107 ("Southern Exposure").

BALL AND CHAIN BLUES. Unidentified Negro convict, State penintentiary, Nashville, Tenn. L of C, AAFS 178 A2.

BALLAD OF F.D.R. Tom Glazer and group. Asch album 200.

BEANS, BACON, AND GRAVY. Gladys, Matilda, and Juanita Crouch, St. Louis, Mo. L of C, AAFS SR 43.

THE BEGGAR DREW NIGH. Mrs. Vera Kilgore, Highlander Folk School, Monteagle, Tenn. L of C, AAFS 2938 B4.

BEN BUTLER. Mrs. A. G. Griffin, Newberry, Fla. L of C, AAFS 955 A4.

BIG ROCK CANDY MOUNTAINS. Harry (Mac) McClintock. Victor 21704.

BLOWIN' DOWN THIS ROAD. Woody Guthrie. Victor album P 27 ("Dust Bowl Ballads").

BOSS MAN, I AIN'T WORKIN' FOR YOU. Victoria Wilson, New Bight, Cat Island, Bahamas. L of C, AAFS 413 A1.

* Hereafter abbreviated L of C, AAFS

BOUND FOR CANAAN. Ed Griffin and the Sacred Harp Singers, Meridian, Miss. L of C, AAFS 3040 A1.

BOURGEOIS BLUES. Huddie Ledbetter (Leadbelly). Musicraft 227; L of C, AAFS 2502 B2.

BREAD AND ROSES. I.L.G.W.U. Record Number Two.

BUFFALO SKINNERS. Woody Guthrie. Disc album 360 ("Struggle").

C.C.C. BLUES.

Washboard Sam. Bluebird B 7993.

Unidentified group of boys, Brawley, Cal. L of C, AAFS 3561 B1.

Jimmy Collins, Brawley, Cal. L of C, AAFS 3563 A2.

Clay Begley, Middlefork, Ky. L of C, AAFS 1454 A3.

CAN'T HELP FROM CRYIN' SOMETIMES. Josh White. Perfect 0285.

CAPTAIN, CAPTAIN, DON'T YOU SEE? Charley Jones, Eatonville, Fla. L of C, AAFS 363 B2.

CAP'N, DID YOU HEAR? James Hale and George James, Atmore state prison farm, Atmore, Ala. L of C, AAFS 943 B2.

CAP'N, DID YOU HEAR 'BOUT? Ed Cobb, Livingston, Ala. L of C, AAFS 1330 A1.

CAPTAIN GOT A LONG CHAIN. George Goram, Culpeper, Va. L of C, AAFS 733 B2.

CAPTAIN, I AM GETTIN' TIRED. Willis Carter and group, State docks, Mobile, Ala. L of C, AAFS 1336 A2.

CAP'N, I HEARD WHAT YOU SAID. George James, Atmore state prison farm, Atmore, Ala. L of C, AAFS 943 A3.

CASEY JONES (THE UNION SCAB). Tom Glazer. "Favorite American Union Songs" album, CIO Dept. of Education and Research.

CHAIN AROUND MY LEG. Woody Guthrie. L of C, AAFS 3415 B2.

CHAIN GANG. Mr. and Mrs. Jack Bryant, Firebaugh FSA camp, Firebaugh, Cal. L of C, AAFS 4148 B1.

CHAIN GANG BLUES.

James Hale, Atmore state prison farm, Atmore, Ala. L of C, AAFS 934 B1.

Kokoma Arnold. Decca 7069.

CHAIN GANG BOUN'. Josh White. Columbia album C-22 ("Chain Gang").

CHAIN GANG SONG.

Vernon Dalhart. Brunswick 2911.

Leroy Ramsay, Frederica, Ga. L of C, AAFS 338 A1, 339 A and B.

CIO UNION SONG. Aunt Molly Jackson. L of C, AAFS 2534 B.

CITIZEN CIO. Tom Glazer, Josh White. Asch album 349 ("Songs of Citizen CIO").

CLOAK MAKERS' UNION. Gladys, Matilda, and Juanita Crouch. St. Louis, Mo. L of C, AAFS 3197 A2.

COAL AND COKE LINE. Addison Boserman, Tygart Valley Homesteads, Elkins, W. Va. L of C, AAFS 2571 B1.

COAL CREEK TROUBLES. Jilson Setters, Ashland, Ky. L of C, AAFS 1017 A.

COAL MINER'S BLUES. Carter family. Decca 46086.

THE COAL MINER'S CHILD. Aunt Molly Jackson. L of C, AAFS 2575 A and B.

COME ALL YOU COAL MINERS. Sarah Ogan. L of C, AAFS 1944 A.

COME ALL YOU HARDY MINERS. Findlay Donaldson, Pineville, Ky. L of C, AAFS 1985 A1

CORN BREAD TOUGH. Huddie Ledbetter (Leadbelly). Disc album 745 ("Work Songs of the U.S.A.").

COTTON FARMER BLUES. Sampson Pittman, Detroit, Mich. L of C, AAFS 2479 B.

COTTON MILL BLUES. Lester the Highwayman. Decca. 5559.

COTTON MILL COLIC. Joe Sharp, Wash., D.C. L of C, AAFS 1629 B2.

COTTON PATCH BLUES. Tommy McClennan. Bluebird 8408.

COTTON PICKIN' BLUES. Robert Restway. Bluebird 9036.

COOLEE (COULEE) DAM. Woody Guthrie. Asch album 347 ("Woody Guthrie").

CROSSBONES SCULLY (T-BONE SLIM). Aunt Molly Jackson. L of C, AAFS 2539 B and 2556 A.

CRYIN' WHO? CRYIN' YOU. Josh White. Columbia album C-22 ("Chain Gang Songs").

CWA BLUES. Walter Roland. Melotone 13103 and Perfect 0293.

DARK AS A DUNGEON. Merle Travis. Capitol album AD-50 ("Folk Songs of the Hills").

DEATH OF HARRY SIMMS. Pete Seeger. Charter C-45.

DEATH OF JOHN HENRY.
Wilby Toomey. Silvertone 6005.
Uncle Dave Macon. Brunswick album B 1024 ("Listen to Our Story").

DEFENSE BLUES. Huddie Ledbetter (Leadbelly), Brownie McGhee, Pops Foster, and Willie the Lion Smith. Disc 5085.

DEFENSE FACTORY BLUES. Josh White. Keynote album 107 ("Southern Exposure").

DEPRESSION BLUES. Tampa Red. Vocalion 1656.

DICKMAN SONG. Gladys, Matilda, and Juanita Crouch, St. Louis, Mo. L of C, AAFS 43 B3 and SR 44 B1.

DIDN'T KNOW I HAD TO BOW SO LOW. James Washington and group, Reid state farm, Boykin, S.C. L of C, AAFS 706 A2.

THE DISHONEST MILLER.
Aunt Molly Jackson. L of C, AAFS 2553 B.
Bascom Lamar Lunsford. L of C, AAFS 1786 B2.

DO RE MI. Woody Guthrie. Victor album P-27 ("Dust Bowl Ballads," vol. I).

THE DODGER SONG.
Almanac Singers. General 5018.
Mrs. Emma Dusenbury, Mena, Ark. L of C, AAFS 3230 B2.
A DOLLAR AIN'T A DOLLAR ANYMORE.
Priority Ramblers. L of C, AAFS 7054 A1.
Union Boys. Asch album 346 ("Songs for Victory").
DON'T TAKE AWAY MY PWA. Jimmie Gordon. Decca 7230.
DOWN IN A COAL MINE. Morgan Jones. L of C, AAFS 1438.
DOWN THE STREET WE HOLD OUR DEMONSTRATION. Alice and Johnny,
St. Louis, Mo. L of C, AAFS 3195 A1.
DRESSMAKERS' VICTORY SONG. I.L.G.W.U. Record Number One.
DRILL, YE TARRIERS, DRILL. Earl Robinson. Keynote album 132
("Americana"). L of C, AAFS 1627 A1.
DUST BOWL REFUGEES. Woody Guthrie. L of C, AAFS 3418 B1, 3422 A.
DUST PNEUMONIA SONG. Woody Guthrie. L of C, AAFS 3420 A2.
DUSTY OLD DUST. Woody Guthrie. Victor album P-28 ("Dust Bowl
Ballads," vol. 2).
THE DYING HOBO. Kelly Harrell. Victor 20527.
EAST BROOKFIELD WOOLEN MILL. Elmer Barton, Quebec, Vt. L of C,
AAFS 3697 B2.
EAST OHIO MINERS' STRIKE. Aunt Molly Jackson. L of C, AAFS 1940 B.
EMPTY POCKET BLUES. Bill Atkins. L of C, AAFS 1922 A.
FARE YOU WELL OLD ELIE (ELY) BRANCH. Aunt Molly Jackson, L of
C, AAFS 1939 B.
FARMIN' MAN BLUES. Luscious Curtin, Natchez, Miss. L of C, AAFS
4004 A1.
FIFTY YEARS AGO. Dick Wright. "Sing a Labor Song" album, Main
Street Records.
FIGHT FOR UNION RECOGNITION. Bert and Ruby Rains, Bakersfield,
Cal. L of C, AAFS 4141 A2.
FRANKLIN ROOSEVELT. Jilson Setters, Ashland, Ky. L of C, AAFS 1010
B1.
FREEDOM BLUES. Earl Robinson. Alco album A2.
FREEDOM ROAD. Josh White. Asch album 349 ("Songs of Citizen CIO").
FRISCO STRIKE SAGA. Ethel Peterson and students of Bryn Mawr Labor
College, Bryn Mawr, Pa. L of C, AAFS 1771 A and B1.
THE GALLIS POLE. Huddie Ledbetter (Leadbelly). Musicraft 227.
GET THEE BEHIND ME. Almanac Singers. Keynote album 106 ("Talking
Union").
GIVE ME BACK MY JOB AGAIN. Jim Garland. L of C, AAFS 1946 B.
GO DOWN MOSES.
Hampton Institute Quartet. Victor album P-78.
Hall Johnson choir. Victor 4553.
Southern Male Quartet. Columbia 8479.
Tuskegee Quartet. Victor 20518.

Go Down Moses—*Continued*
  Edna Thomas. Columbia 1606 D.
  Kenneth Spencer. Sonora album MS-478.
  Carl Sandburg. Decca album A-356.
  Marian Anderson. Victor 1799.
  The Jubilaires. King 4167.
  Paul Robeson. Columbia album M-610.
God Made Us All. Lord Invader. Disc 5080.
Goin' Down the Road Feelin' Bad.
  Tom Glazer. "Favorite American Union Songs," CIO Dept. of
  Education and Research album.
  Ray Melton, Galax, Va. L of C, AAFS 1347 A2.
  Hobart Ricker, Wash., D.C. L of C, AAFS 3903 B5.
  Woody Guthrie. L of C, AAFS 3418 A1.
  Warde H. Ford, Central Valley, Cal. L of C, AAFS 4206 A2.
  Gussie Ward Stone, Arvin FSA camp, Arvin, Cal. L of C, AAFS
  4103 B1.
  Bascom Lamar Lunsford. L of C, AAFS 1805 B1.
  Ollie Crownover and group, Brawley migratory camp, Brawley,
  Cal. L of C, AAFS 3562 B2.
  Rex and James Hardie, Shafter, Cal. L of C, AAFS 3566 A1.
Goin' Home, Boys. Josh White. Columbia album C-22 ("Chain Gang
  Songs").
Goin' to Roll the Union on. *See* Roll the Union on.
Gray Goose.
  Huddie Ledbetter (Leadbelly) and Golden Gate Quartet. Victor
  album P-50. ("Midnight Special").
  Huddie Ledbetter (Leadbelly), Woody Guthrie, Cisco Houston.
  Disc album 726 ("Midnight Special").
  Earl Robinson. Timely 501.
  Alan Lomax. L of C, AAFS 1617 A.
  Augustus (Track Horse) Haggerty and group of Negro convicts,
  state penitenitary, Huntsville, Tex. L of C, AAFS 223 A2 and
  1937 A.
  Huddie Ledbetter (Leadbelly). L of C, AAFS 155 B.
  James (Iron Head) Baker and group of Negro convicts, Central
  state farm, Sugarland, Tex. L of C, AAFS 205 A3.
  Washington (Lightnin'). Darrington state farm, Sandy Point, Tex.
  L of C, AAFS 182 A.
Great Day. Joe Glazer. "Eight New Songs for Labor," CIO Dept. of
  Education and Research album.
Great Day. Michael Loring. Progressive Party record.
The Great Dust Storm. Woody Guthrie. Victor album P-28 ("Dust
  Bowl Ballads," vol. 2)

HALLELUJAH, I'M A BUM. Harry (Mac) McClintock. Bluebird B 11083, Victor 21343.

HALLELUJAH, I'M A TRAVELIN'. Pete Seeger. Charter C-45.

HAM AND EGGS.

Huddie Ledbetter (Leadbelly) and Golden Gate Quartet. Victor album P-50 ("Midnight Special").

Huddie Ledbetter (Leadbelly), Woody Guthrie, Cisco Houston. Disc album 726 ("Midnight Special").

HARD TIMES.

Crockett Ward, Galax, Va. L of C, AAFS 1363 A1.

Liberty High School quartet, near Newton, Tex. L of C, AAFS 2653 B3.

Mrs. Pete Steele, Hamilton, Ohio. L of C, AAFS 1711 A.

Roland Franklin, O. B. Duncan, and Frank Brown, San Antonio, Tex. L of C, AAFS 669 A1 and A2.

Woody Guthrie. L of C, AAFS 3412 A1.

Mrs. Minnie Floyd. Murrell's Inlet, S.C. L of C, AAFS 2719 A.

HARD TIMES BLUES. Josh White. Musicraft album N-3 ("Harlem Blues"), and Keynote album 107 ("Southern Exposure").

HARD TIMES IN COLMAN'S MINES. Aunt Molly Jackson. L of C, AAFS 2532 and 2535 A.

HARD TIMES IN FOXRIDGE MINES. Jim Garland. L of C, AAFS 1950 A2.

HARD TIMES IN KANSAS. George Vinton Graham, San Jose, Cal. L of C, AAFS 3375 B3.

HARD TIMES IN THESE MINES. Finlay (Red Ore) Donaldson. L of C, AAFS 1985 A2 and B1

HARD TIMES, PO' BOY. Gant family, Austin, Tex. L of C, AAFS 70 A3.

HARD TRAVELING. Woody Guthrie. Disc album 610 ("Ballads from the Dust Bowl").

HARLAN JAIL. Unidentified union organizer. L of C, AAFS 1529 A3 and B1.

HENRY FORD BLUES. Huddie Ledbetter (Leadbelly). L of C, AAFS 143 B.

HIGH PRICE BLUES. Brownie McGhee. Encore record.

HIGHROJARAM. Katharine Trusty, Paintsville, Ky. L of C, AAFS 1936 A1.

THE HIGHWAY HOBO. Noel Westbrook, Shafter FSA camp, Shafter, Cal. L of C, AAFS 4112 B.

HIGHWAY 66. Woody Guthrie. L of C, AAFS 3422 B2 and 3423 A1.

HOBO BILL'S LAST RIDE. Jimmie Rodgers. Victor 22421.

HOBO, YOU CAN'T RIDE THIS TRAIN. Louis Armstrong. Bluebird 6501.

HOBO'S LULLABY. Woody Guthrie. Stinson 716.

HOLD ON.

Priority Ramblers. L of C. AAFS 7054 B1.

Union Boys. Asch album 346 ("Songs for Victory").

HOLD THE FORT.
  Tom Glazer. "Favorite American Union Songs," CIO Department of Education and Research album.
  I.L.G.W.U. Record Number Two.
  Union Boys. Asch album 346 ("Songs for Victory").
HORACE GREELEY. Earl Robinson. Timely 501.
THE HOUSE I LIVE IN.
  Earl Robinson. Keynote album 132 ("Americana").
  Josh White. Stinson album 348 ("Songs by Josh White").
HOUSE RENT BLUES. Clarence Williams. Okeh 8171.
HUMBLIN' BACK. Joe Glazer. "Eight New Songs for Labor," CIO Department of Education and Research album.
HUNGRY DISGUSTED BLUES. Aunt Molly Jackson. L of C, AAFS 2538 A.
I AIN'T GOT NO HOME IN THIS WORLD ANYMORE. Woody Guthrie. Victor 26624.
I AIN'T GONNA BE TREATED THISAWAY. Gilbert Fike, Little Rock, Ark. L of C, AAFS 3187 A2.
I AIN'T NO STRANGER NOW. Joe Glazer. "Eight New Songs for Labor," CIO Dept. of Education and Research album.
I AM A GIRL OF CONSTANT SORROW. Sarah Ogan. L of C, AAFS 1945 A.
I'M A LOOKIN' FOR A HOME. Hootenanny Singers. Asch album 370 ("Roll the Union on").
I'M ALL OUT AND DOWN. Huddie Ledbetter (Leadbelly). L of C, AAFS 144 A.
I'M GOIN' TO ORGANIZE, BABY MINE. Sarah Ogan. L of C, AAFS 1952 A2 and B1.
I'M ON MY WAY TO CANAAN'S LAND. Carter family. Bluebird 8167.
I ASKED MY CAPTAIN WHAT TIME OF DAY. Ed Jones, Greenville, Miss. L of C, AAFS 3092 B1.
I'M WORRIED NOW AND I WON'T BE WORRIED LONG.
  Tom Bell, Livingston, Ala. L of C, AAFS 4067 A1.
  Mrs. Lucile Henson, San Antonio, Tex. L of C, AAFS 541 B1, B2.
I BELONG TO THE UNION BAND. Sally Nelson, Riviera, Fla. L of C, AAFS 3381 A2.
I DON'T WANT YOUR MILLIONS, MISTER. Tilman Cadle, Middlesboro, Ky. L of C, AAFS 1401 A1
I'VE GOT A BALLOT. Michael Loring. Progressive party record.
I GOT SHOES. Edna Thomas. Columbia 1863-D.
I'VE JUST COME DOWN FROM THE WHITE FOLKS' HOUSE. Mrs. George White, Saline, Tex. L of C, AAFS 923 A2.
I JUST CAN'T FEEL AT HOME IN THIS WORLD ANY MORE. Group of Negro men and women, Cockrus, Miss. L of C, AAFS 3009 B1.
I.L.G.W.U. ANTHEM. I.L.G.W.U. Record Number One.
IF YOU AIN'T GOT THE DO RE MI. Woody Guthrie. L of C, AAFS 3421 B1.

IN MY HEART. John Handcox. L of C, AAFS 3237 B2.
IN THE LAND OF PEACE AND PLENTY. Gladys, Matilda, and Juanita
Crouch, St. Louis, Mo. L of C, AAFS 3197 B2.
IN WASHINTON. Priority Ramblers. L of C, AAFS 7054 B3.
INTERNATIONALE. I.L.G.W.U. Record Number One.
IT'S A CRUEL WORLD FOR ME. Floyd Tilman. Columbia 20360.
JEFFERSON AND LIBERTY.
Earl Robinson, Keynote album 132 ("Americana").
American Ballad Singers. Bost album ES-1 ("Songs of Early
America").
JERRY.
Josh White. Columbia album C-22 ("Chain Gang Songs").
Stinson album 358 ("Folk Songs").
JESUS CHRIST. Woody Guthrie. Asch album 347 ("Woody Guthrie").
JIM CROW.
Josh White. Decca album A-611 ("Ballads and Blues").
Josh White and the Union Boys. Asch album 346 ("Songs for Vic-
tory").
California Labor School Chorus. CLS record.
JIM CROW TRAIN. Josh White. Keynote album 107 ("Southern Ex-
posure").
JOE HILL.
Earl Robinson. General G-30.
Paul Robeson. Columbia M 534.
Michael Loring. Theme T-100.
JOHN HENRY.
Salty Holmes and his Brown County Boys. Decca 46116.
Riley Puckett. Columbia 14031.
Richard Dyer-Bennett. Asch 461-3.
Earl Robinson. Timely 8.
Spencer Trio. Decca 63779.
Gid Tanner and his Skillet Lickers. Columbia 15019 and 15142.
Henry Thomas. Vocalion 1094.
J. E. Mainer's Mountaineers. Bluebird 6629.
Earl Johnson. Okeh 45101.
Dixieland Jazz Group. Victor 27545.
Wilby Toomey. Silvertone 6005.
Bob and Joe Shelton. Decca 5173.
Paul Robeson. Columbia M-610 ("Spirituals").
Huddie Ledbetter (Leadbelly). Disc 734, L of C, AAFS 2503 B and
2504 A.
Josh White. Keynote K 125 and Decca A 447.
Merle Travis. Capitol 48000.
John Jacob Niles. Victor 2051.
J. E. Mainer. King 550.

JOHN HENRY—*Continued*

Tom Scott. Signature album S-5 ("Sing of America").

Bernard Steffen and Charles Pollock, Wash., D. C. L of C, AAFS 3304 B1.

Farmer Collett, Middlefork, Ky. L of C, AAFS 1429 A2 and B1.

Gabriel Brown, Eatonville, Fla. L of C, AAFS 355 A and B.

John Davis, Frederica, Ga. L of C, AAFS 313 A1.

M. Asher, Hyden, Ky. L of C, AAFS 1519 A2.

Mrs. Winnie Prater, Salyersville, Ky. L of C, AAFS 1593 A3 and B1.

Paul, Wade, and Vernon Miles, Canton, Ohio. L of C, AAFS 4075 B2.

Pete Steele, Hamilton, Ohio. L of C, AAFS 1711 A2.

Chester Allen, Scottsboro, Ala. L of C, AAFS 2943 A2 and B1.

Arthur Bell, Cumins state farm, Gould, Ark. L of C, AAFS 2668 B1.

Aunt Molly Jackson. L of C, AAFS 2551 A1.

Austin Harmon, Maryville, Tenn. L of C, AAFS 2916 B2 and 2917 A1.

Bascom Lamar Lunsford. Leicester, N. C. L. of C, AAFS 3617 B1.

Bill Atkins, Pineville, Ky. L of C, AAFS 1989 B1.

Booker T. Sapps, R .G. Matthews, and Willy Flowers, Belle Glade, Fla. L of C, AAFS 371B

Charles Griffin, Kilby prison, Montgomery, Ala. L of C, AAFS 238 A.

Charley Jones, Eatonville, Fla. L of C, AAFS 365 B2.

Dr. Chapman J. Milling, Columbia, S. C. L of C, AAFS 3789 B.

Fields Ward and Dr. W. P. Davis, with Bogtrotters' Band, Galax, Va. L of C, AAFS 1362 B.

Fields Ward, Galax, Va. L of C, AAFS 4085 A1.

George Roark, Pineville, Ky. L of C, AAFS 1997 A.

Group of Negro convicts, state penitentiary, Parchman, Miss. L of C, AAFS 1865 A2.

Group of Negro convicts, state prison farm, Oakley, Miss. L of C, AAFS 1867 B1.

Group of Negro convicts, work house, Memphis, Tenn. L of C, AAFS 174 B3.

Gus Harper and group, state penitentiary, Parchman, Miss. L of C, AAFS 883 B3.

Harold B. Hazelhurst, Jacksonville, Fla. L of C, AAFS 3143 A2.

Hettie Godfrey, Livingston, Ala. L of C, AAFS 4049 B5.

J. M. Mullins, Salyersville, Ky. L of C, AAFS 1595 A1.

J. Owens, state penitentiary, Richmond, Va. L of C, AAFS 730 A.

Jim Henry, state penitentiary, Parchman, Miss. L of C, AAFS 743 A1.

Joe Brown, state farm, Raiford, Fla. L of C, AAFS 2710 B.

Joe Edwards, state penitentiary, Parchman, Miss. L of C, AAFS 743 A2.

John Henry Jackson and Norman Smith, state penitentiary, Parchman, Miss. L of C, AAFS 3088 A2 and B1.

JOHN HENRY—*Continued*

Jonesie Mack, Nick Robinson, and James Mack, Charleston, S. C. L of C, AAFS 1047 A2.

Julius Clemens, state farm, Raiford, Fla. L of C, AAFS 689 A.

Mrs. Vera Kilgore, Highlander Folk School, Monteagle, Tenn. L of C, AAFS 2939 A1.

Unidentified Negro convict, state penitentiary, Parchman, Miss. L of C, AAFS 1864 B3.

Reese Crenshaw, state prison farm, Milledgeville, Ga. L of C, AAFS 259 A2.

Richard Amerson, Livingston, Ala. L of C, AAFS 1305 B2 and 4045 A2 and B1.

Samson Pittman, Detroit, Mich. L of C, AAFS 2479 A.

Skyline Farms group, Washington, D. C. L of C, AAFS 1629 A.

Thomas Anderson, New York. L of C, AAFS 3636 A2 and B.

Uncle Alec Dunford, Galax, Va. L of C, AAFS 1363 A3.

Veral Hall, Livingston, Ala. L of C, AAFS 1320 A2.

JOHN HENRY WAS A VERY SMALL BOY. Thomas Anderson, New York. L of C, AAFS 3635 B2.

JOHN J. CURTIS. Andrew Rada, Shenandoah, Pa. L of C, AAFS 1435.

JOHNNY, WON'T YOU RAMBLE. Group of Negro convicts, Darrington state farm, Sandy Point, Tex. L of C, AAFS 190 A1.

JOIN THE CIO. Aunt Molly Jackson. L of C, AAFS 1939 A1.

JOIN THE UNION TONIGHT. John Handcox. L of C, AAFS 3237 B1.

KENTUCKY MINERS' DREADFUL FATE (FIGHT). Aunt Molly Jackson. L of C, AAFS 1940 A and 1941 B.

LABOR DAY. Dick Wright. "Sing a Labor Song" album, Main Street Records.

LEAVE HER, JOHNNY. Bluebird B-511; album BC-8 ("Songs under the Sails").

LEAVE HER, JOHNNY, LEAVE HER. Captain Richard Maitland, Sailors' Snug Harbor, Staten Island, N. Y. L of C, AAFS 2533 B2.

LET'S ALL SHED A TEAR FOR THE BOSSES. Dick Wright. "Sing a Labor Song" album, Main Street Records.

LET'S JINE UP. Ruby Rains, Bakersfield, Cal. L of C, AAFS 4141.

LIFT EVERY VOICE AND SING (Negro National Anthem). California Labor School Chorus. CLS record

LISTEN, MR. BILBO. Hootenanny Singers. Asch album 370.

LITTLE MAN ON A FENCE. Josh White. Stinson 622.

LOST JOHN.

Bascom Lamar Lunsford. L of C, AAFS 1801 A3.

Harry Green and group, state penitentiary, Parchman, Miss. L of C, AAFS 885 B1.

Woody Guthrie and Sonny Terry. Disc album 360 ("Struggle").

LONESOME JAILHOUSE BLUES.
Aunt Molly Jackson. L of C, AAFS 2535 B.
Mary Davis, Manchester, Ky. L of C, AAFS 1490 A1.
LOVELESS C.C.C. Tommy Rhoades, Visalia FSA camp, Visalia, Cal. L of C, AAFS 4130 B1.
LUDLOW MASSACRE. Woody Guthrie. Disc album 360 ("Struggle").
ME JOHNNY MITCHELL MAN. Jerry Byrne, Buck Run, Pa. L of C, AAFS 1432.
MIDNIGHT SPECIAL.
Frank Jordan and group of Negro convicts, state penitentiary, Parchman, Miss.
Gus Harper and group, state penitentiary, Parchman, Miss. L of C, AAFS 885 A3.
Gant family, Austin, Tex. L of C, AAFS 647 A.
Huddie Ledbetter (Leadbelly), Angola state prison farm, Angola, La. L of C, AAFS 124 A and 133 A.
Jesse Bradley, state penitentiary, Huntsville, Tex. L of C, AAFS 218.
Woody Guthrie. L of C, AAFS 3410 A1.
Huddie Ledbetter (Leadbelly) and Golden Gate Quartet. Victor album P-50 ("Midnight Special").
Huddie Ledbetter (Leadbelly), Woody Guthrie, and Cisco Houston. Disc album 726 ("Midnight Special").
THE MILL WAS MADE OF MARBLE. Joe Glazer. "Eight New Songs for Labor," CIO Dept. of Education and Research album.
THE MINER'S COMPLAINT. Mrs. Frost Woodhull, San Antonio, Tex. L of C, AAFS 596 B1.
MINER'S FAREWELL. Findlay Donaldson, Pineville, Ky. L of C, AAFS 1985 B2.
MR. CUNDIFF (TURN ME LOOSE). Aunt Molly Jackson. L of C, AAFS 2541 B, 2542 A and B, and 2543 A.
THE MURDER OF HARRY SIMMS. Aunt Molly Jackson. L of C, AAFS 1941 A.
MY NEW FOUND LAND. Woody Guthrie. Disc album 610 ("Ballads from the Dust Bowl").
NEW YORK TOWN. Woody Guthrie. Asch album 347 ("Woody Guthrie").
1913 MASSACRE. Woody Guthrie. Disc album 360 ("Struggle").
NINETY-ONE. I.L.G.W.U. Record Number Two.
NO DEPRESSION IN HEAVEN. Buster Hunt, Yuba City FSA camp, Yuba City, Cal. L of C, AAFS 4156 B.
NO DOUGH BLUES. Blind Blake. Paramount 12723.
NO HOME FOR THE POOR. Mrs. Howard, Tempe, Ariz. L of C, AAFS 3567 A.
NO IRISH NEED APPLY. Pete Seeger. Charter RC 1.
NO KU KLUX OUT TONIGHT. Bascom Lamar Lunsford. L of C, AAFS 1822 B2.

No More Auction Block for Me. California Labor School Chorus, CLS record.

No More Blues. Josh White. Asch album 349 ("Citizen CIO").

No More Mourning. Carl Sandburg. Musicraft album 209 ("American Songbag").

No Restricted Signs. Golden Gate Quartet. Columbia album 145 ("Golden Gate Spirituals").

Nobody Knows de Trouble I've Seen.
Huddie and Martha Ledbetter. L of C, AAFS 2503 A1.
Edna Thomas, Columbia 1863-D.
Dorothy Maynor. Victor album M-879 ("Negro Spirituals").
Mildred Bailey. Columbia 35348.
Hampton Institute Quartet. Victor 27473.
Robert Merrill. Victor 10-1427.

NRA Blues. Billy Cox and Cliff Hobbs. Perfect 13090.

Nutpickers' Song. Gladys, Matilda, and Juanita Crouch, St. Louis, Mo. L of C, AAFS SR 43.

NYA Blues. Pauline, Fanine and Don Reda Lewis, West Liberty, Ky. L of C, AAFS 1562 B2

Oh, You Miners, Don't Go to Raleigh. Group of Negro convicts, state prison camp, Boone, N. C. L of C, AAFS 3993 B1.

Old Man. Huddie Ledbetter (Leadbelly). Disc album 735 ("Work Songs of the U.S.A.").

The Old Miner's Refrain. Daniel Walsh, Centralia, Pa. L of C, AAFS 1734.

On a Monday. Huddie Ledbetter (Leadbelly). Asch 343-3.

On a Picket Line. Dick Wright. "Sing a Labor Song" album, Main Street Records.

On Johnny Mitchell's Train. Jerry Byrne, Buck Run, Pa. L of C, AAFS 1433.

On the Picket Line. Tom Glazer. "Favorite American Union Songs" album, CIO Dept. of Education and Research.

One Dime Blues. Blind Lemon Jefferson. Paramount 12518.

OPA Blues. Ocie Stockard. King 456.

Overtime Pay. Priority Ramblers, Washington, D. C. L of C, AAFS 7054 B4.

Papa Don't Raise No Cotton, No Corn. Gertrude Thurston and group, New Bight, Cat Island, Bahamas. L of C, AAFS 388 B2.

The Passion of Sacco and Vanzetti. Woody Guthrie. Disc album 40.

Pastures of Plenty. Woody Guthrie. Disc album 610 ("Ballads from the Dust Bowl").

Pat Works on the Railway.
Pete Seeger, Charity Bailey. Disc. 604.
American Ballad Singers. Victor album P-41 ("American Folk Songs").

PAY DAY AT COAL CREEK. Pete Steele. L of C, AAFS 4.
PICKET LINE. I.L.G.W.U. Record Number One.
PICKET LINE SONGS. Jefferson Chorus. Union album 100.
PIE IN THE SKY. Gladys, Matilda, and Juanita Crouch, St. Louis, Mo.
   L of C, AAFS SR 43 A3 and A5.
A PIN FOR YOUR LAPEL. Dick Wright. "Sing a Labor Song" album, Main
   Street Records.
PLEASE, MR. BOSS. I.L.G.W.U. Record Number Two.
POOR LITTLE RAGGED CHILD. Vergil Bowman, Cincinnati, Ohio. L of C,
   AAFS 1689 A1.
POOR MINER. Blaine Stubblefield, Washington, D. C. L of C, AAFS
   1848 B.
PO' PRISONER BLUES. Johnnie Myer, state penitentiary, Raleigh, N. C.
   L of C, AAFS 269 A3.
PRETTY BOY FLOYD. Woody Guthrie. L of C, AAFS 3412 B4 and 3413 A;
   Disc album 360 ("Struggle").
PRISON BOUND. Josh White. Musicraft album N-3 ("Harlem Blues").
THE PRISONERS' CALL. Aunt Molly Jackson. L of C, AAFS 1942 B.
PRISONER GIRL BLUES. Negro woman prisoner, old state penitentiary,
   Wetumpka, Ala. L of C, AAFS 225 B2.
PROJECT HIGHWAY. Sonny Boy Williamson. Bluebird 7302.
PUT IT ON THE GROUND. Hootenanny Singers. Asch album 370 ("Roll
   the Union On").
RAGGEDY, RAGGEDY. John Handcox. L of C, AAFS 3237 A1.
RAMBLIN' BLUES. Woody Guthrie. Disc album 610 ("Ballads from the
   Dust Bowl").
RED CROSS STORE. Huddie Ledbetter (Leadbelly). L of C, AAFS 138 B.
   Pete Harris, Richmond, Va. L of C, AAFS 78 B2.
RED CROSS STORE BLUES. Huddie Ledbetter (Leadbelly). Bluebird 8709.
ROLL OUT THE PICKETS. Ruby Rains, Bakersfield, Cal. L of C, AAFS
   4140 B1.
ROLL THE UNION ON.
   Gladys, Matilda, and Juanita Crouch, St. Louis, Mo. L of C, AAFS
   SR 65 A2.
   John Handcox, Brinkley, Ark. L of C, AAFS 3237 A2.
   Hootenanny Singers. Asch album 370 ("Roll the Union On").
   Tom Glazer. "Favorite American Union Sings" album, CIO Dept.
   of Education and Research.
RUNAWAY NEGRO. Group of Negro convicts, Cumins state farm, Gould,
   Ark. L of C, AAFS 244 B2.
SALISBURY MILLS. Mort Montonyea, Sloatsburg, N. Y. L of C, AAFS
   3662 A2.
SAME BOAT, BROTHER. Earl Robinson. Alco album A2.
THE SAME OLD MERRY-GO-ROUND. Michael Loring. Progessive party
   record.

SCOTTSBORO BOYS. Huddie Ledbetter (Leadbelly). L of C, AAFS 2502 A1.

SHINE ON ME. Joe Glazer. "Eight New Songs for Labor" album, CIO Dept. of Education and Research.

SHORTY GEORGE.
Huddie Ledbetter (Leadbelly). L of C, AAFS 149 B and 150 A.
James (Iron Head) Baker, Central state farm, Sugarland, Tex. L of C 210 B and 202 A2.
Smith Cason, Clemens state farm, Brazoria, Tex. L of C, AAFS 2598 A1.

SILICOSIS IS KILLIN' ME. Pinewood Tom (Josh White). Perfect 6-05-51.

SIXTEEN TONS. Merle Travis, Capitol album AD-50 ("Folk Songs of the Hills").

SLAVERY DAYS. Fields Ward and Bogtrotters Band, Galax, Va. L of C, AAFS 1356 A1.

SO LONG, IT'S BEEN GOOD TO KNOW YOU. Woody Guthrie. L of C, AAFS 3410 B2.

SOCIAL WORKERS TALKING BLUES. Asch album 349 ("Songs of Citizen CIO").

SOLIDARITY FOREVER.
Tom Glazer. "Favorite American Union Songs" album. CIO Dept. of Education and Research.
I.L.G.W.U. Record Number One.
Burl Ives and the Union Boys. Stinson 662.

SOME OTHER WORLD. Floyd Tilman. Columbia 20026.

SONG OF 316. I.L.G.W.U. Francis Wertz, Bryn Mawr Labor College,

SONG OF THE NECKWEAR WORKERS. I.L.G.W.U. Record Number Two.

SONG OF 316. I.L.G.W.U. Francis Wertz, Bryn Mawr Labor College, Bryn Mawr, Pa. L of C, AAFS 1771 B2.

SOUP SONG. I.L.G.W.U. Record Number One.

SOUTHERN EXPOSURE. Josh White. Keynote album K-107 ("Southern Exposure").

STARVATION BLUES. Big Bill Broonzy. Broadway 5072.

STATE FARM BLUES.
Claude Cryder, Bloomington, Ind. L of C, AAFS 1721 B3.
Henry Williams, Kilby prison, Montgomery, Ala. L of C, AFFS 235 B2.

STRANGE FRUIT. Josh White. Keynote album K-125 ("Strange Fruit"). Decca album A-447 ("Ballads and Blues").

STRIKE AT HARRIMAN, TENNESSEE. Herschel Philips. L of C, AAFS SR 22.

THE STRIKING MINERS. Henry Garrett, Crossville, Tenn. L of C, AAFS 3175 A1.

SUBCONTRACTOR'S SONG. Henry Truvillion, Burkesville, Tex. L of C, AAFS 3985 A3.

SWING LOW, SWEET ILD. Gladys Matilda, and Juanita Crouch, St. Louis, Mo. L of C, AAFS SR 44.

TAKE THIS HAMMER.

Huddie Ledbetter (Leadbelly). Disc album 735 ("Work Songs of the U.S.A.").

Clifton Wright and group of Negro convicts, state penitentiary, Richmand, Va. L of C, AAFS 726 B1.

TALKING ATOMIC BLUES (OLD MAN ATOM).

Bob Hill. Jubilee 4005.

Ozzi Waters. Coral 64050.

Sam Hinton. ABC 230.

TALKING COLUMBIA BLUES. Woody Guthrie. Disc album 610 ("Ballads from the Dust Bowl")

TALKING DUST BOWL BLUES. Woody Guthrie. L of C, AAFS 3411 A2 and B1.

TALKING SAILOR. Woody Guthrie. Asch album 347 ("Woody Guthrie").

TALKING UNION. Almanac Singers. Keynote album 106 ("Talking Union").

THAT OLD FEELIN'. Sarah Ogan. L of C, AAFS 1945 B2.

THAT'S ALL. Joe Glazer. "Eight New Songs for Labor" album, CIO Dept. of Education and Research.

THAT'S ALL. Merle Travis. Capitol album AD-50 ("Folk Songs of the Hills").

THERE IS MEAN THINGS HAPPENING IN THIS LAND. John Handcox. L of C, AAFS 3238.

THEY CAN ONLY FILL ONE GRAVE. Roy Acuff. Columbia 37943.

THEY LAID JESUS CHRIST IN HIS GRAVE (JESUS CHRIST). Woody Guthrie. L of C, AAFS 3413 B2 and 3414 A1.

THIS OLD WORLD. Hootenanny Singers. Asch album 370 ("Roll the Union On").

THOSE AGONIZING CRUEL SLAVERY DAYS. Elisha Cox, San Angelo, Tex. L of C, AAFS 547 B1.

TOM JOAD. Woody Guthrie. Victor album P-27 ("Dust Bowl Ballads").

TOO OLD TO WORK. Joe Glazer. "Eight New Songs for Labor" album, CIO Dept. of Education and Research.

TRAMP ON THE STREET. Cumberland Mountain Folks. Columbia 20187. Bill Carlisle. King 697.

TROUBLE. Josh White. Columbia album C-22 ("Chain Gang Songs"). Stinson-Asch album 358 ("Folk Songs").

UAW-CIO. Union Boys. Asch album 346 ("Songs for Victory").

UNCLE SAM SAYS. Josh White. Keynote album 107 ("Southern Exposure").

UNEMPLOYMENT COMPENSATION BLUES. Boots Cassetta. Charter RC-1.

UNION BURYING GROUND. Woody Guthrie. Disc album 360 ("Struggle").

UNION MAID.

Woody Guthrie and the Almanac Singers. Keynote album K-106 ("Talking Union")

UNION MAID—*Continued*
  Jefferson Chorus. Union 301-4.
  Tom Glazer. "Favorite American Union Songs" album, CIO Dept. of Education and Research.
UNION MAN. Andrew Morgan, Tamaqua, Pa. L of C, AAFS 1436.
UNION TRAIN.
  Almanac Singers. Keynote album K-106 ("Talking Union").
  Tom Glazer. "Favorite American Union Songs" album, CIO Dept. of Education and Research.
UPRISING OF THE TWENTY THOUSAND. I.L.G.W.U. Record Number Two.
VIGILANTE MAN. Woody Guthrie. Victor album P-28 ("Dust Bowl Ballads," Vol. II).
WALK IN PEACE. Sir Lancelot. Charter RC-102.
WAY DOWN IN OLD ST. FRANCIS BOTTOM. Agnes Cunningham, Tucson, Ariz. L of C, AAFS 3559 A1, 2, and 3.
WE ARE BUILDING A STRONG UNION. Tom Glazer. "Favorite American Union Songs" album, CIO Dept. of Education and Research.
WE'VE GOT A PLAN. Tom Glazer. Asch album 349 ("Songs of Citizen CIO").
WE SHALL NOT BE MOVED.
  Alice and Johnnie, St. Louis, Mo. L of C, AAFS 3195 B1.
  Katharine Trusty, Paintsville, Ky. L of C, AAFS 1396 B2.
  The Union Boys. Asch album 346 ("Songs for Victory").
  Tom Glazer. "Favorite American Union Songs" album, CIO Dept. of Education and Research.
WE WILL OVERCOME. Joe Glazer. "Eight New Songs for Labor" album, CIO Dept. of Education and Research.
WE'D RATHER NOT BE ON RELIEF. Lester Hunter, Shafter migratory camp, Shafter, Cal. L of C, AAFS 3567 B.
WEAVE ROOM BLUES. Dixon Brothers. Bluebird B 6441.
WELCOME THE TRAVELER HOME. Jim Garland. L of C, AAFS 1947 A.
WELFARE BLUES. Speckled Red. Bluebird 8069.
WELFARE SUPERVISOR'S CHANT. Gladys, Matilda, and Juanita Crouch, St. Louis, Mo. L of C, AAFS 3196 A1.
WHEN THE CURFEW BLOWS. Woody Guthrie. Disc album 610 ("Ballads from the Dust Bowl").
WHICH SIDE ARE YOU ON?
  Jim Garland. L of C, AAFS 1951 B1.
  Tilman Cadle, Middlesboro, Ky. L of C, AAFS 1402 A2.
  Tom Glazer. "Favorite American Union Songs" album, CIO Dept. of Education and Research.
WHITE FOLKS IN DE COLLEGE. P. H. Thomas, Jacksonville, Fla. L of C, AAFS 3525 A2.
THE WHITE SLAVE. Jim Garland. L of C, AAFS 1953 A1.
WINNSBORO COTTON MILL BLUES. Pete Seeger. Charter C-45.

WORKIN' FOR THE PWA. Dave Alexander. Decca 7307.

WORKIN' ON THE PROJECT. Peatie Wheatstraw. Decca 7311.

WORKINGMAN'S BLUES. Brownie McChee. Columbia 30027, Okeh 6698.

WORRIED MAN BLUES.

    Carter family. Victor 27497.

    SONNY TERRY. Capitol A-40043.

    Curley Reeves, Brawley migratory camp, Brawley, Cal. L of C, AAFS 3326 B1.

    Woody Guthrie. L of C, AAFS 3416 B1.

WPA BLUES. Big Bill Broonzy. Perfect 6-08-61.

YOU SEE ME LAUGHIN' JUST TO KEEP FROM CRYIN'. James (Iron Head) Baker. L of C, AAFS 719 A1.

Bibliography

Textual Material: Books

Adamic, Louis, *Dynamite*, New York, Viking Press, 1931.
Anderson, Nels, *The Hobo*, Chicago, University of Chicago Press, 1923.
Aptheker, Herbert, *Negro Slave Revolts in the United States 1526-1860*, New York, International Publishers, 1939.
    Essays in the History of the American Negro, New York, International Publishers, 1945.
Archive of American Folk Song, Library of Congress, *Checklist of Songs in the English Language Recorded Prior to August, 1939*, Washington, D. C., 1942.
Beard, Charles A. and Mary R., *The Rise of American Civilization*, New York, Macmillan, 1945.
Botkin, Benjamin A., *Lay My Burden Down: A Folk History of Slavery*, Chicago, University of Chicago Press, 1945.
Brink, Carol, *Harps in the Wind*, New York, Macmillan, 1947.
Brown, Sterling, *The Negro Poetry and Drama*, Washington, Associates in Negro Folk Education, 1937 (Bronze Booklet No. 7).
Burleigh, Harry Thacker, *Negro Folk Songs*, New York, G. Ricordi & Co., 1921.
Carter, Dyson, *Sin and Science*, New York, Heck, Cattell Publishing Co., 1946.
Cayton, Horace R., and Mitchell, George S., *Black Workers and the New Unions*, Chapel Hill, University of North Carolina Press, 1939.
Chaplin, Ralph, *Wobbly*, Chicago, University of Chicago Press, 1948
Chappell, Louis W., *John Henry, A Folklore Stuay*, Jena, Germany. Walter Biedermann, 1933.

Chickering, Jesse, *Immigration into the United States,* Boston, 1848.

Christman, Henry, *Tin Horns and Calico,* New York, Henry Holt, 1945.

Clark, John B., *Populism in Alabama* (Ph.D. thesis), Auburn, Ala., Auburn Printing Co., 1927.

Commons, John R. and associates, *History of Labour in the United States,* 4 vols., New York, Macmillan, 1918-1935.

Davis, Arthur Kyle, *Traditional Ballads of Virginia,* Cambridge, Harvard University Press, 1929.

Donald, Henderson H., *The Negro Freedman,* New York, Henry Schuman, 1952.

Douglass, Frederick, *My Bondage and My Freedom,* New York and Auburn, Miller, Orton, and Mulligan, 1855.

Drewry, William Sidney, *Slave Insurrections in Virginia 1830-1865,* Washington, Neale Co., 1900.

Du Bois, William Edward Burghardt, *The Souls of Black Folk,* Chicago, A. C. McClurg & Co., 1903.

Dulles, Foster Rhea, *Labor in America,* New York, T. Y. Crowell, 1949.

Ellis, David Maldwyn, *Landlords and Farmers in the Hudson-Mohawk Region,* Ithaca, New York, Cornell University Press, 1946.

Foner, Philip S., *History of the Labor Movement in the United States,* New York, International Publishers, 1947.

Fountain, Clayton W., *Union Guy,* New York, Viking Press, 1949.

Fox, D. R., *Decline of Aristocracy in the Politics of New York,* New York, Columbia University Press, 1919.

Gardner, Emelyn Elizabeth, and Chickering, Geraldine Jencks, *Ballads and Songs of Southern Michigan,* Ann Arbor, University of Michigan Press, 1939.

George, Henry, *Progress and Poverty,* New York, Doubleday, 1899.

Gordon, Robert Winslow, *Folk Songs of America,* New York, National Service Bureau, 1938.

Guthrie, Woody, *Bound for Glory,* New York, E. P. Dutton, 1943. *American Folk Song,* New York, Disc Recording Co., 1947.

Harris, Herbert, *American Labor,* New Haven, Yale University Press, 1940.

Henry, H. M., *The Police Control of the Slave in South Carolina* (Ph.D. thesis), Vanderbilt University, Emory, Va., 1914.

Henry, Mellinger Edward, *Songs Sung in the Southern Appalachians,* London, Mitre Press, 1934.

Hicks, John Donald, *The Populist Revolt,* Minneapolis, University of Minnesota Press, 1931.

Jackson, George Pullen, *White Spirituals in the Southern Uplands,* Chapel Hill, University of North Carolina Press, 1933. *White and Negro Spirituals,* New York, J. J. Augustin, 1943.

Johnson, Guy B., *John Henry: Tracking Down a Negro Legend,* Chapel Hill, University of North Carolina Press, 1929.

Johnson, James Weldon, and Rosamund J., *The Root of American Negro Spirituals*, New York, Viking Press, 1937.

Jordan, Philip, *Singing Yankees*, Minneapolis, University of Minnesota Press, 1946.

King, Dan, *Life and Times of Thomas Wilson Dorr*, Boston, King, 1859.

Korson, George, *Songs and Ballads of the Anthracite Miner*, New York, Grafton, 1927.

Minstrels of the Mine Patch, Philadelphia, University of Pennsylvania Press, 1938.

Coal Dust on the Fiddle, Philadelphia, University of Pennsylvania Press, 1943.

Krehbiel, Henry Edward, *Afro-American Folk Song*, New York, G. Schirmer, *ca.* 1914.

Lindsey, Almont, *The Pullman Strike*, Chicago, University of Chicago Press, 1942.

Lloyd, A. L., *The Singing Englishman*, London, Workers' Music Association, n. d.

Lloyd, Arthur Young, *The Slavery Controversy, 1831-1860*, Chapel Hill, University of North Carolina Press, 1939.

Locke, Alain LeRoy, *The Negro and His Music*, Washington, D. C., Associates in Negro Folk Education, 1930.

Lomax, Alan, *List of American Folk Songs on Commercial Records*, Committee of the Conference on Inter-American Relations in the Field of Music, William Berrien, chairman, Washington, D. C., Department of State, 1940.

Lomax, Alan, and Cowell, Sidney Robertson, *American Folk Songs and Folk Lore, A Regional Bibliography*, New York, Progressive Education Association, 1942.

Long, John Dixon, *Pictures of Slavery in Church and State*, Philadelphia, Long, 1857.

MacDonald, Lois, *Southern Mill Hills* (Ph.D. thesis, New York University), New York, Hillman, 1928.

McMurry, Donald Le Crone, *Coxey's Army*, Boston, Little, Brown, & Co., 1929.

Marsh, J. B. T., *The Story of the Jubilee Singers*, Boston, Houghton, 1880.

Milburn, George, *The Hobo's Hornbook*, New York, Ives, Washburn, 1930.

Mowry, A. M., *The Dorr War*, Providence, Preston, 1901.

Odum, Howard W., and Johnson, Guy B., *The Negro and His Songs*, Chapel Hill, University of North Carolina Press, 1925.

Negro Workaday Songs, Chapel Hill, University of North Carolina Press, 1926.

Ottley, Roi, *Black Odyssey*, New York, Charles Scribner's Sons, 1948.

Philips, Ulrich B., *American Negro Slavery,* New York, Appleton, 1918.
Pound, Louise, *American Ballads and Songs,* New York, Scribner's, 1922.
Rochester, Anna, *The Populist Movement in the United States,* New York, International Publishers, 1943.
Siebert, William H., *The Underground Railroad from Slavery to Freedom,* New York, Macmillan, 1898.
Smedley, R. C., *History of the Underground Railroad in Chester and Neighboring Pennsylvania Counties,* Lancaster, Pa., Hiestand, 1883.
Stegner, Wallace, *The Preacher and the Slave,* Boston, Houghton, 1950.
Stroud, George M., *A Sketch of the Laws Relating to Slavery in the Several States of the United States of America,* Philadelphia, Henry Longstreth, 1856.
Talley, Thomas W., *Negro Folk Rhymes,* New York, Macmillan, 1922.
Thomas, Jean, *Ballad Makin' in the Mountains of Kentucky,* New York, Henry Holt, 1939.
Thurman, Howard, *Deep River, An Interpretation of the Negro Spirituals,* Oakland, California, Mills College, Eucalyptus Press, 1946.
Vorse, Mary Heaton, *Strike! A Novel of Gastonia,* New York, H. Liveright, 1930.
Labor's New Millions, New York, Modern Age Books, Inc., 1938.
White, Newman I., *American Negro Folk Songs,* Cambridge, Harvard University Press, 1928.
Woodson, Carter G., *The Mind of the Negro as Reflected in Letters Written During he Crisis, 1800-1860,* Washington, D. C., Association for the Study of Negro Life and History, 1926.
The Negro in Our History, Washington, D. C., Associated Publishers, 1945.
Work, John Wesley, *Folk Songs of the American Negro,* Nashville, Tennessee, Fisk University Press, 1915.
Zahler, Helene Sara, *Eastern Workingmen and National Land Policy, 1829-1862* (Ph.D. thesis, Columbia University), New York, Columbia University Press, 1941.

Textual Material: Periodicals

Balch, Elizabeth, "Songs for Labor," *Survey,* vol. 31 (Jan. 3, 1914), pp. 408-412.
"Ballads of Mine Regions Depict Life of the Workers," New York *World,* Sept. 11, 1927.
Brown, J. M., "Songs of the Slave," *Lippincott's Magazine,* vol. 2 (1868), pp. 617-623.

Cade, John B., "Out of the Mouths of Ex-Slaves," *Journal of Negro History,* July, 1935, pp. 294-339.

Dolph, Edward Arthur, *"Ballads that Have Influenced Ballots,"* New York *Times Magazine,* October 16, 1932, p. 19.

Emerich, Duncan, "Songs of the Western Miners," *California Folklore Quarterly,* July, 1942, vol. 1, p. 216.

Fleming, Walter Lynwood, "Historic Attempts to Deport the Negro," *Journal of American History,* vol. 4, p. 198.

Hand, Wayland D., "The Folklore, Customs, and Traditions of the Butte Miner," *California Folklore Quarterly,* vol. 5 (April, 1946), pp. 1-25; 153-189.

Higginson, Thomas W., "Negro Spirituals," *Atlantic Monthly,* vol. 19 (June, 1867), pp. 685-794.

James, Thelma, "Folklore and Propaganda," *Journal of American Folklore,* vol. 61 (1948), p. 311.

Larkin, Margaret, "Ella May's Songs," *The Nation,* vol. 129 (October 9, 1929), p. 382.

"Ella May Wiggins," *New Masses,* vol. 5 (November, 1929), No. 6.

Lewis, Nell Battle, "Anarchy vs. Communism in Gastonia," *The Nation,* vol. 129 (September 25, 1929), p. 320 ff.

Lindsey, Almont, "Paternalism and the Pullman Strike," *American Historical Review,* vol. 44 (January, 1939), pp. 272-289.

Lomax, John A., "Self-Pity in Negro Folk Songs," *The Nation,* vol. 105 (August 9, 1917), pp. 141-145.

"Some Types of American Folk Song," *Journal of American Folklore,* vol. 28 (1915), pp. 1-17.

Lovell, John, Jr., "The Social Significance of the Negro Spiritual," *Journal of Negro Education,* vol. 8 (October, 1939), pp. 634-643.

Milburn, George, "Poesy in the Jungles," *American Mercury,* vol. 20 (May, 1930), pp. 80-86.

People's Songs, New York, People's Songs, Inc., February, 1946—February, 1949.

Sing Out! New York, People's Artists, Inc., May, 1950—.

Stegner, Wallace, "Joe Hill, the Wobblies' Troubadour," *New Republic,* vol. 118 (January, 1948), pp. 20-24 and 38-39. See also correspondence in vols. 118 and 119 relating to Stegner's article.

Todd, Charles, and Sonkin, Robert, "Ballads of the Okies," New York *Times Magazine,* November 17, 1940.

United Mine Workers' Journal, 1891—.

Ward, Harry F., "Songs of Discontent," *Methodist Review,* September, 1913.

"Which Side Are You on?" *Daily Worker,* June 4, 1941.

White, James Cameron, "The Story of the Negro Spiritual, 'Nobody Knows de Trouble I've Seen,'" *Musical Observer,* vol. 23 (1924), No. 6.

Wimberly, Lowry Charles, "Hard Times Singing," *American Mercury,* vol. 31 (June, 1934), p. 197 ff.

Songbooks and Song Collections Containing Songs of Social and Economic Protest.

Albertson, Ralph, *Fellowship Songs,* Westwood, Mass., Ariel Press, 1906.
Allen, William Francis, *Slave Songs of the United States,* New York, 1867; republished in 1929 by Smith.
Amalgamated Song Book, New York, Amalgamated Clothing Workers of America, CIO, *ca.* 1948.
Balch, Elizabeth, "Songs for Labor," *Survey,* vol. 31 (January 3, 1914), pp. 408-412.
Barton, William Eleazar, *Old Plantation Hymns,* Boston, Samson, 1899.
Beck, Earl Clifton, *Songs of the Michigan Lumberjacks,* Ann Arbor, University of Michigan Press, 1941.
Brown, J. M., "Songs of the Slave," *Lippincott's Magazine,* vol. 2 (1868), pp. 617-623.
Burleigh, Harry Thacker, *Negro Folk Songs,* New York, G. Ricardo, 1921.
CIO Cong Book, Washington, D. C., CIO Department of Education and Research, *ca.* 1949.
Calkins, Alta May, *Cooperative Recreation Songs,* New York, n. d.
Child, Francis James, *The English and Scottish Popular Ballads,* 5 vols., Boston and New York, Houghton, Mifflin and Co., 1882-1898.
Christman, Henry, *Tin Horns and Calico,* New York, Henry Holt, 1945.
Colcord, Joanna C., *Songs of American Sailormen,* New York, W. W. Norton, 1938.
Commonwealth Labor Hymnal, Mena, Ark., Commonwealth College, 1938.
Commonwealth Labor Songs, Mena, Ark., Commonwealth College, 1938.
Dixie Union Songs, Atlanta, Ga., I. L. G. W. U., n. d.
Dobie, Frank, *Follow De Drinkin' Gourd,* Publications, Texas Folklore Society, vol. 7, 1928.
Donn, Holles Elizabeth, *58 Spirituals for Choral Use,* Boston, Birchard and Co., n. d.
Duganne, Augustine J., *The Poetical Works of Augustine Duganne,* Philadelphia, Parry and McMillan, 1855.
Eckstorm, Fannie Hardy, and Smyth, Mary Winslow, *Minstrelsy of Maine,* Boston, Houghton, Mifflin, 1927.
Eight Union Songs of the Almanacs, New York, New Theatre League, 1941.

Emerich, Duncan, "Songs of the Western Miners," *California Folklore Quarterly*, vol. 1 (July, 1942), p. 216.

Everybody Sings, New York, Education Department, I. L. G. W. U., 1947.

Farmers' Alliance Songs of the 1890's, Lincoln, Neb., Federal Writers' Project, n.d.

Favorite Songs of the Farmers' Union, Jamestown, Farmers' Union Cooperative Education Service, n. d.

Fenner, Thomas, *Cabin and Plantation Songs*, in Armstrong, Mrs. M. F., and Ludlow, Helen, *Hampton and Its Students*, New York, Putnam, 1874.

Fitch, Thomas, *Ballads of Western Miners and Others*, New York, Cochrane Publishing Co., 1910.

Foner, Philip S., *History of the Labor Movement in the United States*, New York, International Publishers, 1947.

Gardner, Emelyn Elizabeth, and Chickering, Geraldine Jencks, *Ballads and Songs of Southern Michigan*, Ann Arbor, University of Michigan Press, 1939.

Gellert, Lawrence, *Negro Songs of Protest*, Carl Fischer, Inc., New York, 1936.

Me and My Captain, New York, Hours Press, 1939.

Gibson, George Howard, *Armageddon: The Songs of the World's Workers Who Go Forth to Battle with the Kings and Captains and Mighty Men*, Lincoln, Neb., and London, England, Wealth Makers' Publishing Co., 1895.

Gray, Roland Palmer, *Songs and Ballads of the Maine Lumberjacks*, Cambridge, Harvard University Press, 1924.

Guthrie, Woody, *American Folk Song*, New York, Disc Recording Co., 1947.

Higginson, Thomas W., "Negro Spirituals," *Atlantic Monthly*, vol. 19 (June, 1867), pp. 685-794.

Hille, Waldemar, *The People's Song Book*, New York, Boni and Gaer, 1948.

Horton, Zilphia, *Labor Songs*, Atlanta, Ga., T. W. U. A., Southeastern Regional Office, 1939.

I. W. W. Songs. Songs of the Workers (To Fan the Flames of Discontent), Chicago, I. W. W. Publishing Co., 1st to 28th edition.

Jackson, George Pullen, *Spiritual Folk Songs of Early America*, New York, J. J. Augustine, 1937.

White Spirituals in the Southern Uplands, Chapel Hill, University of North Carolina Press, 1943.

Kennedy, R. Emmet, *Mellows*, New York, Boni, 1925.

More Mellows, New York, Dodd, Mead, & Co., 1931.

Kolb, Sylvia and John, *Frankie and Johnnie, A Treasury of Folk Songs*, New York, Bantam Books, 1948.

Korson, George, *Songs and Ballads of the Anthracite Miner*, New York, Grafton, 1927.
The Miner Sings, New York, J. Fischer & Bros., 1936.
Minstrels of the Mine Patch, Philadelphia, University of Pennsylvania Press, 1938.
Coal Dust on the Fiddle, Philadelphia, University of Pennsylvania Press, 1943.
Labor Sings, New York, I. L. G. W. U. Combined Locals, 1940.
Labor Songs for All Occasions, Madison, University of Wisconsin Songbooks for Summer Sessions, 1938, 1940.
Larkin, Margaret, "Ella May's Songs," *The Nation*, vol. 129 (October 9, 1929), p. 382.
Lawrence, B. M., *Labor Songster; National Greenback Labor Songster*, New York, 1878.
Leavitt, Burton E., *Songs of Protest*, Putnam, Conn., Leavitt, 1906.
Let the People Sing, Madison, University of Wisconsin Summer School for Workers, 1941.
Let's Sing, New York, Educational Department, I. L. G. W. U., n. d.
Lincoln, Jairus, *Anti-Slavery Melodies*, Hingham, Mass., E. B. Gill, 1843.
Look Away, 50 Negro Folk Songs, Delaware, Ohio, Cooperative Recreation Service, n. d.
Lomax, John A., "Self-Pity in Negro Folk-Songs," *The Nation*, vol. 105 (August 9, 1917), pp. 141-145.
Lomax, John A., and Alan, *American Ballads and Folk Songs*, New York, Macmillan, 1934.
Negro Folk Songs as Sung by Leadbelly, New York, Macmillan, 1936.
Our Singing Country, New York, Macmillan, 1941.
Folk Song, U. S. A., New York, Duer, Sloan, & Pierce, 1947.
March and Sing, New York, American Music League, 1937.
Marsh, J. B. T., *The Story of the Jubilee Singers*, Boston, Houghton, 1880.
Milburn, George, *The Hobo's Hornbook*, New York, Ives, Washburn, 1930.
Nebraska Farmers' Alliance Songs of the 1890's, Federal Writers' Project, Nebraska Folklore Pamphlets Nos. 18 and 19, 1939.
Neece, A. C., *The Union Songster*, Sunset, Texas, Neece, 1923.
Niles, John Jacob, *Singing Soldiers*, New York, Scribner's, 1927.
Odum, Howard W., and Johnson, Guy B., *The Negro and His Songs*, Chapel Hill, University of North Carolina Press, 1925.
Negro Workaday Songs, Chapel Hill, University of North Carolina Press, 1926.
People's Songs, New York, People's Songs, Inc., February, 1946—February, 1949.

A People's Songs Wordbook, New York, People's Songs, Inc., 1947.

Randolph, Vance, and Shoemaker, Floyd C., *Ozark Folksongs,* vol. 4, Columbia, The State Historical Society of Missouri, 1950.

Rebel Song Book, New York, Rand School Press, 1935.

Red Song Book, New York, Workers' Library Publishers, 1932.

Sandburg, Carl, *The American Songbag,* New York, Harcourt, Brace, 1927.

Sargent, Helen Child, and Kittredge, George Lyman, *English and Scottish Popular Ballads,* Boston, New York, Houghton, Mifflin, 1904.

School for Workers' Songs, Madison, University of Wisconsin School for Workers, 1945.

Siegmeister, Elie, and Downes, Olin, *A Treasury of American Song,* New York, Knopf, 1943.

Siegmeister, Elie, *Work and Sing,* New York, W. R. Scott, 1944.

Sing a Labor Song, New York, Gerald Marks Music, Inc., 1950.

Sing Along the Way, New York, Womans Press, *ca.* 1948.

Sing Amalgamated, New York, Amalgamated Clothing Workers of America, 1944.

Sing Out! New York, People's Artists, Inc., May, 1950—.

Sing, Sing, Sing, Allentown, Pa., I. L. G. W. U. Cotton Garment Department, 1946.

Sing While You Fight, New York, Recreation Department, Wholesale and Warehouse Employees Local 65, n. d.

Singing Farmers, Chicago, National Farmers' Union, 1947.

Song Book, Seattle, Pacific Coast School for Workers, 1938.

Song Book of the I. L. G. W. U., Los Angeles, Educational Department, I. L. G. W. U., n. d.

Songs for America, New York, Workers' Library Publishers, n. d.

Songs for Labor, Denver, Colo., Research and Educational Department, Oil Workers International Union, CIO, n. d.

Songs for Southern Workers, Lexington, Ky., Kentucky Workers' Alliance, 1937.

Songs of the People, New York, Workers' Library Publishers, 1937.

Songs of the Southern Summer School, Asheville, N. C., 1940.

Songs of the Southern Summer School for Workers, Asheville, N. C., 1940.

Songs of Workers, New York, Workers' Educational Division, Adult Educational Department, W. P. A., 1938.

Songs Our Union Sings, New York, Junior Guards of Local 362, I. L. G. W. U., n. d.

Songs Our Union Taught Us, New York, Educational Department, I. L. G. W. U., n. d.

Station I. L. G. W. U. Calling All Union Songsters, New York, I. L. G. W. U., n. d.

Talley, Thomas W., *Negro Folk Rhymes,* New York, Macmillan, 1922.

Thomas, Jean, *Ballad Makin' in the Mountains of Kentucky*, New York, Henry Holt, 1939.

UAW-CIO Sings, Detroit, Mich., UAW-CIO Educational Department, 1943.

Union Songs, Atlanta, Ga., Dressmakers' Union, I. L. G. W. U., n. d.

United Mine Workers' Journal, 1891—.

White, Clarence Cameron, *40 Negro Spirituals,* Philadelphia, Theo. Presser, 1927.

White, Newman I., *American Negro Folk Songs,* Cambridge, Harvard University Press, 1928.

Wimberly, Lowry Charles, "Hard Times Singing," *American Mercury,* vol. 31 (June, 1934), p. 197 ff.

Workers' Song Book, Numbers I and II, New York, Workers' Music League, 1935.

List of Composers

List of Songs and Ballads

An asterisk before a title indicates that the song or ballad appears with music.

Index

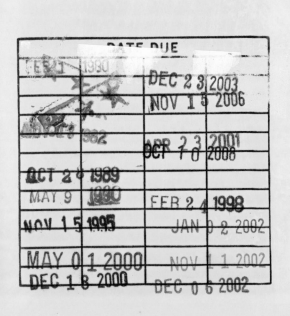